Paragliding – A Pilot's Training Manual, has sold more than 13,000 copies since first published it in 1991.

Mike Meier, one of the owners and executive managers of Wills Wing, is a member of the Society of Experimental Test Pilots, and has been a test pilot for Wills Wing since 1976. Mike does most of the technical writing for Wills Wing, and has written numerous articles for Hang Gliding and Paragliding magazines on safety and technical issues.

Mark Stucky, who began his aviation career in hang gliding, is a professional military and NASA test pilot and SETP member, whose flight test experience ranges from sub-20 mph speeds in paragliders to beyond Mach-3 in the SR-71 Blackbird. He is best known in the foot-launched soaring community for his informative technical articles and flight reviews.

In this, the eighth edition, the manual has been updated throughout with more in-depth information, illustrations and photographs. The book's focus continues to be on presenting technical subject matter in a manner that is easy for the average pilot to comprehend without the need for complex theory or equations. The authors emphasize safety throughout with techniques for risk management and dealing with common emergency scenarios.

Paragliding – A Pilot's Training Manual, is the outstanding single-source document for novice and advanced paraglider pilots alike.

ADVISORY

Paragliding is a form of aviation, with all of the inherent and potential dangers that are involved in aviation. No form of aviation is without risk.

This training manual is intended to be used as one part of a course of professional instruction, and only in combination with personal flight instruction provided by a qualified paragliding instructor. No one should ever attempt to teach themselves to fly.

PARAGLIDING

A Pilot's Training Manual

The Complete Reference

From A to XC

Mike Meier
Mark Stucky

PARAGLIDING
— A PILOT'S TRAINING MANUAL

International Standard Book Number:
    Hardcover version: 0-9754465-2-5
    Softcover version: 0-9754465-1-7
Library of Congress Catalog Card Number: 2006907777
Printed in the United States of America
First Printing: September 2006

Trademarks

All terms mentioned in this book that are known to be trademarks or service marks have been appropriately capitalized. Wills Wing cannot attest to the accuracy of this information. Use of a term in this book should not be regarded as affecting the validity of any trademark or service mark.

Warning and Disclaimer

Every effort has been made to make this book as complete and as accurate as possible, but no warranty or fitness is implied. The information provided is on an "as is" basis. The authors and the publisher shall have neither liability nor responsibility to any person or entity with respect to any loss or damages arising from the information contained in this book or from the use of the DVD.

Bulk Sales

Wills Wing offers excellent discounts on this book when ordered in quantity for bulk purchases or special sales. For more information, please contact:

Wills Wing Inc • 500 West Blueridge Avenue • Orange, CA 92865
• 714 998 6359 • www.willswing.com

Book Acknowledgements

Primary Photographers:
Sarah Char — like none other, her stunning front cover photo captures the beauty and essence of the sport
Andy Stocker — numerous photos
Gene Atkins — photo documentation
Bo Criss — numerous photos
Jeff Goin — powered paragliding photos
Swing Photographers — numerous photos
    Andre Bussmann
    Alfredo Studer
    Peter Wallenda
    AZoom.ch
Svend Eric-Monsen — numerous photos
Mark Stucky — illustration photos
Joan Stucky — illustration photos

Layout and Illustrations
Tim Meehan — edition 7 baseline
Mike Meier — editions 1 - 6
Mark Stucky — illustrations and layout

DVD Acknowledgements

Videographers
Gene Atkins — ground-to-air video
Alexander Caravitis — incident video
Andy Stocker — numerous clips
Mark Stucky — air-to-air video
Joan Stucky — kiting video

Narration:
Joan Stucky

Demonstration Pilots
David Jebb — Torrey Pines instruction
Mitch McAleer — flight techniques and advanced maneuvers
Rob McKenzie — flight techniques and air-to-air tandem pilot
Mike Meier — flight techniques
Mark Stucky — flight techniques

TABLE OF CONTENTS

Chapter One:
ABOUT PARAGLIDING

AN OVERVIEW OF THE NEWEST FORM OF PERSONAL FLIGHT

A beautiful alpine launch overlooking Grindelwald, Switzerland —Andy Stocker photo

Chapter 1 — ABOUT PARAGLIDING
AN OVERVIEW OF THE NEWEST FORM OF PERSONAL FLIGHT

Paragliding is a brand new form of sport flying, which offers perhaps the easiest and most fun way for almost anyone to realize the age-old dream of personal flight.

The basic skills are easy to learn. The equipment is simple, light in weight, and relatively inexpensive compared to any other type of aircraft. While more demanding physically than, say, flying an airplane, paragliding is considerably less strenuous than many other sports, including its close cousin the sport of hang gliding. In actuality, paragliding is a type of hang gliding, but the difference in the equipment used makes a big difference in the ease of learning and the level of physical effort required to practice the sport of paragliding. Like hang gliding, paragliding is free flight, unrestricted by any attachment to a tow or tether line.

Paragliding is not parasailing, which is being towed behind a boat under a vented circular parachute canopy. Paragliders, like hang gliders, can be launched by towing when foot launching from a hill or mountain is not convenient, but they do not depend on the tow line for their ability to fly. Likewise, paragliding is not skydiving — where flight is achieved by jumping out of an airplane and free fall is the primary goal — although the paraglider itself does resemble (in appearance, though not in design, construction, or capabilities) the high performance ram air skydiving parachute canopy from which it is descended. Finally, paragliding is not base jumping, which is a form of skydiving where the skydiver launches from a fixed-to-earth object such as a bridge, building or cliff.

Paragliding is not parasailing, which is being towed behind a boat under a vented circular parachute canopy.

The paraglider pilot launches by "inflating" the paraglider canopy over his head and then running down the slope of a hill, into the prevailing breeze, until the canopy lifts him away from the surface of the earth. Also like hang gliding, paragliding is unpowered flight, with none of the complications that otherwise arise from the use of an engine. In the smooth, calm air of early morning or evening, a paraglider pilot can, with a few easy steps, launch himself from any convenient hillside or mountaintop and glide smoothly and silently to a gentle landing hundreds or even thousands of feet below. And even if this were the only experience offered by the sport of paragliding, it would be well worth it for those of us who have dreamed throughout our lifetimes of imitating the simple, unencumbered flight of the birds.

But like hang gliding and sailplane flying, paragliding offers more. For in the more active air of midday, a paraglider pilot with more advanced skills and experience can launch into soaring conditions, where rising parcels of sun heated air can carry paraglider and pilot aloft, sometimes thousands of feet above the point of launch, and allow for sustained flights of up to several hours. At the right flying site in the right conditions, a pilot with the right skill and experience can even fly cross country, hopping from one thermal updraft to the next, and landing in some distant field miles downwind of his original takeoff spot.

One of the greatest appeals of paragliding is the elegant simplicity of the sport -- from the equipment required to the techniques involved. The paraglider wing itself is a mere 15 pounds of nylon cloth, fabricated into a series of ram air inflatable cells, to which is sewn an array of thin supporting lines which attach to the pilot's harness. The harness is a simple sling of webbing and fabric, fitted with buckles and special clips to secure the pilot in the harness and attach the harness to the canopy. A lightweight helmet and some other simple protective gear, and the pilot is ready to fly. The entire system will fit in a corner of the trunk of your car, or onto a backpack that you can take with you on a hike.

Of course few things are as simple as they first appear, and the design and construction of a paraglider is actually very subtle and very complex. The airworthiness of a paraglider, and hence the safety of the pilot, depend on every aspect of the design, construction and maintenance of the paraglider being exactly right. A small error in design or construction, or an improperly done repair, can easily render extremely dangerous what would otherwise be a safe aircraft. The pilot does, therefore, need to be aware of the complex nature of paraglider design, and the critical importance of proper maintenance. Also, while the beginning skills of paragliding are easy to learn and practice under an instructor's guidance, safe flying on one's own requires a broad range of more advanced skills, and a thorough knowledge of airmanship and weather as well as an accurate understanding of the unique operating limitations of a paraglider as a soaring aircraft. But all that properly taken into account, the paraglider as a finished product is, for the end user, a wonderfully simple and elegant piece of equipment for the achievement of such a lofty goal as personal flight, and paragliding remains probably the most accessible form of personal flight yet developed.

1

NOTES

Learning to paraglide can be fun for anyone with basic physical health and a desire to fly! — *Bo Criss photos*

Chapter Two:

KNOW YOUR ABC'S

GETTING FAMILIAR WITH YOUR EQUIPMENT

— Swing photo

Chapter 2 — KNOW YOUR ABC's

GETTING FAMILIAR WITH YOUR EQUIPMENT

You don't need to know all the details of the design and construction of your paraglider to learn how to fly it, but some level of familiarity with your equipment is essential.

The canopy itself is made of a lightweight cloth of woven polyester or nylon, and consists of a series of parallel cells, open at the front of the chord line (at the leading edge) to admit air and closed at the back. Some older paraglider models have vertical surfaces extending downward from each end of the canopy which are called stabilizers. The canopy is supported by a large number of high strength, small diameter lines, normally made of either Spectra or Kevlar. Internal V-shaped ribbing is used to distribute the loads and reduce the number of line attach points.

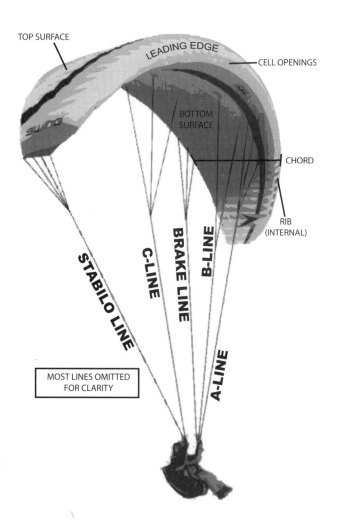

TOP SURFACE
LEADING EDGE
CELL OPENINGS
BOTTOM SURFACE
CHORD
RIB (INTERNAL)
STABILO LINE
C-LINE
BRAKE LINE
B-LINE
A-LINE

MOST LINES OMITTED FOR CLARITY

The lines that attach to the leading edge of the canopy are called the A-lines, while those attaching further back along the chord lines of the canopy are the "B", "C", and D-lines. The lines that attach to the trailing edge are the brake lines, and those that attach to the stabilizers are the stabilizer lines (often referred to as stabilo lines).

The lines cascade down from the canopy becoming fewer in number as two or three upper lines attach to each intermediate line and the intermediate lines may cascade again into a smaller number of lower lines. These lower lines then attach at their lower ends to webbing risers, which connect to the pilot's harness. The exact order of attachment of the lines to the risers depends on the specific canopy. In a general sense, the more forward lines attach to the more forward risers, and thus risers are commonly referred to as "A", "B", "C", and D-risers. Some earlier models may not have a D-riser set.

Note: In this manual we will refer to a four-riser system with a split A-riser. The term outer A-riser refers to the split half of the A-riser that connects to the outer A-lines. Additionally, the B and C risers are "floating" which means their attachment is not fixed at a specific length, but free to move along a looped length of webbing. See Chapter Three for more specific riser diagrams.

The lengths of the lines are extremely critical for the proper aerodynamic shape of the inflated canopy, and for the proper flight characteristics and proper recovery from unusual attitudes. The precise method for sewing the lines is important both for the accuracy of the finished length, and for the strength of the lines. You should never attempt to repair a line yourself, and in particular, you should never tie knots in a line, allow a line to be kinked, or walk on your lines.

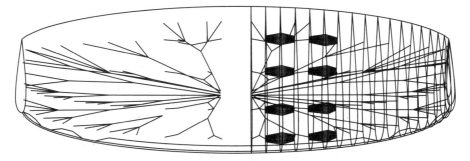

Overhead Computer Aided Design (CAD) graphic illustrates how the lines cascade and distribute loads to the canopy's external and internal structure. Inlets are at bottom. (Some details omitted on one side for clarity).

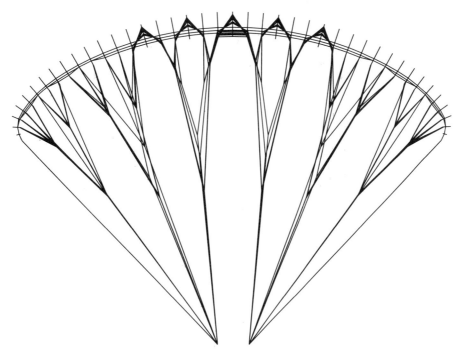

Forward view of line attachments and internal canopy structure — Courtesy of Airwave

2

The lines are attached to the risers with quicklinks which are typically triangular in shape. Each quicklink features a screw gate by which it is secured closed. The quicklink is much weaker with the screw gate open, and the canopy must never be flown with this gate unsecured. The gate itself must be tightened by hand, with no more than one last quarter turn using a wrench. The use of a wrench or pliers to overtighten the link can strip the threads and weaken the quicklink.

The canopy risers attach to the harness by clipping the carabiners to the short, wide webbing loops on either side of the harness. The carabiner gates should face inward, and the carabiners must be locked after attachment. The climbing-style manually locking carabiners of yesteryear have largely been replaced by paragliding-specific self-locking and quick unlocking carabiners.

Compared to harnesses of a decade ago, modern paraglider harnesses offer a significant improvement in safety, comfort, and controllability. Current designs allow for limited weight shift control, have easily adjustable webbing straps with quick release buckles, and include integral back protection. Because of German regulations, most paragliding harnesses manufactured or sold in Europe are certified to DHV standards. These standards include "GH-certified" harnesses which allow for some weight shift control and older "GX" harnesses which have diagonal cross straps to inhibit weight shift control. (Shifting your weight while steering the canopy maximizes your turn performance although at a slight loss of lateral stability.)

Essentially, all current paragliders are certified using GH harnesses and some specifically caution against using the older GX harnesses.

A looser chest strap increases the spacing between the riser attachments, increasing the glider's responsiveness to weight shift. With a wider spacing, turbulence may cause unintended weight shifting which will make a glider feel livelier. To ensure your glider responds as certified, you must ensure you fly with a compatible harness that has been adjusted within the limits used for the certification. If in doubt, consult your Owner's Manual, dealer, or manufacturer.

Your instructor will likely furnish you with a simple harness for your initial low altitude flight training. Training harnesses are normally tuned for maximum stability, do not include a reserve parachute or back protection, and are less encumbering and hence less awkward to run in.

The use of a proper helmet is essential to protect yourself from head injury in the event of a crash or very hard landing. It is recommended that you use a lightweight, but strong hard shell (lexan, fiberglass, or carbon fiber) helmet. The use of full-face helmets (with a lower guard to protect the jaw and face) has become popular in recent years. You will likely see some pilots that choose to fly with common bicycle or hockey helmets, mistakenly feeling they are suitable for dealing with the slow speeds of a paraglider. This is a fallacy. Additionally, unlike hang glider pilots that tend to crash in the prone position with forward momentum, paraglider pilots impact in a much more random manner. It is imperative to have a helmet that provides suitable protection in all quadrants.

A reserve parachute is strongly recommended whenever you are ready to begin making high flights.

The most common injury to paraglider pilots is ankle injury from a hard landing. You should wear boots which protect specifically against this type of injury. Less common but potentially more serious, are lower back and spinal compression injuries due to out of control impact with the terrain. Once you leave the training environment you should ensure your harness

2

is equipped with suitable energy-absorbing and penetration-resistant back protection.

A reserve parachute is strongly recommended whenever you are ready to begin making high flights.

Your instructor can help you with obtaining a proper helmet, boots, parachute and spinal protector.

Equipment Maintenance

The proper maintenance of your equipment is critical to maintaining its airworthiness. Paraglider fabric is specially coated to achieve zero porosity, increase durability and to provide some degree of ultraviolet light resistance. Regardless, the major cause of canopy deterioration is the wear and tear associated with UV exposure and due to impact or rubbing damages during inflation, deflation, and post-flight packing. Taking a few simple precautions can significantly extend the life of your canopy. Follow all maintenance recommendations as stated in the Owner's Manual for your canopy, harness and reserve parachute. (Wills Wing, for example, requires a factory inspection of the canopy every 50 hours or one year of use in order for the canopy to be considered airworthy.) In general, be sure to adhere to the following:

To prolong the life of your canopy you should minimize exposure to UV radiation when not flying.

- Do not expose your canopy to any more sunlight than is absolutely necessary for flying. Keep the paraglider in the bag until you are ready to fly and pack it up as soon as you can after flying. Consider investing in a UV-protective stuff sack or tarp for quickly covering your wing between flights.

- Do not expose your canopy to temperatures in excess of 120 degrees Fahrenheit. The temperature in a parked car with the windows rolled up will quickly reach more than 120 degrees on a warm, sunny day. Do not store your paraglider in your car, or in your trunk, or in the bed of a truck if it will be in the vicinity of the catalytic converter. Extreme temperatures can also degrade the rubber bands used for the proper deployment of your reserve parachute.

- Keep your paraglider dry. Paragliders are flight certified while dry and a wet glider may behave quite differently. If the canopy gets wet, dry it in the shade or indoors. Do not store it packed up wet since it may weaken the fibers and encourage mold and mildew which will degrade the fabric further. If your paraglider gets wet in the ocean, you must flush the salt water out of the paraglider thoroughly, including the insides of the cells, and then dry it thoroughly before packing it up. Crystallized salt may abrade and weaken your lines, and therefore the lines may need to be replaced if soaked in salt water. The canopy can feel dry to the touch while still retaining moisture inside the fibers. If in doubt, release the packing straps and open up the leading edge to allow air to circulate. If you have no choice but to pack up a wet glider then bundle it up loosely and allow it to air out within a few hours. Never allow a wet glider to freeze as this will damage the fabric fibers.

• Avoid washing your paraglider with any soap or detergent; it is normally best to only use water. If dirt gets ingrained in the fabric then a mild non-abrasive detergent may be used with a soft sponge. Never scrub the canopy with anything other than a soft sponge or cloth as you may damage the lightweight fabric and UV protective coating. Using chemicals or steam-cleaning techniques can completely ruin a glider.

• Do not make any attempt to repair the paraglider yourself. The sewing required on the canopy and the lines is both precise and critical. All repairs should be done by a qualified repair technician. An exception to this rule is small (1 inch or less) tears in the fabric that are not located on high-stress areas (seams or line attachment points) may be repaired with special self-adhesive rip-stop nylon sail repair tape. Contact your dealer or manufacturer for sail repair tape and never attempt a temporary fix using duct tape or similar products since the adhesive may permanently bond to the fabric necessitating a major repair. NEVER repair a line by tying a knot; this will greatly weaken the line. Do not walk on or kink the lines.

• To the maximum extent possible, avoid dragging the canopy along the ground and use caution during inflating and deflating to avoid impacting the canopy on the terrain with any more force than absolutely necessary.

• Do not pack up the canopy on a hard surface or any surface with objects that could cause puncture damage (rocks, sticks, thorns, etc.) In such cases it is best to gather the canopy and stuff it in your car for later packing on a grass lawn. If packing your glider on a rough hard surface is unavoidable, do not apply unnecessary pressure (such as kneeling on the fabric) during the packing.

2

• When storing your glider for extended periods, loosen the ties to reduce the stress on the fabric and to allow better air circulation.

Check Your Lines

The precise length of the canopy lines is critical for proper flight characteristics, and particularly for proper recovery characteristics from stalls and canopy collapses. Lines can stretch or shrink over time, which can drastically alter the flight characteristics of your canopy, especially with regard to recovery from stalls and collapses.

The line lengths should be checked by your dealer or the factory as part of regular maintenance inspections.

Never use a knot to tie a broken line together. It changes the line length appreciably and reduces the breaking strength significantly!

The condition of the canopy lines is also critical for safety. The lines and the sewing at the line terminations must be inspected for wear on a regular basis. Each line (except for some unsheathed lines on competition-level gliders) consists of an inner core and an outer sheath. The primary strength of the lines comes from the core, and the core can be damaged inside the sheath without any visible sign of damage on the outside. If you notice that one small section of a line feels much more flexible than the rest of the line, it is a sign that there has been damage to the core and the line must be replaced.

All of the cautions above with regard to you paraglider canopy also apply to your reserve parachute. In addition, your reserve parachute must be inspected every six months and re-packed at least once per year by a qualified person. It is especially important that the rubber bands which secure the line stows in the deployment bag be replaced during each six-month inspection otherwise there is a significantly increased probability that the parachute will not deploy successfully when you need it.

Canopy Airworthiness Certification

There are currently two major testing and certification programs for paragliders; the European Committee for Standardization (CEN) program, which evolved from independent French and Swiss certification programs and the German Hang Gliding Federation (DHV) program.

The testing standards of each organization are continuously evolving, and any written information about the specifics of these programs will almost immediately become outdated. However, the general principles and purposes of canopy testing and certification remain the same. The purpose of testing a canopy for certification is twofold; one is to determine if it meets minimum airworthiness criteria in terms of strength, flight characteristics and performance, and recovery from stalls and collapses. The second purpose is to determine for each model canopy that is deemed to be airworthy, what specific behavior can be expected of the canopy in different circumstances.

Traditionally, this had been expressed by assigning to each canopy a specific level at which the canopy is certified. The level was determined by how the canopy responds in various maneuvers and collapses, and by how much pilot input is required to correct a collapse. Originally, the DHV used a system of three levels, while ACPULS and SHV, the predecessors to AFNOR used two levels. CEN now uses a letter grade with "A" being the most forgiving and "D" being the most demanding (the "F" rating is a failure). The DHV still uses a three level system in which canopies are rated "1" (least demanding), 2 or 3 (expert piloting skills required). However, a canopy might be rated a 2-3, if it has some characteristics of level 2 and some of level 3.

Flight Testing

Flight testing involves a range of maneuvers, including inflation and launch, straight flight, full circle and "S" turns with reversals to the opposite direction, exploring the tendency of the canopy to enter "constant stall", collapsing the canopy by tucking the leading edge (both symmetrically and asymmetrically) and by completely depressing the brakes to cause a full stall, performing spins, and landing. There are specific requirements for the performance and behavior of the canopy in each maneuver in order for the canopy to qualify for certification. In both certification systems, the final glider rating is based on the compilation of the individual tests and the perceived required pilot skill level.

Generally, a canopy suitable for beginners should not take any special skills to fly safely, and it should recover from minor collapses (though not necessarily from well developed spins or full stalls) without the need for special actions on the part of the pilot. This is not as simple an issue as dividing canopies into "beginner" type and "advanced only" type. One canopy might be very resistant to wing collapses from

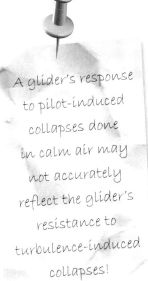

A glider's response to pilot-induced collapses done in calm air may not accurately reflect the glider's resistance to turbulence-induced collapses!

turbulence, but may have a more extreme behavior in a spin. Another may be more docile in or resistant to spins, but may have more of a tendency to collapse a tip in thermals. Currently, the certification standards predict recovery from abnormal flight conditions but they do not predict the tendency or proclivity of a glider to enter the abnormal flight condition.

Testing for Strength

As one example of strength testing, the normal DHV testing method for determining adequate strength of a canopy is to tow the canopy behind a truck (without a pilot). The lifting force of the canopy is measured, and the truck speed is increased until a force of eight times the (maximum) weight of the pilot is measured. The speed is held constant for five seconds, and if the canopy or lines do not fail, the canopy passes the test.

There is also a dynamic test, in which the canopy is inflated and loaded suddenly by accelerating the truck against a slack attachment cable. There is a weaklink calibrated for 6 times the maximum pilot weight in the connection, and if the weaklink breaks without causing a canopy or line failure, the canopy passes the test.

Keep in mind that canopy testing and certification is a young, and not completely exact, science. The minimum strength requirements offer a reasonable safety margin for normal soaring operation within the aircraft's recommended operating limitations, but they in no way preclude the possibility of in-flight structural failure in operation outside those limitations. (Standard type parachute canopies for sport parachuting, for example, are subjected to a shock load test of 5000 pounds, more than three times the shock load administered in paraglider certification.) Furthermore, the results of certification testing are valid only for those individual canopies actually tested, and may not apply to another canopy of the same model if it has been degraded by overexposure to ultraviolet light, or altered by lines stretching, or by an increase in porosity of the fabric over the lifetime of the canopy, or by an improper repair or modification.

Choosing The Right Glider For You

A canopy's response in recovering from various maneuvers during testing, which may be done in smooth air, will not necessarily predict its response in turbulence in a real flying situation. Also, canopy flight testing is somewhat subjective, as it relies to some degree on the impressions of the individual test pilot, and depends on exactly what control actions the pilot takes. Not all canopies with the same rating are exactly equivalent. Certification is a first requirement, but not the only criteria for choosing a canopy. In choosing a canopy you must do more than simply verify that it has been certified; you must take the responsibility to investigate the reputation that the canopy has acquired as a result of its service history in the field. You should fly a very stable, docile and forgiving canopy until you have the skills and the experience and judgment to handle a more challenging canopy. (See *Appendix One – USHPA Paraglider Pilot Rating System*). After that you may fly a more advanced canopy, though you should still choose one that has an established reputation for being well mannered in soaring conditions.

You should follow both your instructor's recommendation and the manufacturer's recommendation with regard to appropriate skill level when choosing a canopy. (That is, do not choose a canopy unless both your instructor and the manufacturer recommend it as appropriate for your skill level.) Also, choosing a canopy which is deemed suitable for a beginner does not mean that the pilot does not need to learn the skills for canopy management and recovery from collapses. Just because a canopy may recover eventually on its own does not mean the pilot will have the luxury of enough time or altitude to wait for it. There are many advanced canopies that are not suitable for beginners, and some older advanced designs which are not suitable for any but the most skilled pilots. In general, paraglider designs have evolved over the years in such a way that the newer designs provide more performance while also being less demanding to fly. Older canopies of the same performance level will often tend to be more subject to spontaneous collapse in turbulence, and less likely to recover on their own. Even the most modern canopies of higher performance are generally too demanding for beginners or even beginning intermediate pilots to fly safely. Small errors in pilot actions during a collapse or the recovery can quickly lead to more serious collapses, or to a spin. Everything happens more quickly on a more advanced canopy, and the pilot's actions must consistently be immediate and correct. Pilots tend to get their best overall performance on a glider they are comfortable flying to its full potential -- not on a twitchy supership they are wary of maneuvering in.

You will get your best overall performance on a glider that is best suitable for your skill, experience, and flying conditions.

2

NOTES

_____

_____

_____

_____

_____

_____

_____

_____

_____

_____

_____

_____

_____

_____

Chapter Three:
LET'S GO FLYING!

BEGINNING SKILLS FOR LAUNCHING, FLYING, & LANDING

— *Sven Eric-Monsen photo*

Light coastal winds blowing up a smooth grassy slope offer ideal novice flying conditions

Chapter 3 — LET'S GO FLYING!
BEGINNING SKILLS FOR LAUNCHING, FLYING, & LANDING

In this chapter we will cover the basic skills for laying out the canopy, pulling it up, ground handling (kiting), launching, flying (including airspeed control and directional control), and landing.

Playing the Harp – What Do Those Lines Do?

Initially you may find the myriad lines to be a confusing jumble of spaghetti. In short order, however, you will learn to quickly recognize which lines go to which risers and you will be able to quickly lay out the lines and risers in the proper order. Most modern canopies aid you in this task by color coding the groups of lines and risers.

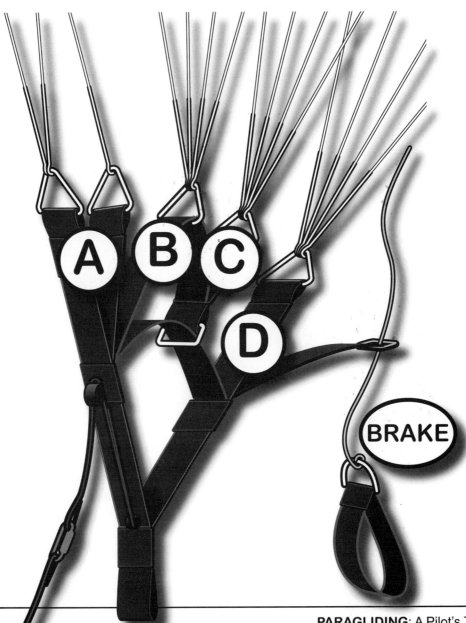

The effect of pulling on risers and lines is dependent upon whether the canopy is already flying overhead or if it is still low in the inflation process. It is also dependent upon how much you pull on a riser, an extreme pull can have the opposite effect of a small pull. As a general rule of thumb, pulling downwards on a riser will decrease lift and increase drag. The further aft the riser, the more the increase in drag, i.e. pulling on a D-riser will increase the drag more than pulling on a C-riser. Note that the brake lines attach to the rear risers but are not, themselves, a riser.

The A-Risers – Used To Lower the Angle of Attack

Kiting – When a canopy is deflated on the ground, it is not providing any lift and is aerodynamically stalled. Pulling on the A-risers will orient the inlets to the airflow, allowing the chambers to pressurize and lift to generate (either some natural wind or forward motion is required). When kiting a canopy, pulling on the A-risers will move the canopy further overhead. Once the wing is kited overhead, additional pulling will move the canopy further forward and start pulling down on the front of the airfoil. If the wing is allowed to travel too far forward, its angle of attack (the angle the air intersects the wing chord line) could lower to the point of losing the lift that keeps the wing overhead and it could fall, showering the pilot with lines. Or perhaps just a section of the wing will fall in an asymmetric collapse causing the wing to fall to the side.

In flight – Once the canopy is overhead, additional pulling will lower the angle of attack causing an increase in speed. This effect is best seen by use of an accelerator (speed stirrup). If you pull too far on the risers the angle of attack will drop below the value required for chamber inflation and the leading edge of the wing will collapse, destroying the airfoil shape. You can get a feel for this point by grasping the A-riser quicklinks and slowly pulling them downward. Initially, you will feel an increase in pressure. With additional pull you will reach the point where the force suddenly decreases. This is the critical point and any additional pulling will cause a collapse of the front of the airfoil (see the discussions on Front Collapse and Front Horseshoe in *Chapter Seven - Advanced Maneuvers*).

The B-Risers – Used For a Wings-Level Vertical Descent

The B-lines attach near the high point of the airfoil. Pulling on a B-riser decreases the camber and the lift of the airfoil. A slight pull will cause an increase in speed but not to the degree as caused by decreasing the angle of attack by pulling on the A-risers. Further pulling on the B-risers will cause the airfoil to bow downward, effectively destroying canopy lift and causing a "B-line stall".

Kiting – There is little reason to pull on the "B's" during kiting.

In flight – The B-line stall is an efficient technique for losing large amounts of altitude or escaping strong lift (see the discussion on B-line stalls in *Chapter Seven - Advanced Maneuvers*).

The C-Risers – Canopy Control During Inflation and Deflation

The C-lines attach just aft of the mid-chord of the wing. Pulling on them disturbs the aft section of the airfoil, causing a decrease in lift as well as an increase in drag.

Kiting – A quick tug on the C-risers during a moderate or high wind reverse inflation is very effective at stopping the rapid forward movement of the canopy while keeping you from getting inadvertently pulled off your feet. It also makes the airfoil more resistant to small differences in lift during the inflation, making it easier to keep the wings level.

In flight – There is little reason to pull on the C-risers in flight. Small pulls on an individual C-riser will cause a turn. Large symmetric pulls will cause a C-line stall, a technique not recommended during the course of normal or emergency flight.

The D-Risers – Emergency Turning Control

Kiting – You can use the D-risers to control a reverse inflation in a similar manner as you would use the C-risers although use of the D-risers increases the drag more and decreases lift less than use of the C-risers. You may find pulling on the D-risers an easy way to quickly collapse the canopy in light winds. In higher winds it is best to use the C-risers to collapse the canopy.

In flight – In the event you have a tangled brake line, the rear risers may be used for gentle maneuvering. Use caution to not pull excessively as this could cause an inadvertent spin entry.

The Brake Handles – For Turning and Pitch Control

Pulling on the lines to the aft of the canopy cause the trailing edge to deflect downward increasing the camber (curve of the wing) and angle of attack. This significantly increases the drag on that side (hence the name "brake" line) while slightly increasing lift. When pulled individually, the increased drag slows the respective side of the canopy and causes a turn in that direction.

Kiting – The brakes make a very effective kiting tool. They may be actuated individually (controlling direction of the wing), or in unison (which moves the wing into or with the wind by changing its angle of attack). Use the brakes individually to lower a wing or use both fully to drop the wing down to the ground in light winds. Because of the high drag caused by pulling both brake handles fully, in higher winds it is best to use the C-risers to collapse the canopy.

In flight – Pulling an individual brake handle will cause a slowing in the corresponding wing and a turn in that direction. Pulling both brake lines to 20-30% of travel (approximately shoulder level depending upon the model of paraglider) will slow the canopy to minimum sink speed. In turbulent conditions "active" piloting technique uses the pressure felt in the brake lines to continuously fine-tune the amount of brake application to keep the wing stable overhead (see *Chapter Seven – Advanced Maneuvers*, Active Piloting section).

3

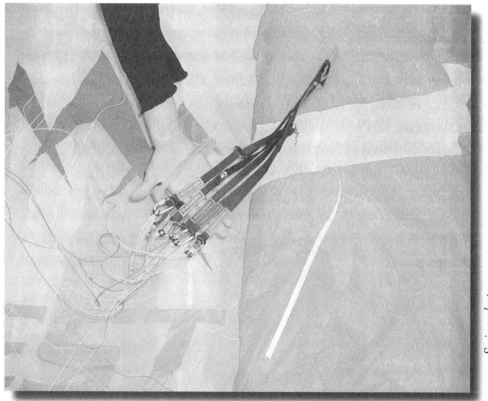

—*Swing photo*

The Speed Stirrup – For Better Penetration

Most paragliders include the provisions for attaching an accelerator (often called speed bar or speed stirrup) to the risers. The pilot places his feet in the stirrup and by extending his legs can increase the glider's speed above the "brakes off" trim condition. A pulley arrangement causes a shortening of the A-risers to reduce angle of attack and, to a lesser extent, a shortening of the "B" (and possibly "C") risers to reduce airfoil camber. The resulting increased speed is useful for maximizing your glide over the ground when flying through headwinds or sinking air.

The speed stirrup is not normally installed for flights on a novice training hill. It should, however, be installed for all flights in moderate or stronger winds or over mountainous terrain. The speed stirrup should be adjusted so that you can get full travel of the risers with full leg extension. Also ensure that there is no tension on the risers when the stirrup is not engaged (either left hanging or stowed for later use). Additional information on precautions and use of the speed stirrup is contained in *Chapter Seven – Advanced Flying Techniques.*

> ### QUIZ:
>
> A speed stirrup increases flying speed by
>
> ☐ increasing
>
> ☐ decreasing
>
> wing camber and angle of attack.

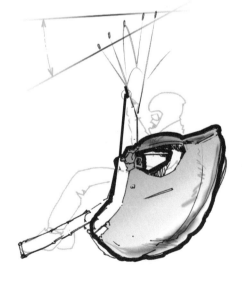

Unaccelerated   *Accelerated*

The accelerator system (speed stirrup) increases glider speed by decreasing angle-of-attack and wing camber

Right Stuff Begins With the Right Site

Learning to fly a paraglider safely begins with the proper training hill. An ideal training hill faces the prevailing wind, is free of obstructions, is tall enough to allow for short flights with gentle turns, is wide enough so the wind is deflected up instead of around it, and it has a large enough landing area so that no turns are required from takeoff to landing.

Santa Barbara's Elings Park training hill

Smooth Norwegian tundra

Note – if you leave your risers connected to the harness or fix the risers during the packup in order to ensure they cannot be twisted or inadvertently looped through a line then it may be appropriate to only shake out the A-riser lines and the brake lines. If these two line groups shake free easily without twists then you can be reasonably assured the remaining lines will shake free during the inflation.

Preflight Checks
— Layout, Inflating, Ground Handling, and Deflating

All paraglider launches require these elements:

- A proper layout of the canopy.

- A proper inflation of the canopy and a visual inspection of the inflated canopy.

- An increase in the canopy's speed of motion through the air sufficient to provide the minimum flying speed necessary.

- Proper control of the canopy from inflation through launch.

If it is your first launch of the day, the following elements will also be added:

- A preflight of the canopy during layout.

- Putting on your harness, helmet and other gear.

- Attaching your harness to the canopy and preflighting the attachment.

Inflating the canopy is accomplished by putting a greater degree of tension on the A-lines than on the other lines. This serves to raise the leading edge into the airflow, fill the cells with air and bring the wing up off the ground and overhead.

If the A-lines are tensioned too much (or for too long) relative to the other lines during the inflation the leading edge of the canopy will collapse and the canopy will deflate. If not enough tension is put on the A-lines the canopy will not rise and fly overhead. The strength and duration of pull that is required to be applied to the A-lines will vary from one model of canopy to another. Some canopies come up very quickly with just slight tension on the A-lines, and may fly overhead past the pilot into a front collapse if tension on the A-risers is not released soon enough. Other canopies require a longer and harder pull on the A-risers to get the canopy fully overhead.

Your first flights will be from a gradual slope, in light winds (6 mph or less). Your instructor will probably make the decision to teach you either a reverse or forward inflation depending upon the strength of the winds. The sequence of steps, from unpacking the canopy to take-off, is described below.

Canopy Layout and Preflight In Calm or Light Winds

1. After removing it from the bag, fully spread the canopy on the ground, with the bottom surface of the canopy facing up and the leading edge behind (relative to the intended direction of launch) the trailing edge. The stabilizers (if so equipped) should be folded over on top of the ends of the canopy, all lines should be visible, and no line should be under any part of the canopy. Check the canopy as you lay it out for any tears or loose or broken stitching. Note: complete, detailed and thorough inspection of every seam and every line in the canopy is not practical on every flight. However, such an inspection should be done on a regular basis. See the PERIODIC MAINTENANCE section of your Owner's Manual for more information.

2. Next bow the canopy into a gentle horseshoe shape, drawing the center of the canopy at the leading edge up the slope or away from your intended launch direction. This is to insure that the center cells will fill first on launch and that the canopy will be most likely to come up square to the wind and to your intended direction of launch.

3. Preflight your harness, checking for any frayed webbing or broken stitches. Check your reserve parachute if so equipped. Put on your helmet. Put on your harness, properly adjusting the leg, chest and shoulder straps.

4. It is flight-critical that the lines and risers be free of twists, tangles, knots, and any debris. Failure to do so can result in anything ranging from simple embarrassment, to a botched inflation, to launching with an unsafe glider. Inspect each riser group starting with the A-risers by holding them clear of the other risers and shake the other lines clear. Work your way through each riser paying particular attention to the "A" and brake lines. Check that each of the quicklinks is secured.

Never use a wrench or other tool to close the quicklink screw gate, because to do so could strip the threads and weaken the link. The link should be closed and tightened by hand, and then tightened no more than 1/4 additional turn with a wrench.

Note—if you discover your risers to be twisted and jumbled, it works best to untangle them by working backward from the canopy to the risers and untangling the A-lines first

3

Forward or Reverse – Choosing the Right Inflation Method

You will learn to inflate your glider while facing forward down the hill with the canopy stretched behind you (forward inflation) as well as the more common reverse inflation in which you face the canopy prior to and during the inflation. Forward inflations are normally performed in calm air (without any threat of the wind blowing the unweighted canopy around) so you have the option of hooking the risers to your harness prior to putting on the harness. For reverse inflations it is best to actually hook-in while facing the canopy in the reverse position. Hooking in while facing the canopy gives you better awareness and a quicker reaction to sudden gusts that might lift the wing.

Historically, forward inflations were used in calm and light wind conditions and reverse inflations were reserved for stronger winds. This has evolved in recent years to reverse inflations being the method of choice with forward inflations saved for those conditions in which a reverse inflation and launch is not practical. Before choosing which inflation method to use you should give consideration to the strength and direction of the wind, the condition of the terrain (slope, footing, obstructions, and launch room), the ability to inspect the canopy prior to launch, and the ability to turn around and face the direction of flight prior to launching. We will categorize wind speed as calm (0-2 mph), light (3-6 mph), moderate (7-12 mph) and high (above 12 mph).

The advantages of a forward inflation are that it is easy to learn, you can see where you are going during the inflation process, and it is easier to quickly get the canopy overhead in absolutely calm conditions on shallow slopes. The disadvantages are you cannot see the canopy until it is up overhead so your must judge the success of the inflation, and any required corrections, by sensing the tension on the risers. Also, if the winds are of moderate or stronger strength, it may be difficult to control the canopy prior to and during the inflation.

An advantage of a reverse inflation is that it puts you in a position to observe the canopy directly as it comes up and to respond as appropriate. In higher winds you have the additional advantages of being in a better position to brace against the pull of the canopy or to run towards the canopy if necessary to moderate the canopy's pull against you. If conditions are smooth, and there is no possibility of being pulled unexpectedly into the air by a gust or sudden thermal, you can kite the canopy while reversed and inspect it easily at your leisure. The disadvantages of a reverse inflation

The proper techniques for canopy layout, inflation and launch depend on how strong and gusty the wind is and the slope of the hill.

are it is initially more complicated to learn, it is difficult to perform if you do not have sure footing, and it is more difficult than a forward inflation in calm conditions on very shallow slopes.

The bottom line is you should strive to be proficient with reverse inflations in myriad conditions and save the forward inflation for conditions in which a reverse inflation may be too difficult. Examples include very shallow slopes where it would be difficult to achieve sufficient speed with enough loading on the canopy to stay inflated during the turn around or on steeper slopes where it would be difficult to maintain your footing during the inflation or spin around due to rocky terrain or snow-slick surfaces.

Beaches offer smooth air and large soft areas ideal for kiting practice

Ground Handling (Kiting) Philosophy

When the winds are blowing strong enough to inflate the glider without forward movement, you can practice kiting. Kiting is a great way to practice canopy inflation, control, and deflation and is a mandatory skill for the advancing pilot. Like all forms of aviation, most paragliding accidents occur during launch and landing. A safe paraglider pilot must be comfortable inflating, launching, and collapsing the canopy in the conditions he wants to fly in. Nothing better prepares you for handling a variety of conditions than kiting practice on varying slopes and in varying winds. You should practice kiting not just in the reverse position but also in the forward position after turning around from a reverse inflation.

Forward Inflation

Tip:
If the winds are calm take the time to layout the canopy and lines carefully the first time!

Layout the canopy, sort the risers and shake the lines free as previously described. Standing in the center of the canopy, and facing in your intended direction of flight, attach the canopy risers to your harness with the carabiners, taking care that the risers are not twisted and properly oriented so that the A-risers will be to the front. Although you will not launch this way, it is usually easiest to hook the risers to the carabiners if you route them under your arms. If you do not have self-locking carabiners then check that the carabiner gates face inward, and that the carabiner gates are locked.

If you are using a speed stirrup, you would fasten it at this time, ensuring the lines are routed directly through the pulleys, so as not to interfere with any other harness straps, and the stirrup is secured (without inadvertently tensioning the stirrup lines) so it will not interfere with your legs during the launch process.

For a forward inflation, follow these steps:

- Use the following technique to avoid launching with a brake line twisted around a riser. Using one hand, reach across your body and hold the opposite riser group away from you without twists. With the correct hand (right hand for right brake), follow the rear riser from the carabiner, detach the brake line handle from its clip or snap which holds it to the rear risers and grasp it securely. Repeat with the other hand and brake handle.

- Lay all of the risers over your forearms as shown and then grasp the front or A-risers in your hands, just below the quicklink. If your risers have split A-risers ensure you have a hold of both A-risers on each side.

- Spread your arms straight out to the sides, and slightly down and slightly back. (To make sure you are centered in the canopy, walk forward slowly holding the front risers in this position until the A-lines just start to go snug, and center yourself until they are equally tensioned on each side. Be careful not to pull the canopy leading edge over onto the rest of the canopy when you do this.

- Before commencing the launch run, check your leg straps (connected and adjusted), your carabiners (closed and locked), your chest strap (secured and properly adjusted), and your brake lines (free to run through the guide or pulley without any wrap or half hitch and without being wrapped around any lines or risers).

- In very light winds, or if there is no wind at all, you will want to take a step back towards the canopy. There is no need to back up several steps for more of a running start because the sudden aerodynamic drag of the canopy during the initial inflation will slow your momentum and make the timing more difficult. Additionally, you are much more likely to cause damage to a line or your canopy if any part of the wing is snagged on a rock or bush. If there is more than 3 or 4 mph of wind, you can start with the lines fully extended, and just push forward firmly and smoothly into your run.

As the lines are tensioned and the canopy begins to rise up, it is important to get a feel for where the wing is as it rises. The pressure of the "B", "C" and D-risers against your arms will tell you how high the canopy is, whether it is centered or off to one side, and how fast it is rising. During this initial pull up of the canopy, at the point where the canopy first clears the ground and is fully inflated, it will exert a strong backward pull on you. It is important in this phase to keep your body leaning forward against the pressure and to shorten and moderate your steps so as to maintain

your balance. As the canopy rises further, allow your arms to come up with it, and as the canopy comes overhead, release the front risers, keep moving forward and be prepared to apply the brakes as necessary to keep the canopy from flying forward in front of you. Flex your knees to keep your body weight loaded on the canopy and maintain your forward motion to keep the canopy inflated and flying.

One of the most important points to learn is the proper forward lean. The canopy has a large amount of aerodynamic drag as it leaves the ground and you must power through this point as it climbs to a lower drag position overhead. Your body position during the run should appear similar to if you were hitting a football blocking sled (bent forward at the waist, leading with you shoulders, and driving with quick powerful steps). The force you are applying to the risers should come from your chest and shoulder straps and not from your arms.

LOOK UP!   At this point you must quickly ascertain, by an appropriate combination of visual inspection and feel, that the canopy is fully inflated, and is symmetrical and square into the wind above you, that all lines are free, and that the brake lines are functional.

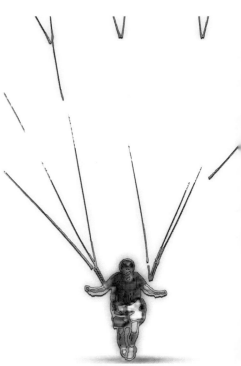

Common Problems and Corrections During a Forward Inflation

The first step to a consistent inflation is to ensure the canopy is laid out square to the wind, in the proper horseshoe configuration and without any line tangles. If the canopy is stalled and languishing low behind you in the high drag position then you are either not providing enough thrust (lean forward and run with powerful steps) or you are slowing the canopy with unnecessary brake input. Remember you cannot use a brake application to correct for a low wing until the wing is raised nearly overhead.

The toughest corrections are in calm winds on shallow slopes. In such situations the canopy is barely loaded and anything that causes loss of thrust or increased drag (such as stepping towards a low wing or applying brake) may be enough to cause the canopy to drop further back and collapse. In such situations you need to run as aggressively as possible and strive for equal riser pressure (felt by the pressure of the risers against your arms).

If the tips come up faster then the center, then the canopy was likely not in enough of a horseshoe. Ensure the A-lines to the center of the canopy pull tight prior to those running towards the wing tips. If it still occurs with a proper horseshoe layout then you may consider folding the outer few feet of each wing tip over on itself.

On steeper slopes the canopy may try to overrun you so keep tension in the A-risers with a good forward leaning run and apply brakes as required to keep the canopy overhead.

Frontal tucks during launch are normally caused by a launch hesitation or failure to stop the canopy overhead. Keep moving forward with a good lean and use brakes as required.

Switching Forward to Reverse (and vice versa)

Perhaps you hooked in facing reverse and decide to do a forward inflation (or perhaps you hooked in facing forward and decide a reverse launch would be more prudent). Whatever the reason, you need to rotate 180° while hooked in. If going from a forward to reverse position you should rotate in the direction opposite that you want to subsequently rotate for launch. Grasp the risers on the side opposite to the direction you will be rotating toward and, using both hands with a wide grip, lift the risers up overhead and rotate beneath them using caution to keep the lines clear of snagging on your helmet or harness. If going from reverse to forward then your risers will be crossed. Lift the risers that are crossed on top and rotate in that direction.

A Note About Canopy Stability on the Ground Versus in the Air

Whenever both you and the canopy are flying in the air, you form a stable pendulum system. If a gust of wind pushes the canopy away from its normal position directly over your head, you will naturally swing back under the canopy and the normal situation will be automatically restored.

When you are on the ground and the canopy is up overhead, you and the canopy form an unstable pendulum system. If the canopy gets off to one side, for example, during your launch run it will then try to fly farther to that side. The proper corrective action is for you to use opposite brake to steer the canopy back over your head. Realize, however, that you will probably have an unconscious tendency to also pull with your body, by running in the direction that you want the canopy to go. This simply will not work. The farther out from under the canopy you get, the harder the canopy will try to fly in the other direction. The complete corrective action in this case is therefore to steer with opposite brake while running towards (under) the canopy.

Your instructor will probably want you to eventually learn to control the canopy completely with the brakes and body lean, without a lot of running sideways back and forth. The reason for this is that as you advance in your flying, you will be launching at sites where your ability to run sideways may be severely restricted, perhaps by the presence of brush or rocks, or by a drop off in the terrain. When you are first learning, however, a few quick lateral steps to get back underneath the canopy can be very helpful in making more of your launch attempts successful.

Note one other thing. Steering with brakes doesn't work when the canopy is behind you rather than above you, because any application of brakes makes the canopy fall back farther. Therefore, if the canopy gets off to one side during the initial part of your pull up, your only option to correct it may be a quick lateral movement. It is important to develop a feel for where the canopy is, by how it is pulling against your harness, and how the risers are pulling against your arms as the canopy comes up, so that you can correct problems like this without being able to see them. Also, remember that when steering the canopy with brakes you must release the brake after pulling it down. If you have the right brake pulled down and want to steer left, let up on the right brake as you pull down on the left. Many student pilots, when using the brakes to steer the canopy, will pull down one brake, then pull down the other, then pull the first one again, never letting either brake up, and as a result end up only collapsing the canopy behind them. On the ground, this is merely frustrating. In the air, it means a complete stall and collapse of the canopy, which is very dangerous.

And finally, note that if the canopy is providing good lift (moderate winds or stronger) then the principle of moving yourself under the canopy works as well in the front to rear direction as it does side to side.

Reverse Inflation

In winds greater than 5 mph on a slope or 7 mph on flatland, the wind is strong enough to fly the canopy while standing still (at zero ground speed), and a reverse inflation is recommended. A reverse inflation is also recommended in lighter winds on slopes that provide for sure footing and have adequate room for the inflation, turn around, and launch.

Anytime the wind is blowing, you should put on your helmet before you do anything else. This will insure that you never find yourself hooked into a canopy in windy conditions without your helmet on.

QUIZ:

When airborne, the paraglider and pilot form a pendulum that is:

☐ stable

☐ unstable

QUIZ:

While still on the ground, the paraglider and pilot form a pendulum that is:

☐ stable

☐ unstable

3

There have been a lot of different techniques developed for reverse inflation over the years, but we are going to recommend and explain three techniques, two for calm or light winds and one for stronger winds. The key to each of these techniques is that the pilot starts with the correct brake handles in the correct hands, and therefore does not have to let go of the brakes and grab them again when turning to face forward. The variations on the technique involve how the pilot holds the risers during layout and initial inflation. Initially, you may find it best to learn a single technique for calm or light winds but once you are comfortable with it you should then learn the other variations.

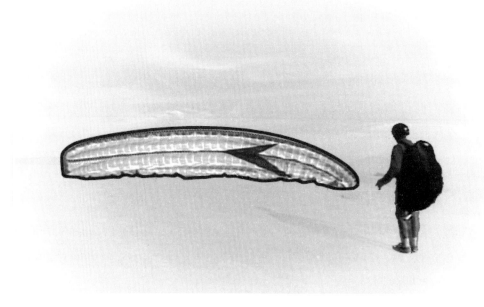

If the winds are more than a few mph you can use them to "build a wall" to ensure the canopy is square to the wind and the lines are free of tangles prior to the launch inflation

Calm or Light Winds (less than 7 mph) - Canopy Layout and Reverse Inflation

Layout the canopy, sort the risers and shake the lines free as previously described. Before you hook up the risers you must decide which direction you are going to turn to face downhill after the inflation. One point to consider is many pilots mount their reserve parachutes on the side of their harness. A right-handed pilot should have the reserve installed on his right side and a left-handed pilot vice versa. A good rule of thumb is to spin around in the opposite direction of your side-mounted reserve. The reason for this is if you ever graduate to tandem flying, you will not want to brush your deployment handle against your passenger when you turn around to launch (and risk accidentally deploying your reserve). So if you are right-handed then you should turn around from a reverse inflation by turning to your left to face downhill.

Using the right-handed pilot as the example, grasp the risers that go to the right wing (which is facing you on your left) and holding them parallel to the ground in front of you, turn them ½ revolution to the left (counter-clockwise when viewed from the end of the riser). Now, hook them into your right carabiner. Next, take the risers to the left wing, turn them ½ revolution to the left and, placing them over the right risers, hook them into your left carabiner. Left-handed pilots would do the exact opposite, risers twisted ½ turn to the right with the right riser crossed over the left riser.

Note that regardless of which hand you use or which direction you will turn, the right riser will always attach to the right carabiner and the left riser to the left! Double check that the risers are hooked in with the A-risers facing away and the brake lines toward you. If you do not have self-locking carabiners then check that the carabiner gates face inward, and that the carabiner gates are locked.

If you are using a speed stirrup, you would fasten it at this time, ensuring the lines are routed directly through the pulleys, so as not to interfere with any other harness straps, and the stirrup is secured (without inadvertently tensioning the stirrup lines) so it will not interfere with your legs during the launch process.

When performing a reverse inflation it is very important that your body is aligned square to the canopy, especially on higher aspect ratio canopies. Otherwise it will be difficult to pull the canopy up squarely and evenly.

Once the canopy is nicely laid out, you can transfer your hands to the proper position for the inflation. There are two variations for holding the risers you can use at this point. The following assumes you are a right-handed pilot and will be turning to your left to face forward. If you are a left-handed pilot and/or will be spinning to your right then the hand positions as well as which riser crosses over the other riser should be reversed.

While you are learning to inflate and kite the glider you will get better results if you first mentally review how you plan to control the canopy *before* you pull the glider up.

For many years flight schools emphasized keeping your torso square to the canopy and controlling the glider by the use of brakes and lateral steps as required. Schools located at sites where ground handling is emphasized (such as Point of the Mountain, Utah and Torrey Pines, California) now teach their students to control the canopy by applying differential pressure to the risers through the use of body lean and torso twist to pull down on the rising wing. Such differential riser control is very effective for canopy control without the added drag caused by excessive brake use, making forward penetration into moderate and stronger winds significantly easier.

If the canopy is banking to its left (right wing rising) then twist your body to pull down on the right riser. If you are facing forward into the wind then this would be a twist to the left, using your right bicep to apply pressure on the right riser. If you are doing a reverse inflation then correct for the rising right wing (which is on your left) by twisting to your right away from the rising wing.

First Variation — Parallel Arms

This variation is normally the easiest to initially learn. You make the initial pull for inflation with your arms parallel and straight out in front of your shoulders, with each hand holding the opposite A-riser (left hand grasping the right A-riser that is naturally in front of it). Once you pull the wing up and it approaches overhead, you release the A-risers and use the respective brake handles for control.

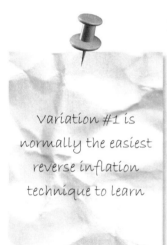

Variation #1 is normally the easiest reverse inflation technique to learn

The disadvantage of this technique is it is difficult to make an immediate correction for a low wing (you cannot pull the A-risers of the low wing while pulling the brake handle of the high wing with the same hand). This is usually not that significant unless you are inflating in a tight spot with a crosswind (then the second variation may work better for you).

1. As you face the canopy, the right wing risers will extend from the right side of your harness out to your left, crossing under the left wing risers which will extend from the left side of your harness out to your right.

2. Use the following technique to avoid launching with a brake line twisted around a riser. Using your left hand, hold the right riser group away from you without twists. With your right hand follow the rear riser from the carabiner, detach the brake line handle from its retaining clip or snap, and grasp it securely. While holding the right brake handle, repeat the process by reaching over the left risers, and grasping and detaching the left brake handle with your left hand.

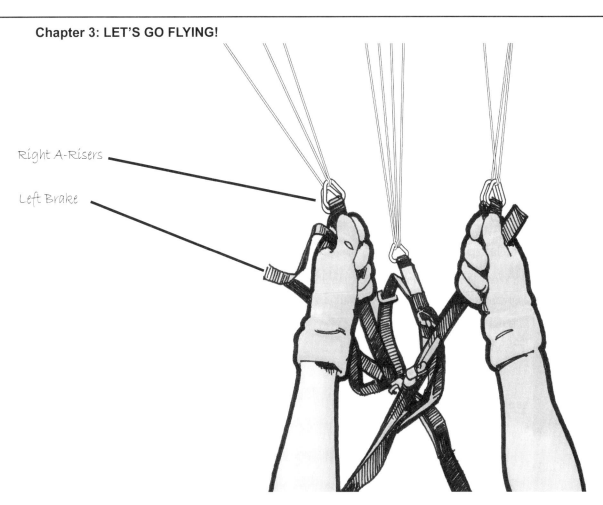

Right A-Risers

Left Brake

REVERSE INFLATION VARIATION #1

3. With your left hand grasp the right wing A-risers just below the quicklinks .

4. With your right hand grasp the left wing A-risers just below the quicklinks in your right hand.

5. Face the canopy squarely and back up until the A-lines are tight.

6. With straight arms, lean back and pull evenly on the A-risers to inflate the canopy and bring it off the ground.

7. As the canopy comes up, release the A-risers and be prepared to use brakes to stop the canopy from flying overhead.

8. If the canopy starts to move off center, step laterally towards the low side while pulling the brake handle that is in your hand on that same side. (For example, if the canopy moves towards your right - canopy's left - you will need to step towards your right and apply brake on the canopy's right side - the handle for which is in your right hand. Twist your torso to the right to help pull down the rising wing.)

Variation #2 (crossed-hand technique) works well in light crosswinds

3

Second Variation — Crossed-Hand Technique

In this variation, you inflate with the right wing risers in your right hand, and vice versa. The advantage is that you can release one riser before the other if you need to apply corrective brake for directional control before the canopy is high enough to release both A-risers (this can be especially advantageous when inflating in a tight spot in a crosswind). The disadvantage is you start the inflation with your arms crossed, which can be more difficult to learn.

1. Disconnect the brake lines from the riser snaps as described in the previous section.

2. Keeping your right hand under the risers, reach all the way under and to the left to grasp the right wing A-risers just below the quicklinks in your right hand.

3. With your left hand over the risers, reach to the right and grasp the left wing A-risers just below the quicklinks.

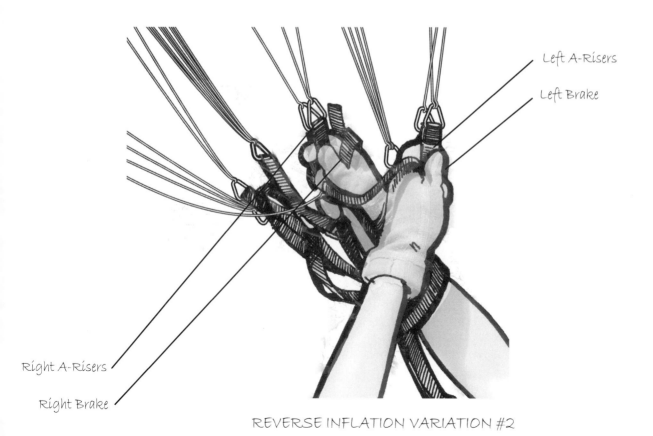

REVERSE INFLATION VARIATION #2

4. Put your hands together at the wrists, facing each other and with your left hand on top.

5. Face the canopy squarely and back up until the A-lines are tight.

6. Lean back and pull evenly on the A-risers to inflate the canopy and bring it off the ground.

7. As the canopy comes up, release the A-risers and be prepared to use brakes to stop the canopy from flying overhead.

8. If the canopy starts to move off center, step laterally towards the low side while pulling the brake handle that is in your hand on that same side. (For example, if the canopy moves towards your right - canopy's left - you will need to step towards your right and apply brake on the canopy's right side - the handle for which is in your right hand. Twist your torso to the right to help pull down the rising wing.)

Common Problems and Corrections During a Calm or Light Wind Reverse Inflation

The first step to a consistent inflation is to ensure the canopy is laid out square to the wind, in the proper horseshoe configuration and with the lines on top of the canopy without any tangles or snags. If the canopy stalls and languishes down low in the high drag position then you are either not providing enough thrust (walk quickly backwards as appropriate) or you are slowing the canopy with unnecessary brake input. Remember you cannot use a brake application to correct for a low wing until the wing is raised nearly overhead. You may, however, increase your pull on the A-riser of the low wing.

If the canopy does not come up square then ensure your hips are square to it so the A-risers pull symmetrically (unless you are consciously making a correction). One common mistake during a reverse inflation is to twist your hips the wrong way.

If the tips come up faster than the center then the canopy is typically not in enough of a horseshoe. Ensure the A-lines to the center of the canopy pull tight prior to those running towards the wing tips. If it still occurs with a proper horseshoe layout then you may consider folding the outer few feet of each wing tip over on itself or using only the inner A-risers for the inflation.

Ground Handling (Kiting) In Calm or Light Winds

Steady kiting of the canopy requires greater than 5 mph of wind so if nature is not providing it you must make up the difference by forward movement of the canopy into the wind. This means that initially you will continue walking backwards as quickly as required to keep the canopy overhead. Continuous backwards walking is difficult and you should practice turning around to face the intended launch direction as soon as the canopy is overhead. Keeping the canopy inflated in such conditions requires a continuous tow force on the canopy during your turn around and is greatly aided if you are moving downhill on a slope because your weight will help keep the canopy loaded and inflated. A small and smooth brake application is normally required to keep the canopy inflated during the turn around to the forward kiting position.

After you spin around you must lean forward and continue moving into the wind with quick thrusting steps while using your shoulders to provide a smooth, continuous pull force on the risers. The canopy should be square overhead and you should use the brakes to keep it there. Too little brake pressure and the canopy will start to depressurize* and you will feel the decrease in the lift and pull on the risers. Too much brake pressure and the canopy will drop behind you and you will feel the increase in drag. If the canopy starts to fall off to one side you will feel a decrease in riser pressure on the side of the lower wing (be cognizant of the force the risers are putting on your biceps). Use a small amount of brake on the higher wing while twisting your body towards the lower wing so your bicep can pull down on the riser of the rising wing while running aggressively. Note — if the canopy drops too far back then the proper correction changes from trying to pull a wing DOWN to trying to pull the other wing UP. So the proper correction would be to pull the lower wing's A-riser forward (into the wind) which you would do by applying forward pressure with that bicep. It sounds very complicated but thankfully, with a few hours of practice is easier done than said!

*It is common for pilots to talk about "pressurizing" the wing, though this is not technically the best way to describe what is happening. Because a paraglider wing has no rigid supporting structure, it assumes the shape of a wing and airfoil only under the influence of a certain minimum positive angle of attack and airflow (airspeed). What pilots experience as, and talk about as "pressurization", is nothing more than the combined affects on the wing of airspeed and angle of attack. If the rate of airflow or angle of attack drops below the minimum required, the canopy will not experience high enough aerodynamic forces to maintain its proper shape. If you think of it in these terms, rather than in terms of pressurization, it will be easier to see the connection between what you do (drive the wing forward for airspeed, pull the brakes down to increase angle of attack), and the result (keeping the wing "inflated" and in its proper shape).

In light winds deflate the canopy behind you by smoothly pulling the brake handles fully while continuing your forward run until the canopy comes down. You can collapse the canopy more quickly if you reach up, grab the most rearward risers and pull them down fully. Lastly, if there is any wind at all, you may want to get in the practice of spinning back around to face the canopy prior to deflating it. It is a good practice to spin back around to deflate the canopy in the opposite direction (right spin if right-handed) that you turn around to launch in. That way the risers will be in the proper configuration for a subsequent inflation.

In winds above 5 mph you can kite the canopy while standing still. You should always have your brake handles in the respective hands prior to inflating for flight, however, it is perfectly acceptable to practice kiting with the brake handles still in their retaining clips. Remember you do not have to pull on a brake handle to pull a brake line, you can simply reach up and pull the rear risers or the brake line itself. If one side of the canopy is starting to drop then pull on the A-riser to that side, if one wing is getting too high then pull on that rear riser or brake line. Learn to intuitively control the glider by using both hands to reach over, around, and behind lines and risers as appropriate. Experiment with pulling alternative lines and risers to control the wing. Doing so will get you more in tune with your glider and make you a more precise and safer pilot.

Perhaps you had an unsuccessful inflation or perhaps a small gust moved a wing tip, regardless the cause, your canopy is no longer laid out in a beautiful horseshoe so now what to do? If the winds are less than 5 mph then you will have to physically reposition the canopy prior to the next inflation. If you have an instructor or assistant then they can unfold a wing tip or pull the center section back up the hill to reform the horseshoe. If you do not have the luxury of a helper then you need to be able to do it yourself. You can always unhook from your harness, reposition the canopy, and hook back in but you can reposition it while remaining hooked in by walking to the offending wing tip. Lift up the lines and risers as you walk around them to the tip. If you find the lines to the opposite wing tip pulling tight then you did not have enough of a horseshoe. Ignore it for the time being, fix the tip you are at and then go back down and around and fix the other tip. To keep from inadvertently getting a riser twist you should avoid walking around the wing tip towards the top of the canopy. You may have to do just that, however, if the canopy needs to be repositioned up the hill a few feet. To avoid twisting the risers when you walk around the tip keep your body oriented so that it always faces the canopy. Pull the center section uphill as required and then retrace your steps back to the front (do not walk completely around the canopy or you will twist the risers).

One trick you may find useful in light winds is kiting the canopy by holding both A-risers in one hand and both D-risers in the other. By applying light pressure on both risers you can increase the camber of the wing without significantly affecting the drag and will be able to kite the canopy in about one or two mph less wind than normal. This is a useful trick for kiting the glider back up the training hill while others are forced to ball it up and carry it on their back. You can make lateral corrections without releasing the risers, simply move your A-riser hand laterally towards the rising wing and your D-riser hand laterally away it. (In light winds it works best to pull up the A-riser of the low wing and pull down the D-riser of the high wing.)

If you need to reposition the canopy a short distance and do not have sufficient wind to kite it then, using both hands, lift one riser and turn in the opposite direction to face the canopy (if you are not already facing it). Grasp the tops of the risers and hold the lines with one hand. With your free hand encircling the lines, slide it towards the canopy until you reach full extension. Grasp the lines and pull them back to your other hand, making a coil. Continue this process until you reach the canopy. It should now be gathered into a tight rosette which you can heave over your shoulder. If you need to reposition back up to the top of a training hill then it can be less time consuming (as well as significantly less taxing) if you repack the canopy into a back pack. Large UV-resistant stuff sacks complete with shoulder straps are available just for this purpose.

Moderate Winds (7-12 mph)- Canopy Layout and Inflation (Variation #3)

As the winds increase in strength and/or the launch slope becomes steeper, the possibility increases for either getting dragged downwind during the inflation or pulled off your feet prematurely – either event being potentially dangerous. The canopy can best be controlled in these situations by using a launch technique that begins with the correct brake lines in each hand and one hand controlling the initiation of inflation with the A-risers and the other hand controlling the rate of inflation with the C-risers. We will refer to this launch technique as "variation #3."

In winds of more than 10 mph, or in gusty winds you may be pulled off the ground before you are ready to fly. Use extreme caution in these conditions. Do not attempt to launch in high or gusty winds until you have mastered kiting the canopy in these conditions.

You will not normally start the reverse inflation process with the canopy laid flat on the ground in a nice horseshoe as you did in lighter winds. For one thing, the wind is probably strong enough to blow the canopy around somewhat, and rearrange your nice initial layout. Or you may have pulled the canopy straight from a stuff bag and just dropped it in a ball on the hill. In this section we explain how to use the wind to lay out your canopy in the proper manner prior to inflation.

Place the canopy in a "rosette" which is a loosely shaped ball, oriented so that the center section is downwind (uphill) and facing the wind. Pull the tips out from the center several feet so that the wind will be able to inflate the center section. Gently pull the risers as you walk away from the canopy, freeing the lines. Sort the risers and

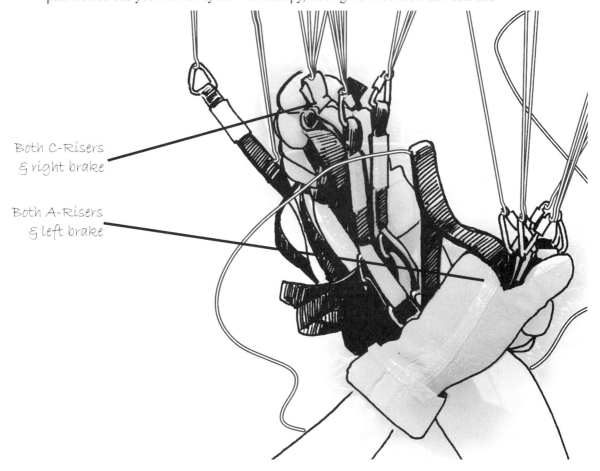

Both C-Risers
& right brake

Both A-Risers
& left brake

REVERSE INFLATION VARIATION #3

lines as best you can, ensuring the A-risers and lines are on top and the brake lines are on the bottom. You should not open the wing up fully to verify that all the lines are free of snags until later, after you have hooked the risers to your harness and you are better able to control the canopy.

Hook the risers to the canopy in the reverse position described previously. Facing the canopy, with the brake handles attached to the rear risers, grasp all A-risers in your left hand and both C-risers in your right. Each set of risers should be aligned at the quicklinks, and you should hold them just below the quicklinks. In higher winds you will likely find it works best to hold only the inner A-lines of a split riser system (consult your Owner's Manual).

Back away from the canopy until the A-lines go tight, and then by pulling on the A-risers, tease the leading edge of the canopy up into the wind to start it inflating. Do not raise the canopy fully off the ground, just bring the leading edge up three to five feet and fill the cells to make the canopy spread out spanwise. If the canopy starts to fly off the ground, release pressure on the A-risers while stepping towards the canopy and, if necessary, pull on the C-risers to bring the canopy back down. Stepping towards the canopy will keep the leading edge from folding forward over the rest of the canopy, which would close the cell openings and make the next inflation more difficult. In stronger or gusty winds, or if you are on anything steeper than a gentle slope, maintain a strong grip on the C-risers, and be ready to pull hard on the "C's" while moving quickly toward the canopy to prevent a full inflation.

You should maintain pressure on the A-risers with a backward lean while keeping the canopy anchored with a firm grasp and pull on the C-risers. Do not attempt to keep the canopy down by leaning forward to relieve pressure on the A-rises as doing so may cause the trailing edge to lift off the ground and the canopy will flap about like a flag, being difficult to control.

If the canopy begins to inflate asymmetrically, let go of the A-riser of the inflated side while pulling on the deflated side. If one wing begins to rise off the ground then bring it back down by pulling that C-riser. If you catch it early enough you do not have to let go of an individual "A" or C-riser to correct for one wing lifting more than the other, simply move your A-riser hand laterally towards and your C-riser hand laterally away from the rising wing (see illustration).

If the canopy shows a tendency to inflate more at the tips than in the center, you will need to correct this before attempting the full inflation. You can do this by alternately pulling each C-riser about 2 feet towards the opposite wing. This will pull down the outer portions of the wing and raise the center, improving the layout for inflation and preventing the wing from entering a forward horseshoe configuration on inflation. You may also consider using only the inner A-risers for the inflation.

As the canopy builds into a wall, you will be able to fully verify the risers and lines are correctly routed and free of snags. If you discover that is not the case then collapse the wing, bundle it back into a loose rosette (as required) and fix the problem.

1. At this point the risers should be hooked to your harness, you have verified the lines and risers are clear and routed correctly to the harness, and the glider should be inflated spanwise in a low wall.

2. Bring your right hand towards your left under the risers and grasp and detach the right brake with your right hand.

3. Keeping your right hand under the risers, grasp both C-risers with your right hand.

4. Bring your left hand towards your right, above the risers and grasp and detach the left brake with your left hand.

5. Keeping your left hand above the risers, grasp all the A-risers with your left hand.

6. When ready, tug lightly on the A-risers to start the inflation. As the canopy comes up it will pull hard against you. Moderate the rate at which the canopy comes up and the canopy's pull on you by using pressure on the C-risers and stepping quickly towards the canopy as necessary.

> **Note** – You may see some pilots using a nearly identical technique that uses the D-risers instead of the C-risers. We feel that using the C-risers to control the inflation works better over a wider range of wind and slope conditions. Aside from moderating the rate of inflation, use of the C-risers helps decrease the sensitivity of the canopy to one wing rising faster or the tips starting to horseshoe forward.

Variation #3: If the winds are stronger or the slope is steeper then initiate a reverse inflation by pulling both A-risers with your front hand and modulate the canopy's rapid forward movement by pulling both C-risers with your rear hand.

Ground Handling (Kiting) In Moderate Winds

Your first kiting attempts in moderate winds should be on flat or shallow slopes. You should practice controlling the wing using brakes as well as differential "A" and C-riser control. You should not attempt kiting in moderate winds on anything steeper than a shallow slope until you are fully proficient at the latter.

Remember to also practice kiting while facing forward, maintaining an exaggerated forward lean to keep tension on the A-risers and bent knees for greater traction.

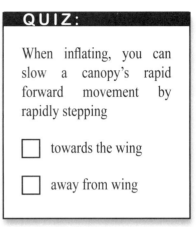

QUIZ:

When inflating, you can slow a canopy's rapid forward movement by rapidly stepping

☐ towards the wing

☐ away from wing

Remember:

In strong or gusty winds, the canopy will want to inflate harder and faster, and may inflate unexpectedly. Pay attention all the time, keep a firm grasp on the C-risers and use them to keep the canopy on the ground until you are ready to perform the inflation.

To collapse the canopy, spin around to the reverse position (if you are not already there) and then pull fully down on the C-risers. In winds above ten mph you may find it helpful to take a quick step or two towards the canopy as it comes down.

You can laterally reposition the canopy by pulling the wing up in a slight turn in the direction you want to go. If you are using the reverse inflation technique of individual A-risers in each hand (variations #1 or #2) then hold the risers of the side you want to raise first about a foot higher than the other A-riser. If you are using variation #3 (both A-risers in the same hand) then offset your A-riser hand away from the side that you want to raise while offsetting your C-riser hand in the opposite direction. Turn your body slightly so you face in the direction of intended travel. Pull the wing up and control the amount of turn by turning your body towards the low wing as you move in the desired direction.

Common Problems and Corrections During Moderate to High Wind Reverse Inflations

As the winds increase in strength you need to get the canopy off the ground and overhead quickly. Any hesitation while the canopy is in the high drag region can result in pulling you off your feet. By the same token, failure to check the canopy as it moves rapidly overhead can result in you being lifted off your feet momentarily with the canopy overshooting into a forward tuck. The best way to gain confidence is to practice inflations and kiting in these conditions on varying slopes on a smooth training hill.

High Winds (greater than 12 mph) - Canopy Layout and Inflation

You will use the previously described moderate wind technique (Variation #3) in strong winds. Start out with the canopy in a tighter rosette to ensure no wind gets into the center section of the canopy until you are ready. Additionally, you must maintain a firm grasp on the C-risers for safety reasons, so that you can collapse the canopy at any point in the sequence.

Remember that in strong or gusty winds, the canopy will want to inflate harder and faster, and may inflate unexpectedly. Pay attention all the time, keep a firm grasp on the C-risers and use them to keep the canopy on the ground until you are ready to perform the inflation.

Ground Handling (Kiting) In High Winds

Use caution as you progress to stronger winds and do not attempt kiting on slopes until you have demonstrated proficiency on a large unrestricted grassy field. As the winds approach the limits of the canopy you will need to keep the canopy weighted as much as possible. Regardless of whether you are reverse or forward kiting, maintain a strong lean away from the canopy and an exaggerated knee bend.

Always be ready for small gusts that may momentarily lift you off the ground. If you are reverse kiting strive to maintain your body position. If you get spun around, lean forward aggressively to keep as much weight as far forward as possible. Maximum forward lean is achieved by leaning between the risers with your upper body nearly horizontal and your arms stretched upward behind you maintaining minimal brake pressure.

If you ever start to lose control of your position then quickly reach up and pull both C-risers fully while spinning to face the canopy and running towards it. Gathering up the canopy into a rosette can be very difficult in high winds unless you run laterally around (abeam) the canopy as you are gathering up the lines.

Some Extra Tricks for Handling the Canopy on the Ground

There are a couple of tricks for handling the canopy on the ground that can make you look like a real pro (or at least keep you from looking like a complete fool) once you master them.

Clearing a Tangled Canopy

Sometimes, despite your best efforts, you find yourself with a canopy tangled up with itself. Avoid the temptation of grabbing a tip and pulling it out of the jumble – it will likely make matters worse. Instead, locate the center section of the canopy and work each wing outwards to the tip using a hand-over-hand motion at the leading edge. Once the canopy is straightened out check the risers to make sure they are free of twists. Straighten riser twists by working from the canopy towards the risers, starting with the inner A-risers and working outwards and then working backwards through the rest of the risers.

The Brake Line Fly Over

Sooner or later, while you're trying to inflate or control the canopy on the ground, it's going to come down with a partial twist, with one wing tip flying over the top of the canopy, the leading edge hitting the ground first in a partial inverted wall. If no more than approximately 50% of the canopy is inverted and there is at least seven mph of wind, simply pull on the brake line on the side of the canopy which flew over the top. This will inflate the canopy from the trailing edge just on that side, the canopy will fly backwards up and back over itself back to its normal position. As it does so, run laterally towards the flying tip as necessary to keep yourself directly upwind of the canopy. This technique may even work on older canopies with shorter wingspans that are completely inverted on their leading edge. On newer models if more than half of the wing is twisted over then it is usually easiest to walk over and grab the offending wing tip and walk it back to the proper position.

The Partial Wing Inflation

Occasionally you will find yourself in the position of having one wing inflated and the other partially crumpled in front of it. You can inflate the collapsed portion by letting more air into the inflated portion. Do this by applying more tension to the A-riser of the inflated wing while keeping it from rising by simultaneous application of brake to that side. This is best done by pulling on the brake line itself with the opposite hand (you can easily do this while maintaining the brake handles in the appropriate hands).

The Single Line Save Your Life (and Dignity) Maneuver

In strong winds, when handling the canopy on the ground, you may get into a situation where control of the canopy has gotten away from you, you have been or are about to be dragged off your feet, and are trying to avoid being dragged across the ground. In this case, grab one line (whatever you can get your hands on) and reel it in hand over hand as you run towards the canopy until you have canopy cloth in your hand. In this configuration, the canopy cannot inflate and drag you.

A Note about Assisted Inflations in Strong Wind

When inflating in winds of more than 10 mph some pilots have used a technique involving an assistant or two holding on to the pilot's harness to anchor the pilot to the ground. We have come to the conclusion over the years that this technique is too difficult to execute properly to be reliable, and is unnecessary if proper canopy handling techniques are mastered. With the exception of windy cliff launches, we now feel that a pilot should not attempt to inflate or launch in winds which are too strong for the pilot to handle unassisted.

QUIZ:

☐ true

☐ false

In stronger winds you should normally use a launch assistant to help control the canopy.

Remember:
Launches are optional.
Landings are mandatory...

Think about it.

Taking Flight
Launching in Calm or Light Winds

Prior to committing to launch you must first ensure you are ready to take flight, the canopy is cleanly overhead, and there is nothing that will interfere with proper control.

If you determine that there is any problem with proceeding with the launch, abort the launch by stopping your run. In light winds, on a shallow slope, you may collapse the canopy behind you by either pulling both brakes or the rear risers fully.

Once you have ascertained that the canopy is flyable, release some brake pressure as you smoothly accelerate into an aggressive launch run. Use the brakes sparingly to help control the canopy direction (too much brake will drop the canopy behind you). To ensure a clean flyaway you should achieve maximum speed during your run. Maximum speed can be attained by weighting the canopy with a good forward lean and bent knees with whatever brake application is required to keep the canopy stable overhead. If you are not yet flying after you have attained your maximum running speed, apply brakes gently to attain lift off. If brakes are used to lift off, let them off slowly once airborne and clear of the ground to gain flying speed.

Other benefits of an exaggerated forward lean is it places your weight forward with respect to the canopy. This allows for more launch speed and a cleaner lift off and flyaway from shallow slopes. With the canopy overhead, the forward lean puts your shoulders well in front of the risers. To keep from inadvertently pulling on the brakes, your arms should be extended to the rear, parallel with the ground. It is important that you learn to feel the proper amount of brake application by the pressure in your hands not by the position of your arms. If your glider has long brake line travel or light brake pressure you may find it beneficial to take one wrap of the brake lines around your hands after the glider is fully inflated and you are into your run.

Lastly, an exaggerated forward lean helps your upper body to counterbalance your legs immediately after liftoff. This helps keep your feet beneath you (and ready for action) instead of rotating to a reclined position while still at low altitude.

Launching in Moderate and Strong Winds

If you need to abort a launch in breezy conditions then collapse the canopy by grasping and pulling down hard on both C-risers since attempting to use the brakes to collapse the canopy could result in your being lifted off the ground.

If the inflation is good, release the "A" and C-risers and turn immediately to face forward.

Note: Just because you turn forward immediately in this situation does not mean you have to launch immediately. It is still wise to kite the canopy on the ground until you have completed your visual inspection and are assured that everything is ready to go. You should have ample practice kiting the canopy while facing forward so you feel comfortable doing this.

The same exaggerated forward lean used to launch in light winds is also important in stronger winds. Keeping your weight forward adds a couple of mph of speed to your wing and can help you penetrate forward during launch. Failure to do so in strong conditions can result in being raised and blown backward into the region of increased wind speed above the apex of the hill, making forward penetration even more problematic.

— Andy Stocker photo

Bareback Mt., Tehachapi, CA

3

Sitting Back In Your Harness

On any slope launch, keep your feet underneath you and be prepared to run again if you come back down. Once you are safely away from the ground you can sit back in your harness. During the training hill phase you will likely fly in a more upright position with your feet underneath you. As you progress to longer flights you will find that a more reclined position is more comfortable, more streamlined, and may help you react faster to canopy deflations. Regardless of your final position, you should not rush to sit back in your harness.

By leaning forward during the launch you can use bicep pressure on the risers to actually push yourself into the seat. Never reach down with both hands to adjust yourself in the seat while holding the brake handles as you will stall the canopy. If you must use your hands to get back in your seat, put both brake handles in one hand, and reach down with the other hand to push the seat forward so you can slide back into the seat.

If you experience difficulty getting into your seat then your harness may simply need better adjustment. Take the time to suspend yourself from a sturdy support and properly adjust not just the amount of recline but also the seat depth and angle. You should suspend yourself at a low enough height that you can lean forward and put your legs on the floor and practice reclining and getting back upright for landing. If you still have difficulty then you may find you can slide into your seat without shifting your hands from the brakes by simply leaning back and crunching both knees to your chest. You can help push yourself back by pushing forward on the risers (while holding the brakes at their normal level).

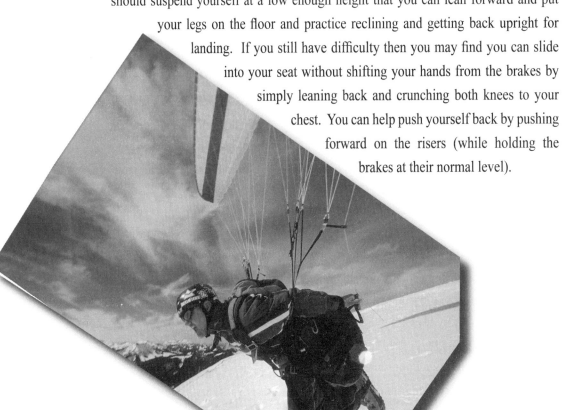

Launching On Varying Slopes

Your initial flight experience should be on the gentle slopes of a training hill. As you gain experience you will want to fly larger and more varied sites and you will need to be able to inflate and launch your paraglider on shallow as well as steeper slopes. The slope of the terrain will effect both your inflation as well as your launch techniques.

Launching on gentle slopes in calm or light winds requires an aggressive run and light touch on the brakes. As the slopes become steeper there are two readily noticeable effects. First, the canopy will pull upward more during inflation and second, the canopy will seek an aerodynamic equilibrium position that will be more forward than on a shallower slope. On steeper slopes the canopy will actually seek a position forward of straight up and you will need to use the appropriate amount of brakes to keep the canopy from getting so far forward that gravity will force it further forward. Because of these two factors, in moderate or stronger winds you should use the high wind reverse inflation technique (variation #3) on moderate or steeper slopes to initially control the upward rate of the canopy and then be ready to stop the canopy with judicious use of brakes.

As slopes become steeper, it gets progressively harder to layout the canopy and keep it in the proper horseshoe shape as it will tend to slide over on itself. Even light winds may cause the canopy to lazily float off the ground and fold over forward. An assistant standing behind the canopy and gently holding the center section upright is invaluable in such cases. They should hold the fabric gently using a light "pinch" grip and let the canopy pull free when you initiate the inflation.

If used, the launch assistant should hold the center of the canopy from behind using a light pinch grip, allowing the glider to pull free once the inflation starts

If you do not have the luxury of a launch assistant, you can make an inexpensive aid by securing a clothespin to a small rod. If there are bushes or trees immediately behind the inflation spot you may secure the clothespins to a short lanyard anchored to a branch. If you do not have assistants or clothespins then small rocks can be placed on the trailing edge of the canopy to help hold it in place.

Crosswind Launches

The effects of a crosswind during inflation depend on the canopy specifics (span, sweep, and anhedral), the slope of the terrain, and the wind speed. On shallow slopes the upwind wing tip may tend to collapse and drop which can be self-correcting. On steeper slopes in stronger winds, the effects of the crosswind may be masked by the wind gradient effects (one wing getting up into the higher velocity air quicker and wanting to continue to rise). You should avoid trying to inflate and launch near the lateral edge of a hill because of the naturally occurring crosswind caused by the venturi effect. The canopy will be more difficult to control as it seeks to follow the flow around the corner.

Regardless of the slope, you should strive to lay out and pull up the canopy as directly into the wind as possible. It normally works best if you inflate on the top of the hill and once the canopy is inflated, controlled, and checked, turn to proceed directly down the slope to launch. Use the appropriate brake pressure to keep the canopy centered overhead on your desired ground track.

If you must inflate on a slope and the winds are strong enough to kite the canopy then consider inflating with a "pre-correction" already applied. You should get a feel for which wing will try to rise first when you are building a wall. If you are using the reverse inflation technique of individual A-risers in each hand (variations #1 or #2) then hold the risers of the wing you expect to rise first about a foot lower than the other A-riser. If you are using variation #3 (both A-risers in the same hand) then offset your A-riser hand towards the wing that will rise while offsetting your C-riser hand in the opposite direction.

Once the canopy is inflated, keep it overhead with appropriate use of the brakes and body twist while you curve your takeoff run more directly downhill.

Launching With Complications

Perhaps you made a mistake or perhaps nature threw you a curve and you find yourself in the midst of launching with twisted risers or before you are ready to take flight. This section deals with handling such emergencies.

Launching While Still Reversed

Usually it is best to spin around and launch forwards but there are a few situations where advanced pilots may find it preferable to launch backwards. In strong winds at a cliff site you may be able to get better initial penetration if you lean way back and push yourself off while still reversed. Another situation is when the winds are light and switching. In these conditions it can be very difficult to keep the canopy square during the spin around to face forward. Lastly, in stronger winds on moderate slopes you may be able to keep from launching prematurely by pulling on the C-risers but the moment the canopy is square and you let go of the risers you will be flying. If that's the case then plan for it ahead of time since it's better to launch backwards than off balance halfway through the spin around to face forward. Remember, you do not have to launch backwards in any scenario, in fact, if the conditions require such skill then it may be prudent to not launch at all!

If you are ever pulled off your feet while still facing the hillside then your first priority should not be turning around but to instead keep the canopy straight and level and tracking away from the hill. The risers will tend to unwind naturally and you should resist this by maintaining light brake pressure and increasing your rotational inertia by leaning back and sticking your legs forward. If you have the presence of mind you can help lock yourself in position by reaching upward and holding the A-risers apart. When safely away from the hill you can lean forward and unwind to face the direction of flight. And next time you are launching in similar conditions remember to use the A-riser and C-riser (variation #3) inflation technique!

Remember:
It is much better to be on the ground wishing you were in the air than to be in the air wishing you were on the ground!

Turning the Wrong Way and Launching With a Full Riser Twist

Occasionally it happens – someone does a reverse pull-up, spins around the wrong way, and is faced with risers wrapped together in a full 360° twist. The best way to keep this from ever happening to you is to learn a correct, precise, and repeatable method for hooking the risers to your harness, inflating, and launching (in other words, use the procedures in this book!).

Some situations can be conducive to inadvertently reversing the riser layout (e.g. the left riser group going under instead of over the right riser group). These situations include aborted launches, side hill and top hill landings. It is usually best if you collapse the wing in any of these situations by turning in the opposite direction of your launch spin. Sometimes, however, other factors such as canopy position, crosswinds, and terrain will naturally affect the direction you spin to gain control or collapse the canopy. When this happens you may well have set yourself up with reversed risers for your next launch.

Anytime you are preparing to reverse inflate you should verify the proper riser group is on top. If it is not, then you can either spin around in a complete revolution in the direction of the top risers (right riser group on top, spin right 360°) or choose to go ahead and inflate while remembering to spin the other direction to face forward. If you are using inflation variations #2 or #3, then you can help ensure you will spin the correct way for the riser layout by reversing your hands so that the arm that is on top of the risers matches the direction you will spin (right riser group on top then right hand should be on top of the risers). Obviously you should occasionally practice such an "opposite" inflation as part of your kiting.

If, despite these precautions, you somehow find yourself facing forward to launch with a full riser twist then it is usually best to reverse spin back around to face the canopy. If the canopy is still under control then you may choose to continue your spin another 180° and launch. If not, then collapse the wing. Never accept launching with a full riser twist since the decreased control effectiveness and pilot disorientation will make a transition to safe flight extremely difficult.

Launching With An Individual Riser Twist

This situation normally arises due to hooking up the risers incorrectly and may not even be noticed until after launching. Flying with a single riser twist usually has negligible effect but if you do notice such a twist after facing forward to launch then you should abort the launch, investigate the problem, and double check for any other errors. Do not panic if you find yourself airborne with a riser twist. Your brake lines will still be effective; however, they will rub against the risers. Be conservative and head out for a landing.

Note— a common way to inadvertently put a half twist in both risers is to leave your harness hooked to your canopy and have it roll through the risers prior to strapping it on. This is easy to do if you lay the wing and harness out facing forward on a moderate to steep hill.

A Swing test pilot demonstrates a forward inflation. Can you spot the problem?!

The left brake line is entangled with some D and A-lines

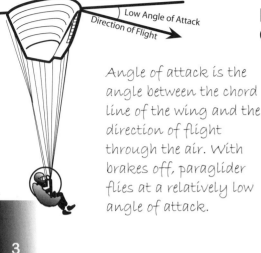

Angle of attack is the angle between the chord line of the wing and the direction of flight through the air. With brakes off, paraglider flies at a relatively low angle of attack.

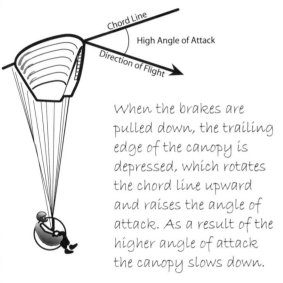

When the brakes are pulled down, the trailing edge of the canopy is depressed, which rotates the chord line upward and raises the angle of attack. As a result of the higher angle of attack the canopy slows down.

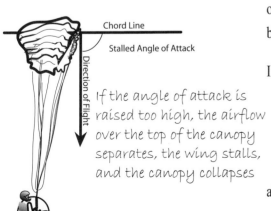

If the angle of attack is raised too high, the airflow over the top of the canopy separates, the wing stalls, and the canopy collapses

Flying the Canopy
Controlling Your Flying Speed

The angle of attack of the canopy, (which we talk more about in the next chapter on aerodynamics) and as a result the flying speed of the canopy through the air, are controlled primarily by the use of the brakes. Pulling down on the brake lines increases the canopy angle of attack (as well as the camber of the canopy) and reduces the airspeed. Pulling down too far, too rapidly, or for too long will lead to separation of the airflow from the top surface of the canopy (i.e. a stall of the canopy), and to an increase in descent rate. (See *Chapter Seven – Advanced Maneuvers* for a more complete discussion of stalls and recovery from stalls).

The rapid application of brakes will cause a greater initial increase in angle of attack, because of pendular action; the sudden slowing of the canopy results in the pilot swinging out in front and thus dynamically rotating the canopy to a higher angle of attack.

In your early flights, you will generally fly with the brakes most of the way or all of the way off (brake handles all the way up) except when turning or when landing. Later on, you will use the brakes to fly more slowly when you want to obtain your slowest sink rate, and you will use the brakes to make the canopy more stable and resistant to collapses when flying in turbulence.

Modern gliders are trimmed to achieve their best glide through the air with the brakes fully off. If you are trying to soar in light lift then you will likely want to fly at the speed that provides for your lowest sink rate which is slower than best glide speed. This usually occurs at about 20% of brake travel (the brake handles near the bottom of the risers).

If you are flying into a headwind or through sinking air then you should fly at an airspeed faster than your no-wind best glide speed (the theory for this is provided in *Chapter Six – Getting High* and *Chapter Eleven – Down the Road*). This is what your speed stirrup is designed for. More discussion on the use of the speed stirrup is also provided in *Chapter 7 – Advanced Flying Techniques.*

How to Turn the Canopy

Turning the canopy can be accomplished by a combination of shifting your weight in your harness and applying brakes - both on the side towards which you wish to turn. For your early flying, your instructor may want you to make all of your turns using only the brakes. Turning control using brakes is achieved by pulling down smoothly on the brake on the side of the desired turn. That is, to make a left turn, pull down on the left brake. The further you pull the brake down, the steeper the bank angle and the more rapid the turn. Also, the more quickly you pull down the brake, the greater the initial bank angle and turn rate, though you will not maintain that bank angle without further brake application. The relationship between initial bank angle and speed of brake application is due to the pendular action described above but acting in the roll axis (banking of the wing) instead of the pitch axis (nose up and nose down rotation).

You should be using only relatively shallow and slow turns, with only small changes in flight direction in your early flights. Hold the brake down until you have turned to just short of the direction you wish to go, and then smoothly let it up.

If you are flying with both brakes on to some degree, then you may want to both pull down on one brake and let up on the other to turn.

If you are flying at or near the edge of stall (both brakes pulled down to or past the carabiners), attempting a turn by the aggressive use of brakes as described above may result in a spin, with a dangerous loss of control. Do not fly near stall in close proximity to the terrain. Until you learn exactly where the stall point of your canopy is, you should never pull either brake handle below the bottom of the carabiner unless landing is imminent.

Weight shift control is another method of turning which is achieved by leaning the body and rolling the hips in the direction of the desired turn. To turn using weight shift you will want to lift your weight off of the seat on one side so as to weight the harness seat as much as possible on the side towards which the turn is desired. In fact, you may want to cross your legs in the desired direction of turn. The most effective turns are made using a combination of brakes and weight shift. For your early flights your instructor will probably have your harness configured for maximum stability, and will probably have you using the brakes exclusively for turning control. Relatively tight adjustment of the chest strap on your harness will provide this extra stability to the harness and canopy, which may be preferable at this stage to increased weight shift response. As you gain experience, you may choose to open up your chest strap to allow more lateral rocking in the seat.

Landing the Canopy

The purpose of a proper landing is to arrest both your descent and your forward motion just as you reach the ground, so that you touch down on your feet as nearly motionless relative to the ground as possible.

The most important rule about landing is to always try to land into the wind. Flying into the wind gives you your slowest speed over the ground and this makes your landing easier and safer.

You should not be sitting in the seat of your harness when you land. You should instead be rocked forward in a standing position, hanging from your leg straps with your feet underneath you, having slid forward and out of the seat. If you are sitting back with your feet in front of you, you will likely lose your balance and fall back hard on the base of your spine, especially if your landing flare causes you to swing forward. Also, if you are standing upright in your harness and accidentally stall your glider then you will tend to rotate backwards, impacting on your back protection. If you are already sitting back in your harness and accidentally stall then you will tend to rotate and land on less-protected areas such as the back of your neck or head.

During your early flights, you may be ground skimming along a slope which closely parallels your gliding slope. You will probably never be more than six to ten feet off the ground, as you glide at a more or less constant altitude following the slope of the hill. When in this situation, use this rule: "Ground coming up, brakes coming down. Ground falling away, brakes going up." In this manner, you will insure that anytime you are descending towards the ground you will be applying the brakes to slow your descent, and soften your impact if you do land. Often times, you will find that as you apply the brakes a little gust or thermal bump will pick you up again, and in this case you want to ease up on the brakes to keep flying speed and again give yourself a reserve of brake travel to use in arresting your descent when you come down again. The brakes should never be let up abruptly, but they should sometimes be applied abruptly. The speed of application of the brakes depends on your rate of descent and how close to the ground you are. If the ground is close and coming up fast, quickly apply whatever brakes you have left. (This is assuming you are not in a state of "constant stall" or "parachutage" in which case applying the brakes would make things worse. You will learn about constant stall in a later chapter, but during your early flights you should never be in constant stall and should not have to be concerned with it.)

If you are flying from a steeper training hill you will want to hold the brakes at a constant position, perhaps just slight brakes applied, to maintain a constant speed as you glide towards your landing.

As you progress in your flying, you will be making your landing approach from much higher up, gliding into a landing over flat ground. It is often difficult for student pilots to judge altitude as they approach for landing in this situation. A two-stage application of brakes works well in this situation. Make your approach with brakes full off or just slightly applied (to make your canopy more resistant to a gust induced collapse, and to give you some ability to speed up if necessary). As you approach within about ten to 15 feet of the ground, smoothly pull on half brakes (to just above your waist) to slow your descent and forward speed. Then, depending on your rate of descent and forward speed, at between two and six feet of the ground, pull both brakes smoothly as far as necessary to arrest your descent and forward motion and make a light touch down. You will need a greater and quicker application of brakes in zero or light winds, and less if there is more wind. Once you have your height judgment

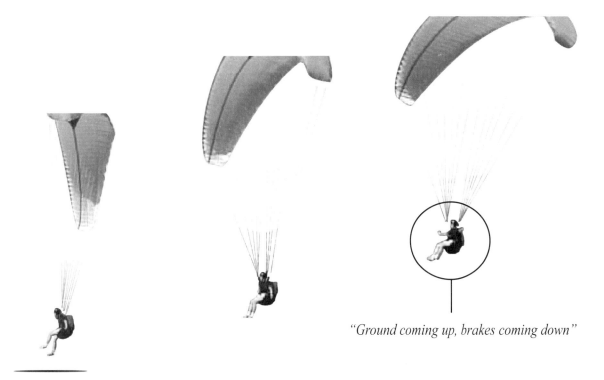

"Ground coming up, brakes coming down"

3

fully developed, the ideal landing "flare" is a smooth application from 0% brakes (or whatever your initial brake setting is) to 100% brakes over a period of about 2 seconds, beginning when your feet are about 5 to 8 feet off the ground.

Collapsing the Canopy After Landing

The goal after landing is to collapse the canopy behind you, under control. Unless the winds are very strong or gusty, there should be no hurry to collapse the canopy. In light to moderate winds, bring the brakes back up after touchdown to bring the canopy back overhead. (In stronger winds, you may also want to take a quick step or two backwards to get the canopy quickly back overhead so that it doesn't drag you backwards off balance.) In very light winds, where you cannot kite the canopy overhead standing still, continue to walk forward as necessary to keep the canopy loaded and inflated. When the canopy is stable overhead, tilt your head back, spin quickly to your right 180 degrees, grasp the rear risers and pull down sharply while walking downwind towards the collapsing canopy.

In strong or gusty winds, it may be difficult to control the canopy and there is a danger in getting pulled off your feet and then dragged along the ground. If possible, release the brake handles immediately on landing and look for and grab the C-risers as you turn to face downwind. Pull down hard on the C-risers as you run as necessary towards the collapsing canopy to keep from being pulled off your feet. If you find yourself completely losing control and in danger of being dragged, grab any one line, and reel it in hand over hand as you run downwind towards the canopy until you have canopy fabric in your hand. The canopy will collapse completely from that one side, and produce no further lift or drag. This will prevent you from being dragged across the landing area by the wind, which can be dangerous.

Composite launch sequence — Swing photo

Landing Approach Safety

The most important aspect of landing is to always keep a safe landing area within your gliding range while you are flying. On the training hill, this will always be the case as the entire area in front of you will be suitable for landing. Later on, you will have to pay more attention to the terrain and obstacles between you and your landing point, and your relative angle of elevation above the place you wish to land. This requires special care if there is any wind, as your effective glide ratio relative to the terrain will go to zero as the wind speed approaches the maximum speed of the canopy, i.e. in a strong enough wind you will descend straight down with no ability to move forward. Also, flying the canopy at or near its maximum speed can be dangerous close to the ground if there is any turbulence, because the canopy becomes more likely to collapse when flown at higher speeds. Therefore, you must always set up your approach high when there is any significant wind, so that you can have some brakes applied during the approach for added canopy stability and still have sufficient penetration to reach your intended landing point.

Keep in mind that physical obstructions upwind of your landing point will cause rotor turbulence in the presence of significant wind. Also remember that power lines are essentially invisible from the air.

We recommend the use of a standard aircraft approach for landings where you reach the landing area with a lot of altitude and the winds are 8 mph or less. The aircraft approach will be discussed in detail in the chapter dealing with intermediate skills, *Chapter Six – Getting High*. In stronger winds a "figure eight" approach with alternating turns while flying into the wind works well.

> **QUIZ:**
>
> Always keep a suitable
>
> ☐ landing area
>
> ☐ windsock
>
> ☐ spectator
>
> within your gliding range.

LANDING APPROACH SAFETY

You must always monitor your angle of descent to the landing area and stay within a safe volume of air space as defined by the cones shown below. In the first case, there is little or no wind and a symmetrical cone whose sides make an angle of 30 degrees elevation above the ground will give you a safety margin of glide to overcome up to a 10 mph wind and up to 500 feet per minute sinking air. (Assuming a canopy with a 7:1 L/D at 22 mph. Lower performing canopies need a cone with steeper sides.) Pilots A and B, even further from the landing area than C or D, are within the safe region, while pilot D is not.

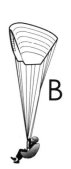
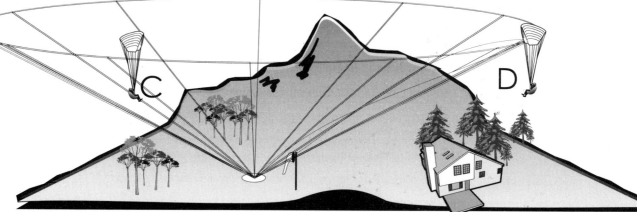

In the situation below, there is a significant wind. This tilts the cone of safe air space towards the direction from which the wind is blowing. (You can glide much farther down wind than into the wind.) Pilot B is still within the safe region but Pilots A and C are each in a location that was within the cone in no-wind, but outside in this situation. With the tailwind, Pilot D is now within reach of the target.

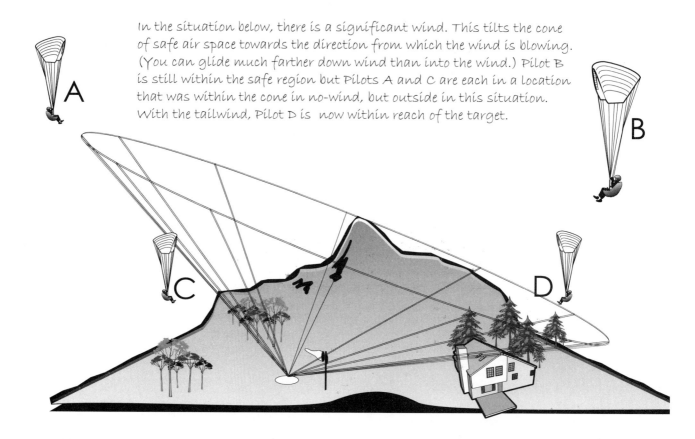

Side Hill Landings

You may want or have the need on occasion to land on the side of a hill. Provided that the slope is not too steep, this is not a problem if done properly. The idea is to make your approach directly across the hill, close in to the hill and exactly parallel to the slope, traveling neither uphill nor downhill.

If you are traveling downhill at all, you will gain ground clearance as you pull on the brakes and stall the canopy, and then you will fall from a significant height.

On the other hand, **DO NOT LAND DOWNWIND UPHILL OR INTO THE HILL**. The act of flaring (pulling the brakes) for landing will cause you to swing forward, which in combination with your higher downwind groundspeed will cause you to hit very hard. If the wind is crossing the hill at all, land in the direction more into the wind, to minimize your ground speed.

Make a normal flare, more aggressive if there is less wind, less so if there is more wind. In wind, try to turn just slightly into the wind just as the canopy stalls, to bring your groundspeed to zero just at the moment of touch down. (It is better not to turn into the wind at all, than to turn too much too soon, for the reasons stated above, but in any case do not let yourself get turned downwind.)

Packing Up The Canopy

Pack up the canopy as soon as possible after landing. Exposure to sunlight is one of the most damaging things you can do to your paraglider. A large stuff bag that you can stuff the canopy into easily without folding and packing it is a handy way to protect your canopy from UV exposure when you take a break from flying. As an alternative, you can gather the canopy together, and throw a blanket over it to shield if from the sun.

1. After landing, clip the brake handles into their retainers, gather the canopy into a rosette by reeling in the lines, and proceed to an area out of the way suitable for packing up the canopy.

2. Remove your harness, leaving the canopy attached for the time being to the harness.

3. Spread the canopy on the ground, bottom surface up, in a rectangle.

3

4. Disconnect the harness from the canopy, and run a line clearing check on each side to ensure that the lines are not tangled. Holding the riser base in your hand, flip the lines up onto the surface of the canopy.

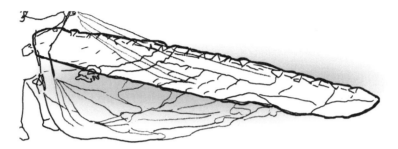

5. Secure the risers in a manner that will ensure they will not inadvertently get twisted, flipped or looped through a line. A riser "sock" or small duffel bag is a good idea. Lay the risers centered at the base of the canopy.

6. Grab a wing tip and walk it to the center of the canopy making sure all lines are on top of the canopy, and get folded into the canopy as you proceed. Continue successively folding the wing in half until it is only a couple of feet wide. Repeat the process with the other wing.

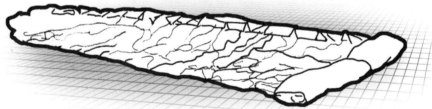

7. Fold one half of the canopy over on itself as shown, place the risers on top, and then fold the canopy from the trailing edge to the leading edge, taking time to force the air out of the canopy as you fold it. Avoid placing any undue pressure on or creasing the mylar in the leading edge. Place the canopy in your bag, along with your harness.

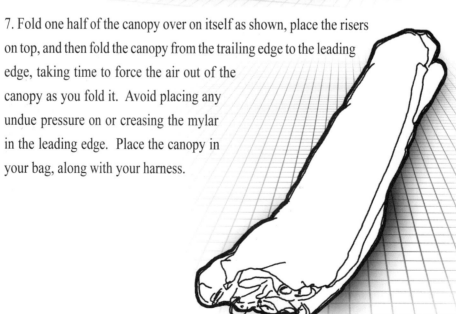

As an alternative to packing the canopy in this manner, if you have a large capacity stuff bag you can simply gather the canopy into a loose bundle by progressively sliding your hand up the entire line array. Carefully coil the lines (but do not "daisy chain" the thin lines of modern gliders). Do not allow either carabiner to pass through between any lines (one way to do this is to leave the canopy hooked to the harness) and then place the bundle of canopy into the stuff bag. Slowly press the air out of the canopy and close up the bag.

In moderate winds you may find it easier to fold the canopy if you lay it out parallel with the wind. Fold the upwind side towards the center, then spin the canopy around so the unfolded wing is now upwind, and repeat.

There are advantages and disadvantages to keeping your risers attached to your harness while packing up. The advantages are: reduced chances of tangled lines or risers and less chance of making a preflight mistake. The disadvantages include: it's more difficult to pack up and the finished product has more volume.

When preparing for a calm wind forward inflation,
take the time to ensure your lines are clear of debris.

Tip—
Taking an extra couple of minutes to ensure your lines are clear of tangles while packing up will save you both time and aggravation on your next flying day!

*Accordion folding
the trailing edge*

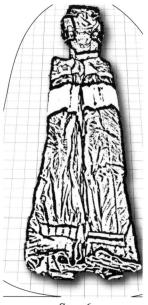

Step 4 Complete

The Accordion Fold — Preserving the Mylar Ribs

The ease of inflation in calm winds is proportional to the quality of the leading edge. Some manufacturers recommend extra care be taken with the mylar ribs to avoid creasing them during pack up and storage. Instead of folding the wings in successively narrower bundles, they use an "accordion" style fold, gathering the mylar ribs together so that they will lay flat against one another in a smooth bundle. If you want to preserve your glider as well as keep the risers attached to your harness then try the following technique:

1. Rosette the canopy normally.

2. Instead of looping the lines onto the canopy, daisy chain them starting from the risers and going upward until they start to pull the wing tips. Use a hardware store mini-carabiner to lock the final daisy chain link to the lines. Daisy chaining the lines isn't required but it keeps the lines from getting caught on things and makes it impossible for the risers to get twisted if you decide you need to unhook them from the carabiners (if you want to remove the risers from the harness, hook them to another mini-carabiner to maintain their proper orientation).

3. Starting from the 3rd cell seam from the center, pick up the cell at the rib, reach two ribs outboard (towards the wingtip) and accordion fold the trailing edge of one wing by laying the seam of every other cell (the 5th, 7th, 9th, and so forth) on top of the 3rd cell in a reasonably flat pile. Unless you have an assistant it will be difficult to keep the accordion fold exact. Don't worry about it, it's the leading edge that needs the emphasis. If there's any wind, then place your harness on the bundle to hold it in place while you repeat with the other wing. Place the two trailing edge bundles on top of each other and under the harness.

4. Starting from the 3rd cell from the center, gather the leading edge mylars together, holding them flat against each other. Lay them in a stack on their side. Use your helmet or some other weight to hold them down. Repeat with the other wing.

Step 6

5. Fold any extra canopy material on top of the stacked mylars and fold the two wings into each other so they touch at the centerline.

6. Lift your harness and place it next to and facing the leading edge. The line bundle to the risers should be going out the top center of the canopy and the risers should now have a half twist.

7. Fold one of the wings on top of the other. Squeeze the excess air out of the canopy (from the trailing edge to the leading edge).

8. Now move the harness so that it is perpendicular to the canopy (directly across the roll/fold line).

9. Roll the canopy from the trailing edge toward the leading edge leaving 2 to 3 feet remaining unrolled.

10. Fold the leading edge down towards the roll (this helps protect it). Continue rolling up the canopy and secure it with a strap. The lines will now extend from the side of the bundle. Pull the storage bag over the glider from the side opposite the risers.

11. Secure the bag within the harness.

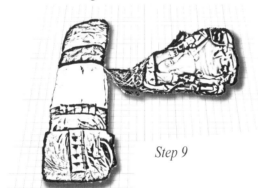

Step 9

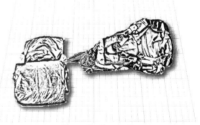

Step 9 Complete

Step 10

Step 11

NOTES

AERODYNAMICS

WHAT HOLDS YOU UP?

Land's end — soaring a coastal mountain range in Norway.

Chapter 4 — AERODYNAMICS

WHAT HOLDS YOU UP?

One of the most common questions asked in the landing area by spectators unfamiliar with paragliding or hang gliding is, "What do you do when the wind stops?" More than one pilot, after hearing this question once too often, has put tongue firmly in cheek and responded in mock panic, "You plummet man, you just plummet!" Of course the question itself betrays a lack of understanding of the mechanics of flight, which is what sometimes leads to frustration on the part of the pilot being questioned. The spectator is obviously equating the paraglider or hang glider with a kite on a string, and assumes that when the wind stops you must fall out of the sky.

In truth, the comparison is not all that inaccurate; a string kite and any type of glider do fly on much the same principle. They both depend on the flow of air over a wing surface to create a lifting force to balance the force of gravity and hold the aircraft aloft. The difference is that in the case of the kite, the aircraft is held stationary (by the string) in a moving body of air (the wind) and it is only the motion of the air itself which creates the required flow of "relative wind" over the surface of the kite.

A kite is held motionless in the sky by the balanced forces of the wind, the string and gravity. If the wind stops, the kite, which is not designed to be able to glide, falls.

Force of wind on kite

String pulling on kite

Gravity pulling down on kite

In just the right conditions, a paraglider can emulate a kite. A paraglider which is descending along a glide path at 20-mph in a wind which is blowing up a slope at exactly the same speed, can hang motionless in the sky. If the wind stops, or the wind speed becomes less, the paraglider simply begins to glide forward.

Paraglider flight path

In a glider, whether it is a paraglider, a hang glider, or a sailplane, the aircraft is not tethered, and must, therefore, always fly forward through the air mass in which it is flying, maintaining by virtue of this constant forward motion the required "relative wind" or flow of air over the wing surface. A paraglider flying in wind may emulate a kite and hang motionless in the sky, if its flight direction is exactly into the wind and its forward speed of flight through the air exactly matches the speed of the wind into which it is flying.

(This would be analogous to you going to the passenger terminal at an airport and walking the wrong direction on the moving sidewalk at exactly the speed that the sidewalk itself was moving. Although walking at a steady three or four miles per hour on the sidewalk, you would remain motionless within the terminal itself.)

In the case of our "motionless" paraglider, unlike the kite, if the wind stops the paraglider will simply begin moving forward again, at its normal flying speed.

So what is it that holds us up when we fly? It is the upward pressure exerted by air moving over our wings as we fly forward through the air. And why is this force necessary? To balance us against the constant pull of gravity.

Any object subjected to an unbalanced force will accelerate in the direction of that force. As long as the imbalance in the force acting on the object continues, the object continues to accelerate. We all learn at an early age about the effect of gravity, a force which acts on every object pulling it towards the center of the earth. An object that is unsupported against the pull of gravity accelerates toward the earth, with its speed increasing at a rate of about 20 mph per second. You don't have to fall very far under the pull of gravity to build up enough speed to hit pretty hard when you reach the ground.

Of course, even without a wing of some kind, we would eventually stop accelerating under the influence of gravity. As soon as our speed built up to the point where the aerodynamic drag on our body was as strong as the pull of gravity, the acceleration would stop and the speed would remain constant. The only problem is that for the human body this "terminal velocity", where the force of aerodynamic drag equals the body's weight, is about 150 mph, straight down. This makes for a short flight and a very hard landing.

Balance of Forces

A body falling at terminal velocity; drag force and gravity force are balanced. The body stops accelerating and falls at a constant speed. Note that the balanced forces do not result in the body hanging motionless because the aerodynamic drag force only exists because of the high speed of descent. Balanced forces do not result in lack of motion, they result in unaccelerated (constant speed) motion.

Aerodynamic Drag force

Force of Gravity

Since a wing can produce lift at right angles to its motion through the air, a wing gliding horizontally can be in a balanced equilibrium of forces except...

Lift

Direction of motion

Force of Gravity

...that

it is not possible to make a wing (or any object) that can move without experiencing a force of drag or resistance in the direction opposite to its motion. Because of drag, the wing slows down, and because it slows down, the lift

Lift

Direction of motion

Drag Force

Force of Gravity

produced

diminishes and the unbalanced force of gravity makes the wing accelerate downward.

In an airplane, the engine and propeller provide the thrust force to balance the drag force.

Lift

Direction of motion

Drag Force

Thrust Force

Force of Gravity

Enter the wing. What makes a wing special, is that it has the ability to create an aerodynamic force in a direction other than the direction of the airflow over it. A falling object like a rock or a human body creates only drag, a force of aerodynamic resistance (friction with the air if you will) that is in the direction of the flow of air over the body or object. Because of this, drag can only work against gravity (which always pulls straight down) if the object is falling straight down. But flying, in most people's imagination, should include the idea of gliding around in the horizontal direction. Falling straight down is not most people's idea of flying.

The wing, on the other had, has the ability to create a force which is perpendicular to the flow of air over it. In contrast to the force of drag, this special aerodynamic force is called lift.

NOTE: Soaring pilots use the term "lift" to refer to two completely different and distinct things. Do not get these two confused! The first is aerodynamic lift produced by a wing, as we are discussing here. The second use of the term "lift" refers to any upward moving parcel of air in the atmosphere, which a pilot may use to gain altitude, and/or extend the duration of his flight. The use of the same word for these two distinct things is merely a coincidence; the two have nothing to do with one another.

Now imagine a wing, moving forward horizontally through the air, and producing lift. You should be able to see how, since the direction of lift is perpendicular to the direction of airflow, the wing can use lift to balance the force of gravity as long as it continues to move forward. In this way, we can avoid the downward acceleration that would result from gravity acting with no force to balance it. And this is how aircraft fly; the wing moves forward through the air, producing upward lift, which balances downward gravity. Except for one minor problem.

The problem is drag. Unfortunately, no aircraft wing has ever been invented which can produce only lift, without producing some drag as well. (In fact nothing has ever been invented or discovered that can move over the ground or through the air or water without producing some form of friction or drag. That is why all unpowered objects eventually come to rest.) When you add drag to our lift-producing gliding wing, acting as drag always does in the direction of the airflow over the wing, you will see that the drag now represents an unbalanced force in a direction opposite to the direction the wing is moving. The result is the wing "accelerates" backwards, which, since it is moving forwards, is another way of saying that the wing slows down.

But the wing's forward motion through the air, and in particular the specific speed of that forward motion, was what produced the necessary amount of lift required to balance gravity's downward pull, so as the wing slows down the lift it produces decreases and now is no longer strong enough to balance the pull of gravity. So, we are back to accelerating downwards towards the earth.

What to do?

Well, one answer is to put an engine and a propeller on the aircraft, and create a forward force of thrust from the propeller to balance the backward force of drag. Now we are back in a completely balanced force system. We have invented the airplane!

OK, but how does a glider manage it, without an engine? Well, here's what we do. Instead of trying to fly horizontally, we tilt the flight path downwards slightly, so that the aircraft glides "downhill." This has an interesting and profoundly important effect on our lift and drag forces. It tilts the lift force forward, so that part of it balances the drag force, and it tilts the drag force upwards, so that part of it is used to balance gravity. And we once again have a completely balanced force system, and so we once again avoid the downward acceleration. Note that we do have a downward motion; we are descending downwards along a shallow sloped glide path. In fact we must glide downwards; without thrust from an engine we cannot fly horizontally through the air without losing speed. But we do not have a downward acceleration; our speed is both moderate, and constant. We are analogous to the rider of a bicycle without pedals; we must move forward to keep from falling over, but to keep our speed up against the inevitable losses to friction we are forced to ride continuously downhill. It can, however, be a shallow hill; we do not need to go plummeting off of a cliff!

LIFT

A wing gliding down a sloping flight path, being acted on by a balanced system of forces. By definition, the drag force acts exactly opposite to the flight path & the lift force is perpendicular to it. The force due to gravity always points toward the center of the earth (straight down).

DRAG

Distance Flown

Altitude Lost

Flight Path

GRAVITY

In the top example, the lift force depicted is eight times higher than the drag force but not quite as strong as the force due to gravity. The lift and drag forces, when added together as vectors, produce a resultant force exactly equal and opposite to the force of gravity.

LIFT

DRAG

Distance Flown

Altitude Lost

Flight Path

GRAVITY

In the lower example the drag force has doubled. In accordance with the rules of vector addition, the lift to drag ratio is slightly more than halved and the wing's descent angle is slightly more than doubled. (See Chapter Six for more information on vectors and vector addition.)

You can see something else here, if you look carefully. The slope of the glide path depends on the relationship between lift and drag. In fact, any object can function as a wing and produce lift. (Even the human body of a skydiver in free fall before he deploys his parachute can do so if oriented properly. Contrary to what our simplified explanation earlier implied, a falling human body can develop some small amount of lift.) But what separates a good wing from a poor one is how efficiently the wing produces lift. In other words, what is the ratio of the amount of lift produced by the wing to the amount of drag? It is a simple result of the definition of lift and drag that the ratio of lift divided by drag equals the ratio of distance flown to altitude lost along the slope of the glide path of the wing. A wing that produces equal amounts of lift and drag descends along a glide path with a one to one slope; i.e. a glide path angled downwards at 45 degrees. Such a wing can glide forward only a distance equal to its altitude, and has a rapid descent rate that is 71% of its speed through the air. This is about what a skydiver's body is capable of if aligned just right to the airflow. It is considered extremely poor performance in aerodynamic terms.

On the other end of the Lift to Drag ratio (usually written as L/D and sometimes called the glide ratio) performance spectrum are the sailplanes, some of which produce lift forces that are fifty times as high as their drag forces. Such a glider could fly for a mile with only 100 feet of altitude, and would have a descent rate of only 2% of its speed through the air.

Paragliders are in between, having glide ratios of between five and nine to one.

The Basis of Soaring

It is important to note here that L/D and glide ratio are not the same thing in the real world. In completely smooth and unmoving air, the glide ratio is the L/D ratio. In actuality, however, the L/D is only the glide ratio relative to the airmass in which the glider is flying. If the air mass is moving - whether horizontally (wind), or vertically (lift or sink) - the glider's glide ratio relative to the ground will be different than its L/D ratio. Flying in lift, or flying downwind will increase the glide ratio relative to the ground above the value of the L/D, while flying into the wind or in sink will decrease the glide ratio relative to the ground below the value of the L/D. The term L/D has only one meaning as it refers to a pure performance parameter of the aircraft. But when you use or hear the term "glide ratio", make sure you know whether you are referring to glide ratio relative to the ground or glide ratio through the air.

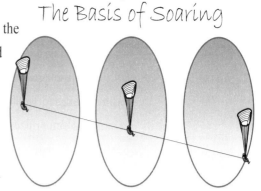

A paraglider descends within the air mass at its lift to drag ratio

However, if the airmass is rising faster than the paraglider is descending, the paraglider will gain altitude relative to the ground

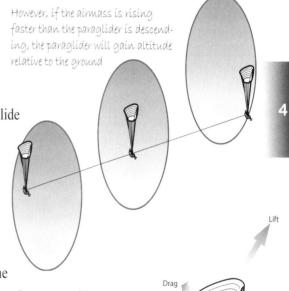

Lift

Drag

Gravity

While we are speaking of how to measure the performance of a wing, let us look at the other important measure of performance for a soaring aircraft. Soaring pilots are concerned not just with how far they can glide with a given amount of altitude, but also with how long they can stay in the air, and in what conditions. The most important measure of performance with respect to these two questions is the aircraft's sink rate. The sink rate (and in particular the aircraft's minimum sink rate) is the rate at which the aircraft is losing altitude. This is such an important number because it determines what conditions must be present for the aircraft to stay in the air. The atmosphere is filled with randomly distributed parcels of rising and descending air. To stay up, the pilot of any non-powered aircraft must find, and stay within a parcel of rising air that is rising faster than he is descending. Now parcels of air that are rising at 300 feet per minute are relatively common on an average soaring day. But parcels of air that are rising at 600 feet per minute are much more rare. So an aircraft with a minimum sink rate of 200 feet per minute has a good chance of finding soarable air, while a glider that sinks at 500 feet per minute has a much poorer chance.

4

Sink rate depends on two things. One is the L/D ratio; the flatter the slope of your glide path the more slowly you are descending. But equally important is your flying speed; if you fly slower, you also descend more slowly. In fact, while top performing sailplanes have L/D ratios of as much as ten times that of entry level paragliders, their sink rates are only about two times slower because paragliders fly so much slower.

Beyond that, flying slowly as paragliders do has another advantage for soaring. Thermal lift exists in a limited volume of air; in order to stay in the thermal column the aircraft must circle within the region of lift. Also, a typical thermal is not of uniform strength; it may be five times stronger near the center than it is at the outer edges. The radius of the turn that an aircraft can make depends on its speed. Faster flying sailplanes (and to a lesser extent hang gliders) are forced to fly larger radius circles around the outer edges of the thermals where the lift is weaker. Paragliders, flying slower, can circle more tightly in the stronger core of the thermal, and therefore can often climb faster even with a higher sink rate.

Getting back to aerodynamics, so how does a wing produce lift? If you've read any aviation books or studied aerodynamics at all, you've probably heard several explanations for this. One of the most popular in books on the subject refers to Bernoulli's Principle, which states that when air speeds up it drops in pressure. The typical aviation book explanation then goes on to refer to the normal cross sectional shape of a wing, which is curved on top and flatter on the bottom, and states that the air molecules which pass over the top of the wing must speed up to travel the longer distance along the curved surface in the same time, and therefore the pressure drops on top of the wing and lift is produced.

The problem is that this explanation does not explain how such a wing can fly quite well upside down where the "shorter" flat surface is on the top. The fact is that wings can and do fly perfectly happily in an inverted state. (The Grob 103 Twin Acro sailplane is one good example; its L/D is actually higher at some speeds upside down than right side up!). The traditional Bernoulli explanation cited above also does not explain the source of lift on a symmetrical wing, and symmetrical wings also produce lift quite happily and reasonably efficiently.

The problem is not that Bernoulli was wrong, but that the explanations of Bernoulli that are geared to the level of understanding of aerodynamics required by a pilot are overly simplified; so much so that they, in fact, become incorrect. Beyond that, such explanations are unnecessary for a pilot's understanding of lift production by a wing.

QUIZ:

The glide ratio through the air is equal to the

_____

to

_____

ratio.

Besides, as soon as you get Bernoulli figured out, a real aerodynamicist will come along and tell you that unless you understand the mechanics of the circulation theory involving the rectangular vortex ring, then you really don't understand at all how a wing produces lift.

Let's leave it at this: The wing produces lift by deflecting air downwards. The reaction force on the wing that results from the wing pushing the air down is the air pushing upwards on the wing, and this is what the wing experiences as the lift force.

Also, wings produce lift most efficiently (with the highest ratios of lift produced to drag incurred), when the flow of air over the wing is as smooth as possible. All of the vast complications of the technical process of wing design (and it is a process of extreme complexity) in the end boil down to these considerations; how to make a wing which pushes air down without creating large disturbances in its flow.

Regardless of the glider's pitch or roll attitude, you must maintain an acceptable angle of attack in order to maintain stability and control — Swing photo

We need one more concept to complete our pilot's understanding of aerodynamics; the concept of angle of attack.

Angle of Attack

The angle of attack is the angle between the wing itself and the airflow over the wing.

Note: Don't think here in terms of the actual airflow over the wing surface; that tends to adhere to and follow the surface of the wing, and there is really no angle between it and the wing.

Think instead of something one might refer to as the "remote free stream," that is the direction of the relative airflow for the air that is remote from and not yet disturbed by the wing. Think of the angle of attack as the angle between this remote flow, and the chord line of the wing; the chord line being a straight line from the forward most edge of the wing to the rearward most edge, aligned with the direction of flight. Realize also that the angle of attack is not the attitude of the wing, which is its angle relative to the horizon. A wing can have a nose high attitude and a small angle of attack, or it could have a nose low attitude and a large angle of attack. This single confusion, between attitude and angle of attack has probably killed more pilots that any other single misunderstanding.

In simple terms, think of the angle of attack as "how much of a bite" the wing is taking from the air as it moves through the air. Now at large angles of attack the wing takes a big bite, deflects a lot of air, and produces large amounts of lift and drag. At small angles of attack the wing takes a small bite, deflects a little bit of air, and produces a small amount of lift and drag.

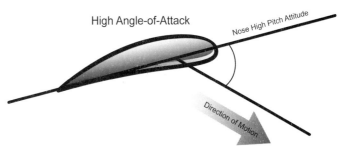

Angle of Attack is the angle between the wing and its direction of motion through the air. AoA is not the same as pitch attitude to the horizon.

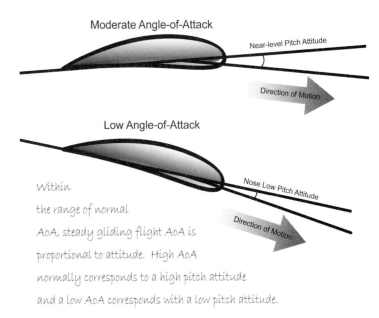

Within the range of normal AoA, steady gliding flight AoA is proportional to attitude. High AoA normally corresponds to a high pitch attitude and a low AoA corresponds with a low pitch attitude.

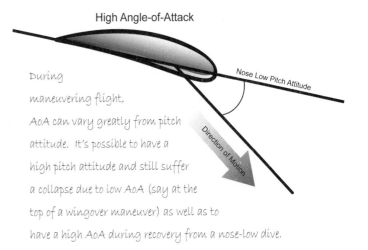

During maneuvering flight, AoA can vary greatly from pitch attitude. It's possible to have a high pitch attitude and still suffer a collapse due to low AoA (say at the top of a wingover maneuver) as well as to have a high AoA during recovery from a nose-low dive.

OK. Let's start with a wing at a moderately high angle of attack, gliding downwards along its characteristic glide slope at a constant speed. Lift and drag forces combine to exactly balance gravity, and the aircraft is in equilibrium; not stationary (because only the movement through the air is producing the lift and drag) but flying at a constant speed and in a straight line.

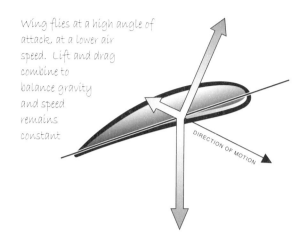

Wing flies at a high angle of attack, at a lower air speed. Lift and drag combine to balance gravity and speed remains constant

Now let us lower the angle of attack by somehow rotating the wing nose down. What happens? Well, at the new lower angle of attack, the lift and drag produced are less, and now they no longer completely balance the force of gravity. With an unbalanced force in the downward direction, the aircraft begins to accelerate downwards, picking up speed. As the speed increases, however, lift and drag (which depend also on the speed of the airflow over the wing) build up again, until at some new higher speed they again balance the force of gravity and the speed again stabilizes.

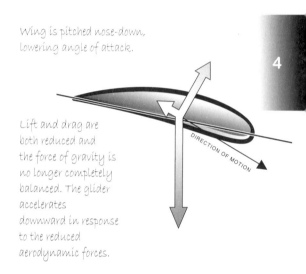

Wing is pitched nose-down, lowering angle of attack.

Lift and drag are both reduced and the force of gravity is no longer completely balanced. The glider accelerates downward in response to the reduced aerodynamic forces.

So what do we have? Simply this: control of the angle of attack is what controls flying speed. For every angle of attack there is one speed at which the aircraft will be in force equilibrium, and it will speed up or slow down until it reaches that speed. Lower angles of attack give rise to higher speeds, and higher angles of attack give rise to lower speeds. Every (steady state) speed has one corresponding angle of attack.

What are the limits? Well ultimately, on the bottom end, when the angle of attack is low enough that no lift is produced, the aircraft is diving straight down at its terminal velocity, where drag alone balances the force of gravity.

But what about at the upper end? How slow can you go?

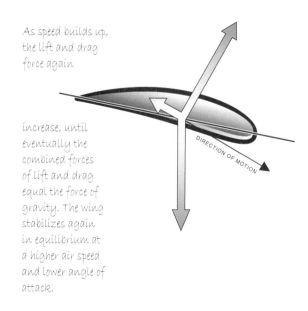

As speed builds up, the lift and drag force again increase, until eventually the combined forces of lift and drag equal the force of gravity. The wing stabilizes again in equilibrium at a higher air speed and lower angle of attack.

Well, there is one fundamental limitation on the operation of the wing; it only works up to a certain angle of attack. At angles of attack higher than this limiting angle, the airflow over the wing separates from the top surface of the wing and becomes turbulent, leading to a loss of lift and an increase in drag. This phenomenon of turbulent flow separation above the limiting angle of attack is known as the "stall".

This is another of those unfortunate uses of a word we have other meanings for. The "stall" in an airplane has nothing to do with the engine stopping; that is referred to as "engine failure." A stall in aviation means that the pilot has raised the angle of attack above the critical limiting angle, and that as a result the wing will no longer fly. The misunderstanding that has killed many pilots that was referred to earlier is when the wing has a high angle of attack in combination with the nose being at a very low attitude to the horizon. The nose low attitude prevents the pilot from recognizing the stall for what it is, and causes the pilot to continue to try to "raise the nose" which only locks the glider farther into the stall.

Since the phenomenon of the stall sets an upper limit on angle of attack, and since higher angles of attack correspond to lower airspeeds, the stall is what sets the lower limit on how slowly an aircraft can fly. If you attempt to fly below the stall speed you will raise the angle of attack of the wing above the stall angle of attack and the wing will cease flying.

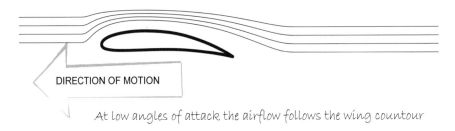

DIRECTION OF MOTION

At low angles of attack the airflow follows the wing countour

If the angle of attack is increased too high, the airflow will no longer be able to follow the wing countour. The flow seperates in turbulent eddies, the wing stalls and stops generating lift.

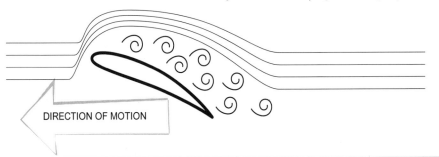

DIRECTION OF MOTION

Since the stall is caused by too high an angle of attack rather than too low an airspeed, it is possible to create a stall at a higher speed than the normal stall speed. In an airplane or sailplane for example, a sharp sudden increase in angle of attack can stall the wing before the aircraft has a chance to slow down to the normal stall speed. This type of high speed stall is not a factor in paragliders, although there is one situation in which the stall in a paraglider can occur at a higher than normal speed, and that is the steep turn. Any aircraft is loaded more heavily in a steep banked turn due to centrifugal force, and as a result the speeds at all angles of attack, including the stall angle, become higher.

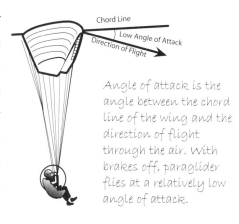

Angle of attack is the angle between the chord line of the wing and the direction of flight through the air. With brakes off, paraglider flies at a relatively low angle of attack.

The angle of attack on a paraglider is controlled primarily by use of the brake lines. Pulling down on the brakes pulls down the trailing edge of the canopy, raising the angle of attack and slowing the canopy down. Letting up on the brakes allows the trailing edge to return to its normal position, lowering the angle of attack and increasing flying speed. (Pulling down on the brakes also changes the shape of the wing, which also is part of what causes the wing to fly slower). If the canopy is fitted with a speed stirrup or other pitch control device, further adjustments in the angle of attack can be made. Pressing down on the speed stirrup pulls down on the leading edge of the canopy, lowering the angle of attack. (The stirrup also pulls down on the canopy in the mid-chord area, flattening the camber of the airfoil and making it fly even faster.)

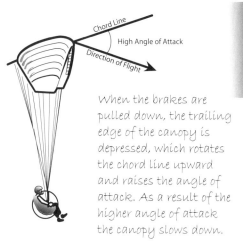

When the brakes are pulled down, the trailing edge of the canopy is depressed, which rotates the chord line upward and raises the angle of attack. As a result of the higher angle of attack the canopy slows down.

In practice, the paraglider has significant limitations associated with high and low angles of attack. Because a paraglider is a completely flexible wing which is kept inflated and therefore maintains its shape by ram air pressure, it is subject to deflation and collapse of the canopy if operated at too high or too low an angle of attack. Special caution needs to be used with the speed stirrup as its use makes the canopy more susceptible to a spontaneous, turbulence-induced collapse.

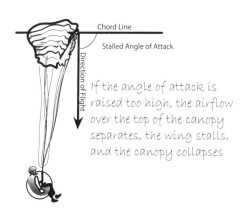

If the angle of attack is raised too high, the airflow over the top of the canopy separates, the wing stalls, and the canopy collapses

Paraglider Design Considerations

The design of a paraglider is a combination of art and science with designers using a mix of aerodynamic and layout software as well as intuition and trial-and-error to achieve their goals. Designers are sensitive about sharing trade secrets but a good deal of information is available from NASA studies. Vertigo, an aerospace company located in Lake Elsinore, California, has a rich history of scientific work involving flexible wings and parafoils (paraglider and hang glider pilots abound throughout their corporate structure). Roy Haggard, Vice President of Vertigo, graciously offered up some generalizations which are summarized here.

Like all aircraft design, a paraglider must target the proper mix of stability and control. In order to have either, the canopy must have sufficient internal pressure to hold the canopy shape. Maintaining proper internal pressure requires a minimum airspeed which varies according to the loads on the lines (only a few mph of wind is required to kite a canopy but significantly more is needed if the canopy is weighted) as well as the proper angle of attack. A typical parafoil section starts to collapse when the AoA is less than 3 degrees and begins to stall when the AoA exceeds 10 degrees. Inlet size, shape and location affect how well the parafoil maintains its shape across the speed range as well as how it responds to collapses.

Tailless aircraft must achieve pitch stability through a combination of airfoil reflex (upturned trailing edge) and pendular stability (achieved by a vertical distance between the wing and the overall center of gravity). Airfoil reflex tends to reduce glide performance so paraglider designers emphasize pendular stability. The paraglider is statically stable because if the wing gets in front of or behind the pilot then the pilot's weight will tend to swing back under it, restoring level flight. In order to be dynamically stable the wing must maintain angular limits so that the static stability does not cause excessive rates that would exceed either the positive or negative AoA limits. (This is one of the reasons why aerobatics in a paraglider requires skill to do properly and safely.)

Roll stability is achieved through a combination of dihedral effect and pendular stability. Wing dihedral is the inclination of the two wing halves to each other, evident in many conventional aircraft. To maintain its shape, a parafoil must have anhedral (negative dihedral) but achieves a positive dihedral effect due to the wing being so far above the center of gravity.

Conventional aircraft use a vertical stabilizer for yaw stability. The paraglider's downward sloping wingtips provide such vertical surfaces. When the relative airflow no longer meets the wing head on (sideslip), it causes an increased angle of attack on the downwind wingtip causing a rolling and yawing moment into the sideslip. At higher sideslips the upwind wingtip's AoA can be reduced enough so as to cause a collapse (a common cause of asymmetric collapses). A swept leading edge also contributes to yaw stability but to much less of a degree. Leading and trailing edge sweep together define the wing planform. Proper lift distribution along the lateral axis is important to reduce buckling during maneuvering flight. As paraglider design has matured, the wing planforms used by different designers have converged so that only subtle differences exist between most designs.

The arch of the parafoil is a major contributor to how the canopy responds after a partial collapse. Modern paragliders are designed so that the drag and loss of lift of the collapsed side is at least partially countered by the reorientation of the lift vector of the flying side.

Paragliders turn by changing the lift and drag distribution between the two wings. The relative amounts of lift and drag changes are very dependant upon the relative lengths of the brake lines and how they alter the shape of the wing. Some gliders actually change the wingtip shape to add additional parasitic drag to the inner wing. The balance of the forces in turning flight is beyond the scope of this book but it is the unbalancing of these forces that determine the specifics of how an aircraft turns and how and when it will transition from a turn into a spiral dive.

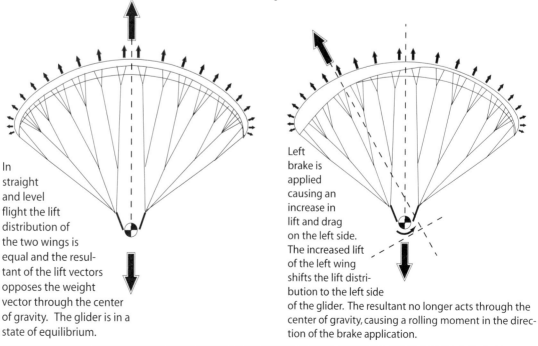

In straight and level flight the lift distribution of the two wings is equal and the resultant of the lift vectors opposes the weight vector through the center of gravity. The glider is in a state of equilibrium.

Left brake is applied causing an increase in lift and drag on the left side. The increased lift of the left wing shifts the lift distribution to the left side of the glider. The resultant no longer acts through the center of gravity, causing a rolling moment in the direction of the brake application.

NOTES

QUIZ:

A stall occurs when your flying speed is too low to generate the required lift.

☐ True

☐ False

QUIZ:

A stall occurs when your angle of attack is too

☐ low

☐ high

WIND & WEATHER

THE AIR AND THE ATMOSPHERE

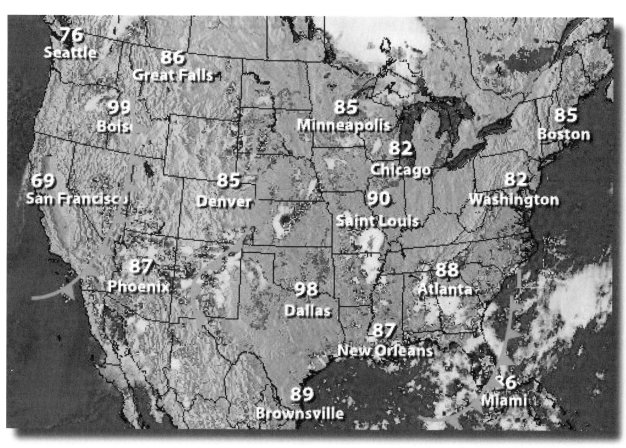

You need at least a casual understanding of the weather in order to safely practice the sport of paragliding. This chapter takes you from the basics to advanced soaring forecasting.

Chapter 5 — WIND AND WEATHER
THE AIR & THE ATMOSPHERE

This manual will not attempt a comprehensive treatment of meteorology—the study of weather. There are excellent books available on the subject which you are urged to study. See the appendix of reference sources at the back of this manual for further suggested readings.

Bill Cosby, in an early comedy routine, claims to have dated a philosophy major in college who used to walk around asking questions like, "Why is there air?" To which Bill replied indignantly, "Any phys-ed major knows why there's air: There's air to blow up basketballs with, to blow up volleyballs!"

A paraglider pilot might add to that, "There's air so we can fly paragliders!" And indeed, air, and its special properties are fundamental to our ability to fly. Consequently, an understanding of the air, and how and why it does what it does is a great help to anyone aspiring to be a pilot.

Because air is invisible, odorless and tasteless (except for some summer days in the Los Angeles area), we tend to think of it as not really there, or as not having any substance. At walking speeds, it offers no impedance to our progress through it. Unlike water, it provides only an insignificant amount of buoyancy to our bodies against the pull of gravity. And yet we are all aware that air has sufficient substance to exert tremendous force—the destructive power of a hurricane being perhaps the most graphic and familiar example.

And in fact, the large and small scale motions of the air that we call "wind" is the most important thing about the air that we as pilots need to be concerned with. The nature of the wind on any given day is the key to whether or not we will decide to fly, and what we can expect from our flying if we do fly. We need to know what direction the wind is blowing (because we need to take off and land into the wind), how strong it is blowing, how much variation there is in the wind speed, and whether or not the wind is expected to get stronger or change direction as the day goes on.

It is helpful to think of the air as a fluid, like water, but much less dense, and more elastic. Motion of this fluid is what we experience as wind. Random or chaotic fluctuations in the motion of the fluid are what we experience as gusty wind conditions or, during flight, as turbulence.

In flight, we as pilots are supported against gravity by a force which results from the "relative wind," or the relative motion of air over our wings as we move through the air. Therefore, the strength and direction of the ambient wind, and changes in the direction and speed of the wind are very important to our flying.

There are many causes of turbulence. Most of them are associated with the dynamics of weather, and will be discussed below. One important cause of turbulence is not directly weather related, however, other than the fact that it results from wind. This type of turbulence is called "mechanical" turbulence (sometimes referred to as a rotor, especially when the axis of rotation is horizontal), and it occurs whenever wind flows over or around an obstruction. Imagine putting your hand into a moving stream of smooth water. As the water flows past your hand (the obstruction) the pattern of flow becomes turbulent; it breaks up into little circular eddies and vortices. The same thing happens in the air; swirling chaotic motion in the air exists downwind of any significant obstacle in any significant wind. The larger the obstacle, and the stronger the wind, the greater the turbulence. Rotor turbulence downwind (on the "lee" side) of a mountain in a strong wind can produce a strong enough down draft to send a small airplane into the ground. As a pilot, you want to avoid flying into the lee of a large object in a significant wind.

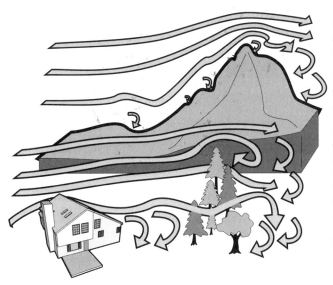

Wind flowing around structural or terrain obstacles becomes turbulent on the lee side of obstacles. Avoid flying in the lee of obstacles in any significant wind.

Larger obstacles or terrain produce larger and stronger areas of turbulence on the lee (downwind) sides. Lee-side turbulence surrounding mountains in strong winds has forced light airplanes into the ground!

Keep in mind that all turbulence is potentially dangerous to a paraglider pilot, more so than to pilots of other aircraft, because it can cause spontaneous collapses and loss of control of the canopy. Paraglider pilots should not fly in any significant amount of turbulence until they have completely mastered the advanced skills of canopy collapses, canopy control, and canopy re-inflation.

If we think of the air as a fluid, we can then picture ourselves living at the bottom of an ocean of air (the atmosphere) that is about 50 miles deep. At the bottom of this ocean, the pressure of the air is greatest, just as the pressure on your ears becomes greater as you swim down towards the bottom of a swimming pool. The source of this pressure is the weight of all of the air above you. (The weight of a column of air which is one inch square and as tall as the atmosphere is about 15 pounds Thus we say that the normal sea level air pressure is 15 pounds per square inch.) You are not normally aware of this pressure because it is equalized inside and outside your body. But you will notice it sometimes when driving up or down a mountain road, or climbing or descending in an airplane; your ears will "pop" as the air pressure inside your head equalizes with the outside pressure.

Because of the elasticity of the air, and the pressure difference with altitude, the air density also changes with altitude. The air is most dense at the surface, and becomes more and more rarefied with increasing altitude. Because of this, the air exerts less force at the same speed at higher altitudes, so all aircraft have to fly faster at higher altitudes.

This is normally not important for flight itself, but can be very important for takeoffs and landings, especially when dealing with an aircraft on which you must run to reach your flying speed. Takeoffs in light winds on a hang glider or paraglider from a very high mountain will require a much stronger run than will the same launch at a lower altitude.

And finally, the air also has a temperature gradient with altitude; that is, it gets cooler as you go higher, at the rate of about 3.5 degrees (F) per thousand feet of increased altitude for the first ten miles or so.

If the atmosphere were a static entity, that would be all there was to it; an ocean of air with decreasing pressure, density, and temperature as we climbed to higher altitudes. In such an atmosphere we could still fly, but soaring would be impossible, because there would be no vertical movement in the air to carry us to higher altitudes. In reality, however, the atmosphere is dynamic; it is constantly changing, and further it is not uniform even at a given altitude. The pressure and temperature vary from place to place at the same altitude, and the distributions of temperature and pressure throughout the atmosphere are constantly changing. This constant change of temperature and pressure, and the movement of air that results, along with the condensation of water vapor from the air in the form of snow and rain, is what we refer to as our weather.

In order to understand something about the mechanics of weather, you have to understand just a few additional facts about how gases behave. Air is a mixture of gases; almost 80% of it is nitrogen, about 20% is oxygen, which is the part we need for breathing, and the rest is trace amounts of hydrogen, helium, and other gases, one of which is water vapor, or water in the gaseous state. (Water vapor is not what you see coming out of a boiling tea kettle. What you see is condensed water vapor; i.e. gaseous water that has returned to the liquid state as tiny droplets, having been cooled by contact with the air in the room. Water vapor itself is invisible, just like the other gaseous components of the air.)

As a mixture of gases, air behaves like a gas. Gases have some interesting properties; one of which is the relationship of temperature, pressure and volume. Unlike solids or liquids whose volume changes only slightly with changes in temperature or pressure, gas is highly elastic, and its volume is directly proportional to its temperature, and inversely proportional to its pressure. If you have some gas in a closed cylinder, and you change the temperature or pressure, you will change the volume of the gas. Likewise, if you change the volume, it must result in a change to either the temperature or the pressure, or both.

The key aspect of this relationship to remember for weather, is that when a gas is compressed, it heats up, and when it is allowed to expand, it cools.

A related aspect of atmospheric behavior relates to the concept of atmospheric stability. Simply stated, an air mass is stable when the cooler air is on the bottom and the warmer air is on the top. This is a stable state because cooler air is denser, and therefore heavier, and therefore tries to get to the bottom, while warmer air is less dense and therefore lighter and therefore tries to rise to the top. If you invert this picture, the air mass has now become unstable; the cooler air at the top is heavier and wants to move down, while the warmer, less dense air at the bottom is lighter and wants to rise.

How Air Changes Temperature with Changes in Volume:

In a high pressure system, air descending to lower altitudes where the pressure is higher, becomes compressed and heated. Since warm air can hold more water vapor, this results in cloud dissipation and clear weather.

In a low-pressure system, air rising to higher altitudes where the pressure is lower, expands and cools. Since cooler air cannot hold as much water vapor, this results in cloud formation and precipitation.

In actual fact, the air temperature does not need to actually increase with increasing altitude in order for the air mass to be stable. It is enough if the drop in temperature with increasing altitude is less than a certain rate. This is true because as a given parcel of heated air rises, it cools due to its expansion. It will only continue to rise if the air it is rising into remains always cooler than the rising parcel of air. In general, the environmental lapse rate, or the rate at which the surrounding air mass becomes cooler with increasing altitude, must be greater than 5 degrees (F) per thousand feet for a rising parcel of warmer air to continue rising. When the environmental lapse rate is greater than this minimum required value, the air is said to be unstable.

A final fact about air you need to understand is the concept of relative humidity, and its relationship to temperature. We have said that air contains some amount of gaseous water. The actual amount can vary, but at any given temperature there is a limit to how much water vapor a volume of air can hold. Warmer air, however, can hold more water vapor than cooler air. A 20 degree (F) rise in temperature about doubles the amount of water vapor a volume of air can hold. Relative humidity, expressed as a percentage (the humidity is 45%, for example) is a measure of how much water vapor is in the air relative to the maximum amount that the air can hold at that temperature.

Again, the key aspect of this relationship for understanding weather is to remember that as air is cooled, it loses its ability to hold water vapor as gaseous water. If warm, moist air is cooled, some of the water must condense out, in the form of water droplets or ice. This is the source of clouds, of rain, and of snow.

In pilot weather briefings provided for airplane or sailplane pilots, the concept of relative humidity is dealt with by reference to a special temperature known as the dew point. This is the temperature to which the present air mass would have to be cooled to reach the saturation point, i.e. 100% humidity. For example, if the temperature is 70 degrees, and the dew point is 64 degrees, the pilot knows that there will be fog or precipitation if the temperature drops 6 degrees.

We said awhile back that the atmosphere was not static. The thing that prevents it from being static is uneven heating by the sun. The density of solar radiation in the middle latitudes near the equator is higher, and the earth's surface is heated more in this area. This causes the air above the surface near the equator to become warmer, and therefore to expand and become less dense. This expanded, less dense air rises, and air flows into the area from the regions north and south of the equator to replace it. This sets up a global circulation of the air, with air rising at the equator, flowing north and south towards the poles, and returning towards the equator along the surface. However, the actual pattern of airflow becomes much more complicated than that. Because of the effects of the earth's rotation, moving air tends to be deflected to the right in the northern hemisphere, and to the left in the southern hemisphere. (This is known as the Coriolus effect). Seasonal and daily fluctuations in solar radiation at a given location add complexity to the pattern of temperature distribution. Finally, there is additional uneven heating due to the irregular distribution of land masses and ocean on the earth's surface. The temperature of the ocean is much less affected by the sun shining on it, and so land mass temperatures fluctuate above and below those of the ocean during periods of increasing and decreasing solar radiation.

> **QUIZ:**
>
> Mechanical turbulence that occurs behind a hill or object is often referred to as
>
> _____
>
> turbulence.

A pilot enjoys the waning lift at Torrey Pines as sunset nears

Pressure Systems and Weather Fronts

As a result of the uneven heating of the surface, areas of low pressure and areas of high pressure tend to develop in the atmosphere above the earth's surface. Air tends to flow into an area of low pressure, assuming a cyclonic rotation due to the Coriolus effect as it flows inward toward the center of the low (counter-clockwise flow in the northern hemisphere). As the air flows into the low pressure area from all directions, it is forced upward. As the air rises into higher altitudes, it enters an environment of surrounding air where the pressure is lower (remember that pressure drops with increasing altitude), and therefore the rising parcel of air expands. As a result of the expansion, the air cools, (remember that gases cool when allowed to expand). As a result of the cooling, the air may become too cool to hold all of its water vapor, and some of the water vapor may condense out into clouds. If enough condenses out, rain or snow may result. Low pressure areas are therefore associated with cloudy weather and precipitation.

When a high pressure develops, the air tends to rush outward from the center of the high, assuming an anticyclonic rotation due to the Coriolus force (clockwise rotation in the northern hemisphere). Air descends in the center of the high to replace the outward rushing air. Descending air is moving into a lower altitude region of higher pressure, and is therefore compressed and therefore heated. This air becomes capable of holding greater quantities of moisture as gaseous water vapor as it heats up, and therefore high pressure areas are associated with the dissipation of clouds and with clear weather.

Most of the large-scale weather patterns that we experience are associated with frontal systems. A front is a boundary between two masses of air of different temperatures. Such air masses tend not to mix at their boundaries, but instead retain their individual characteristics. When cold air moves into a region and displaces warmer air, we refer to it as a cold front. On weather charts a cold front is delineated by the color blue with small triangles extending outward along the front line. When it is a warm air mass moving in to displace colder air, we call it a warm front. Warm fronts are delineated on weather charts by the color red with small semi-circles extending outward along the front line. Note that a warm front and a cold front are in one sense the same thing; a boundary between a mass of cold air and a mass of warm air. Which type of front we label it, and many of the properties associated with it depend on which way it is moving relative to a fixed point on the ground; i.e. which air mass is displacing the other.

Whether hot or cold, a front always extends from an area of low pressure. In the U.S., most low pressure systems originate to the northwest and move in a southeasterly direction. During summer months the great plains states and Atlantic coastal states may also be influenced with fronts that come northward from the Gulf of Mexico or northwestward from the Atlantic Ocean. In all cases the front stretches in a curving path outward from the center of the low pressure. Irrespective of the overall cyclonic flow, immediately ahead of the front, the prevailing winds sweep parallel to the front towards the center of the low pressure while the winds will be perpendicular to the front (pushing it) immediately behind the boundary. You can therefor identify frontal passage with the switching of the winds and the bottoming out and reversal of the barometric pressure (which falls as the front approaches).

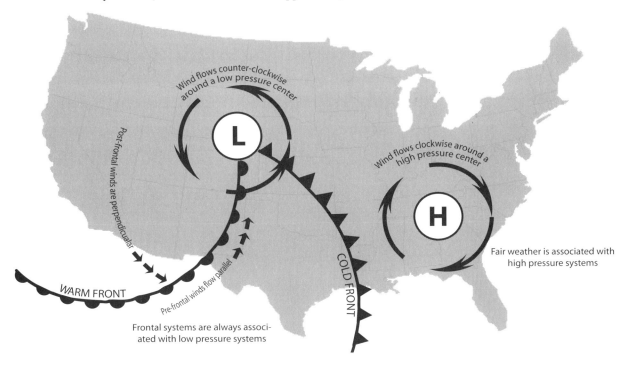

As you would expect, some amount of clouds and perhaps precipitation are to be expected along a front due to the cooling of the warmer air at the frontal boundary. The cold air acts like a wedge underneath the warm air mass, lifting it and thus causing cooling and precipitation. Normally more violent weather is associated with cold fronts; the slope of the frontal boundary is usually steeper, and the front usually moves more rapidly. Cold fronts are also normally associated with cumulus clouds with strong vertical development, with strong and gusty winds, with heavy rain and with turbulence. The air is usually unstable, and visibility outside of the clouds and precipitation is usually good. Warm fronts are usually slower moving, and are associated with stratus clouds, light rain or drizzle, stable air, poor visibility, and lighter winds.

Although weather fronts are usually associated with periods of worsening weather, soaring pilots keep an eye open for cold fronts. Cold front passage is typically characterized by rapidly clearing skies and fair weather cumulus clouds. In areas that often suffer from hot, stable weather, the new colder air mass offers a chance for a day or two of unstable air with cumulus clouds marking the tops of the thermals.

COLD FRONT

Cold air moves in replacing warmer air causing instability, cumulous clouds, possible rain and thunderstorms.

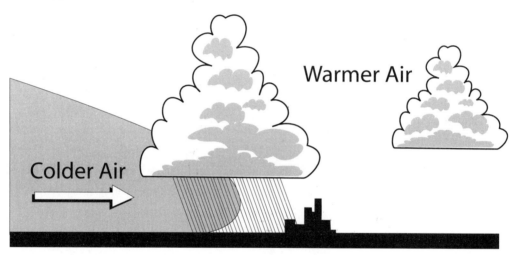

WARM FRONT

Warm air moves into to replace cooler air. Air mass is stable, clouds are stratus, visibility is poor, and precipitation is drizzle.

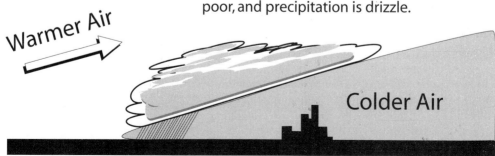

The jet stream is a localized area of high velocity flow normally located in the upper regions of the troposphere. Wind speeds within the jet stream can exceed 200 mph and cause areas of severe turbulence. During summer months in the U.S., the jet stream normally flows eastward across the northern portion of the country at altitudes of approximately 40,000-ft. During winter months the jet stream is pushed further south, often dipping down into lower altitudes. The high velocity flow accelerates the air beneath it and is therefor of special concern to paragliders. Many weather maps depict the current and forecasted position of the jet stream.

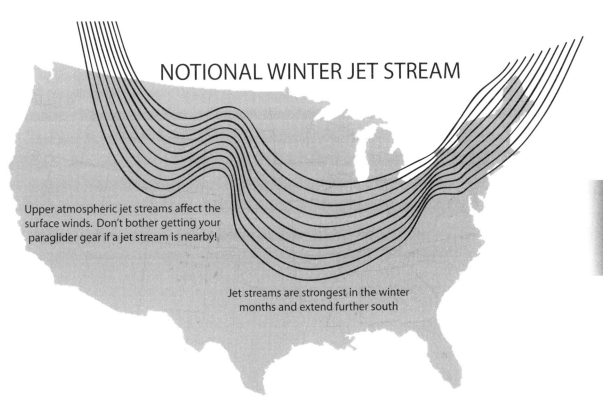

NOTIONAL WINTER JET STREAM

Upper atmospheric jet streams affect the surface winds. Don't bother getting your paraglider gear if a jet stream is nearby!

Jet streams are strongest in the winter months and extend further south

5

QUIZ:

Weather fronts are associated with

☐   low

☐   high

pressure systems.

The Cycling of Onshore and Offshore Winds

Solar heating of the land during the day raises its temperature to above that of a neighboring body of water. Air above the land is warmed and rises, drawing cooler air in off the water.

At night the land cools more quickly than and becomes cooler than the water. Air over the water remains warmer than the air above the cooler land. the air over the water rises, while the air over the land descends, resulting in an offshore flow.

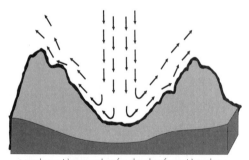

Upslope thermal winds during the day

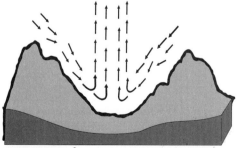

Downslope flow in the evening, with air rising over the middle of the valley

Micrometeorology - Weather on a Smaller Scale

The same dynamics of temperature differential that give rise to large scale weather patterns also cause similar patterns on a much smaller scale. When the sun shines on the ground, some types of terrain grow hotter more quickly. Damp ground or vegetation which contains water tends to heat up more slowly, while bare dirt or rock faces heat up faster. The air above a hotter surface like a rock face becomes hotter than the air over surrounding cooler terrain. This hot air expands, becoming less dense and therefore buoyant, and eventually breaks free and begins to rise. This is the birth of a thermal updraft, one type of rising air or "lift" that allows pilots of unpowered aircraft like paragliders to soar. As the thermal releases from the surface and begins to rise, air rushes in from the surrounding area to fill the void, and normally picks up a rotational flow. On a hot summer day you may see "dust devils" which look like miniature tornadoes, rising from a bare patch of ground or a plowed field. These are thermals in their early stages of generation. How fast and how far the thermals rise will depend on the level of stability or instability of the air.

Another small scale effect of local differential heating occurs at the boundary between land and water. Normally during the day the land heats up to a higher temperature than the water. Air over the land rises, and air flows in from off the water to replace it, leading to an onshore flow of air. We experience this as wind blowing onshore. In the evening, the temperature of the land surface falls faster than that of the water, and the water ends up being warmer than the land. Now the air rises over the water, leading to an offshore wind direction.

And finally, air in the vicinities of valleys and hillsides will tend to flow up the slopes out of the valleys during the day, when the sun warms the air adjacent to the hillsides and in the valleys. In the evenings, when the air next to the ground cools rapidly, the air will tend to slide down the slopes into the valleys, causing a downhill flow.

The Wind Gradient - The Slowing of the Wind Near the Ground

Another important phenomenon involving the motion of air is called the wind gradient. This is where the speed of the wind is slowed in the vicinity of the ground because of the friction between the ground and the moving airmass.

On landing approach, when flying into the wind at any given airspeed, your speed of forward motion over the ground is reduced by the speed of the wind. Your inertia (the tendency of any mass to continue to move at a constant speed) will cause your ground speed to have a tendency to remain constant. If, as you descend, the wind speed is suddenly reduced because you are descending into the gradient, then you will experience a sudden loss of airspeed, and will suddenly descend more quickly. If this happens very close to the ground, you may hit the ground more quickly and harder than you expected. As your canopy responds to the changing wind speed condition it will accelerate forward attempting to regain normal flying airspeed. As a result, you may also land with more forward speed, and further along your approach path than you expected to.

The solution to problems caused by wind gradient on landing are to be aware of the possibility of it and to be prepared to deal with it. Keep an eye on the windsock or streamer which is at or near ground level (if there is one) as you approach. If your forward progress over the ground indicates a significant wind, while the streamer indicates little wind, there is a significant wind gradient. Approach with some extra speed so that your descent into the gradient will not result in a stall and so that you

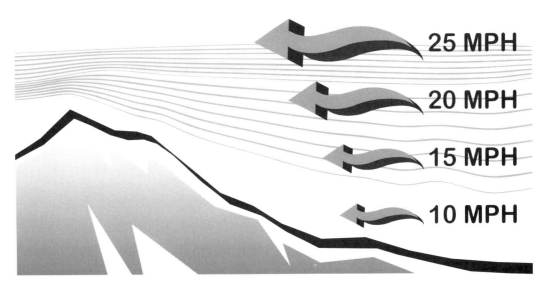

Wind Gradient

25 MPH

20 MPH

15 MPH

10 MPH

have some reserve of brakes to use to slow your descent and forward speed prior to landing touchdown.

Another important aspect of wind gradient is that when you measure or judge the wind speed while standing on launch, you are measuring the wind from within the gradient. The true speed of the wind just 20 or 30 feet higher could be much greater. If the wind measured at launch is on the border line of being too strong to fly in, it is almost certainly too strong at the altitude to which you will immediately be lifted after launch.

Wind gradients tend to be most severe in stable air conditions, where there is little vertical mixing of the air masses and there tends to be horizontal shearing action between different vertical layers of air. In unstable conditions, the vertical air movement tends to mix the layers and eliminate sharp boundaries and strong gradients.

Venturi Effect – The Acceleration of Airflow

The flow of air accelerates when it is forced to squeeze through a narrow opening. This can happen to the flow of air passing between rising terrain and a stable air layer above, or when air passes through a gap in a ridge. In either case there can be accelerated local horizontal wind. In a manner similar to the accelerated flow over the top of a curved wing, the air flow will also speed up around the sides of a hill which can make it difficult for an unsuspecting paraglider pilot to return back to the front.

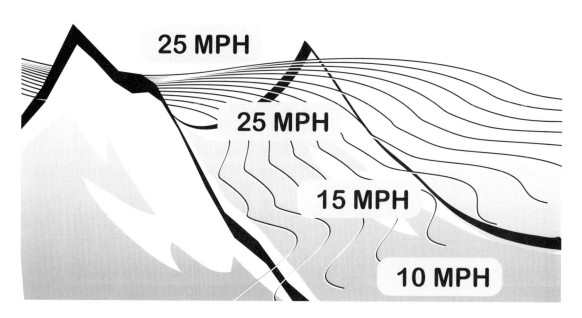

Venturi Effect

25 MPH

25 MPH

15 MPH

10 MPH

Forecasting Soaring

The single most important factor for whether or not a day will be soarable is wind velocity (speed and direction). If you are looking for thermals then you will want to get an idea of the lapse rate, the cloud cover and the potential for over-development.

So how do you get good wind information? Television weathermen usually gloss over the wind forecast, often omitting the wind direction and only mentioning the speed if it will be breezy. Additionally, the wind direction, if given, may not be exactly the same at your local flying site due to the terrain influences on the local flow. Luckily, there are plenty of sources available for wind direction. You can use your phone for access to FAA weather briefers, Automatic Weather Observation Services (AWOS), Air Traffic and Information Services (ATIS), and more. If you have internet access then you have an extraordinarily wide range of information and services at your disposal.

Before you start searching for weather information you need to learn a bit of the language. Aviation forecasts are normally given in Zulu time (also known as "Z", "UTC", Greenwich Mean Time or "GMT") which is the standard time in Greenwich, England, located at 0° longitude. You need to convert Zulu time to your local time so subtract 8 hours for Pacific Standard Time (7 hours if daylight savings).

Flying sites near major metropolitan areas often have automatic "wind talkers" installed. You simply dial the phone number to get a real time readout of the wind speed, direction, and temperature with maximum gust values and averages over the last hour. A list of wind talkers is included in Appendix Four.

If your flying site is near an airport with a control tower then you can get wind and temperature information from the AWOS or ATIS. Look in your local telephone book for airport listings. Typically direct numbers are not listed, however, the airport manager or local flying school will be able to refer you to the correct number.

5

Even though they may not be designed specifically for soaring pilots, you can often find good sources for local wind data from internet sites that support sailing, wind surfing, kite surfing, or even kite flying: The Intellicast web site is a good source for free graphical maps.

An easy source for rough lapse rate information is the "winds aloft forecast" available from your nearest Flight Service Station or many internet sites. This forecast shows the wind velocity and temperature at 3,000 feet intervals above various locations. If you know the predicted surface temperature for when you will be flying then you can compute the lapse rate to an altitude above it. If the rate of change is >5° F per thousand feet then you could have a good unstable day. If you are flying in areas that are conducive for thermal streeting (such as mountain ranges or convergence zones) then a lapse rate >4° F may be acceptable for good soaring. One limitation, however, of the winds aloft forecast is it will not pick up changes in the lapse rate between the reporting levels. For you trivia buffs out there, the forecast winds aloft are also given in true heading which will differ from your magnetic compass heading by the amount of the local magnetic deviation.

To get a better idea of the local lapse rate we need a more precise temperature profile. Until recently, the only way to get this was from rawinsonde data. A rawinsonde is a small disposable instrument package that is carried aloft by a weather

EXAMPLE AVIATION WINDS ALOFT FORECAST

```
FDUW02 KWBC 191416
DATA BASED ON 191200Z
VALID 191800Z    FOR USE 1700-2100Z. TEMPS NEG ABV 24000

FT  3000    6000    9000    12000   18000   24000   30000   34000   39000
BIH         1607    1607+19 1812+11 1723-06 2019-19 241334 242340 253049
BLH 1611 1710+21 1407+15 1409+07 1211-07 1410-18 160733 990039 351449
FAT 1706 1508+21 1615+16 1721+09 1921-05 1917-19 222033 232941 244048
FOT 3618 9900+20 9900+14 1506+07 1909-07 1914-21 202838 203346 214750
ONT 9900 1611+23 1716+16 1814+09 1707-07 1707-19 351131 321638 301450
RBL 9900 1810+20 1814+15 1819+09 1919-07 1918-20 204037 214344 225350
SAC 2207 1711+21 1718+14 1725+08 1820-06 1919-19 203635 214042 225549
SAN 1810 1511+23 1813+16 1610+09 1306-07 0905-19 021331 361738 361350
         1711 1516+22 1718+16 1819+09 1915-05 2006-18 271332 252140 242949
                  735+08 1919-06 1925-19 203535 214442 225849
                              223638 214546 225250
```

balloon. The data is transmitted down to ground stations and an accurate profile of the atmosphere is generated. Rawinsonde data is limited, however, since these balloons are only released from certain airports around the country. The balloons are released twice per day at 0000Z and 1200Z. We are usually most concerned with the 1200Z observation as this is the most recent profile of the atmosphere prior to the day's solar heating. This data may be useful to you if your flying site is within a reasonable distance of a rawinsonde site (so as to fall within the same overall air mass). If your flying site is located between two sites then you may want to interpolate the data from the two sites.

Now if you know the predicted high temperature at your flying site then it is relatively easy to compute the maximum height of thermals. You can find the predicted high temperature from your local weather forecast or numerous web sites such as the University of Wyoming's site at http://weather.uwyo.edu/models/mos/mos.html. At temperatures above the local dew point, a thermal will cool as it rises at the dry adiabatic lapse rate of 5.4° per thousand feet. If you start at the predicted surface temperature and plot a line upward at the dry adiabatic rate you can graphically see the point at which a thermal will cool and reach the same temperature as the surrounding air. The difference between the atmospheric temperature and the temperature of the

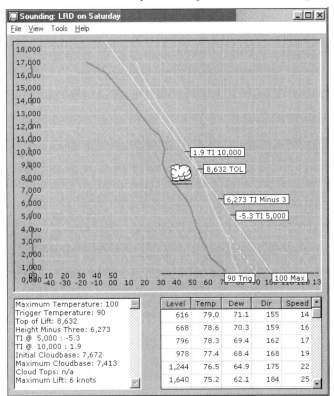

The freeware SOARCAST program allows the user to graphically predict thermal and cloudbase heights

thermal at any given altitude is called the Thermal Index (TI). The thermal will lose its buoyancy where the TI equals zero. Remember, though, that a soaring glider is always sinking relative to the rising air and thus can never truly reach the top of a thermal, instead topping out when the thermal's rate of climb equals the glider's rate of descent (approximately 200 feet per minute).

The difference between the maximum height of a thermal and the maximum usable (soaring) height is usually on the order of one to two thousand feet but is dependent on lapse rate as well as local topography and can be much more or less. You can approximate the maximum soaring height by finding the altitude that equates to a thermal index of -2°F. Remember, this is only an approximation of the maximum soaring height expected over flat terrain on a cloudless day. You can expect higher altitudes for a given thermal index over elevated terrain and beneath vertically developed clouds. In fact, you may want to establish a different thermal index that works best for your local site.

A freeware software program called SOARCAST plots out graphical representations of the above information and gives other useful information such as the trigger temperature (the minimum temperature that will trigger a thermal to 4000 ft AGL).

Due to the recent developments in modern day supercomputers and weather data collection, soaring pilots no longer are forced to rely on rawinsonde data from distant sites. The Forecast Systems Laboratory (FSL) of the National Oceanic and Atmospheric Administration (NOAA) has a program that splits up the U.S. in a 20-km grid pattern. The Rapid Cycle Update (RUC) program uses Mesoscale Analysis and Prediction System (MAPS) data from atmospheric soundings generated by conventional rawinsondes as well as atmospheric profilers, data-linked aircraft, and more. Using an internet interface any user can request the sounding for any location for time periods up to 36 hours in the future.

The graphical interface allows the user to point and click on expected maximum surface temperatures and instantly see the top of the lift, cloudbase, and wind profile. One of the nice features of the interactive interface is you can click on increasing ground level temperatures to see what temperatures will trigger thermals to the altitude of interest. When the pink lapse rate line intersects the black horizontal (cloudbase) line then you will know the trigger temperature for a thermal to cloudbase. Note that if the adiabatic lapse rate line touches the red temperature profile but instead of crossing it, begins separating vertically then the atmospheric profile is saturated and is now cooling at the moist adiabatic lapse rate of 3.3°F/1000 ft. You should note the altitude the moist lapse rate eventually intersects the temperature profile. This intersection signifies the top of the clouds. Remember, the thickness of a cumulus clouds is the biggest indicator of the level of lift beneath it and the potential for cloud suck and overdevelopment.

The RUC website is http://maps.fsl.noaa.gov. Once there, click on the "interactive/java" soundings link.

It is important to note the RUC plots do not depict lines of constant temperature vertically but instead extending upward to the right at a forty-five degree angle. These plots are referred to as "Skew-T" plots (skewed temperature). You need to know what type of plot you are looking at so that you can properly interpret the lapse rate.

Dr. Jack Glendening, a meteorologist with the Naval Research Laboratory has devised a series of analysis tools that make use of NOAA's RUC data for individual locations and displays the data (Boundary Layer Information Predictions – BLIPMAPs) in a group of useful thermal soaring parameters over a graphical map. For a nominal annual subscription fee you can select BLIPMAPS for your regional area and a quick perusal will provide valuable information on the thermalling potential to include the predicted best locations, intensity, height of the thermals; their buoyancy to shear ratio, areas of local convergence and thunderstorm potential. To maximize the utility of the information you should read the provided background explanations and caveats.

The hourly-updated BLIP forecasts are available on the web at:

`http://www.drjack.net/BLIP/index.html`

Additional local weather information is available at the weather underground web site at:

`http://www.wunderground.com`

A good generic weather site for forecasting the potential for overdevelopment and thunderstorms is:

`http://www.intellicast.com/`

Last, and certainly not least, are the National Oceanographic and Atmospheric Agency (NOAA) National Weather Service (NWS) sites at:

http://www.nws.noaa.gov/

Some NWS regional sites, especially in the southwestern U.S., offer daily soaring forecasts that offer information such as thermal strength and top of lift. These regional sites do not have standardized home pages so you may need to do a local browser search to find what you are looking for.

Government sites tend to be less user friendly than commercial sites but offer more information to the discerning pilot (they also don't flood your computer with pop-up ads and spyware!). Their sites continue to develop in sophistication and utility. This page gives numerous weather forecasting links as well as graphical links to show you locations of any FAA Notices to Airman (NOTAMs) and Temporary Flight Restrictions (TFRs) where paragliding would be illegal due to hazardous conditions:

http://aviationweather.gov/std_brief/

The FAA has Flight Service Station (FSS) offices throughout the country that provide for weather briefings, the filing of flight plans, and the checking of Notices To Airmen (NOTAMs). If you dial the toll-free number 800-WX-BRIEF (800-992-7433) you will automatically be connected to your local briefer. In some areas of the country, the briefers are familiar with gliding operations (even hang gliding and paragliding) and may even be able to provide soaring forecasts. In other parts you will have to ask specifically for the information you need. Do not be scared off if the briefer asks for your "N-number" (aircraft registration), they simply need to justify their existence as well as keep records of who they provided service for. Do not make up a number but do introduce yourself as a paraglider pilot that is looking for the following information:

1. Soaring forecast (if available)

2. Local forecast for the time period of _____ to _____ Z.

3. Surface winds

4. Cloud coverage to include base height and thickness

5. Winds aloft forecast for the appropriate altitudes (it is given in 3,000 ft. intervals to 12,000 ft; then 6,000 ft. intervals)

6. Any significant weather (SIGMETs, AIRMETs, Weather Watches & Warnings)

7. Any NOTAMs for your area of flight (all VFR aircraft, including paragliders, are required to be familiar with NOTAMS and temporary flight restrictions along their route of flight). Ask the briefer for any NOTAMS or Temporary Flight Restrictions (TFRs) in your area of flight.

Light winds and clear skies dotted with puffy cumulus clouds signify a beautiful soaring day.

Rules-of-Thumb For Thermal Prediction

You can actually learn some simple rules-of-thumb to predict the strength and abundance of thermals by paying attention to some basic indicators. Since thermals are born from solar heating, a good indicator of the potential for heating is the forecasted difference between the minimum and maximum temperature for the day. A rule of thumb (rough because it is without regard to lapse rate) is to multiply the forecasted temperature difference by 200 ft per degree to reach an estimate of thermal tops (e.g. nightly low was 55°F and the forecasted high is 75° then this rough guestimate would predict thermals reaching to 4,000 ft. AGL).

An indicator of thermal strength is the height of thermal tops (or cloud base) -- the higher the rise, the stronger the thermals. Generally, you need thermal heights and cloud bases above 2000 ft. AGL to have usable lift. A simple rule-of-thumb is to subtract one from the height of the cloud base (in thousands of feet) to arrive at average thermal strength (in hundreds of feet per minute), e.g. a cloudbase of 4,000ft would indicate 300 fpm thermals.

Another indicator of thermal strength is the vertical development of the cumulus clouds. Development of more than 1,000 – 3,000 ft indicates good thermal strength. Greater than 3,000 ft is cause to pay attention for signs of rapid development and possible cloud suck as the cloud can literally begin feeding upon itself because of the release of latent heat due to condensation. Pay special attention to clouds with vertical development greater than 7,000 ft (give yourself lateral and vertical room for an escape route, if required). A cloud with greater than 15,000 ft of vertical development is likely a developing thunderstorm and should be avoided at all costs (you do not want to be under, close to, or even landing anywhere near a thunderstorm). Vertical development of thunderstorms has been measured at over six thousand feet per minute. When such lift is present, so is extreme sink, microbursts, and sudden gust fronts that can reach outwards for tens of miles at gale-force strength.

Note that it is impossible to judge the height of a cloud when you are directly underneath. Observe clouds as you approach them and watch for the signs of darkening bases indicating increasing vertical development.

You can predict cloud base by noting the difference between the temperature and the dew point. Divide this difference by 4.4 to arrive at the altitude that moisture will condense and form clouds (e.g. temperature of 72° F and dew point of 54° would equate to a cloud base of 4,000 ft AGL).

The sky coverage is also a soaring indicator. Thermals tend to be stronger with scattered to broken cumulus clouds (3/8 to 6/8 coverage) than on days without cumulus clouds ("blue thermals"). Too much cloud coverage, however, causes shading that will impact the sun's ability to heat the terrain. Add a couple of hundred feet per minute to your lift estimation for scattered clouds and subtract the same amount for broken cloud cover. A thin layer of high altitude cirrus clouds usually has minimal effect on the solar heating but a layer of altostratus will greatly decrease thermal intensity for the shaded area.

Bo Criss followed this cloudstreet on his way to a 117-mile flight

An average thermal will rise until it cools to the temperature of the surrounding air and loses its buoyancy. Remember, however, that soaring aircraft cannot reach the top of the thermal because they are continuously sinking within the rising air.

Thermals will reach greater heights than the TI index will predict over locally raised terrain. By recording your predicted maximum height with the actual height you achieved you can come up with empirical data to better predict future soaring at your specific site.

NOTES

QUIZ:

Check the predicted wind

_____ and

_____ rate

to predict if it will be

soarable.

Chapter Six:

GETTING HIGH

LANDING APPROACHES & OTHER SKILLS FOR INTERMEDIATE FLYING

Setting up for a landing in a beautiful alpine village — Andy Stocker photo

Chapter 6 — GETTING HIGH

LANDING APPROACHES AND OTHER SKILLS FOR
INTERMEDIATE FLYING

For the purposes of this training manual, we will consider beginner level flying to be that part of your early flying that takes place on the training hill. We will define a training hill as a flying site where there is a continuous open slope from launch to landing area, where no turns are required to set up a landing approach, and where there is no possibility of flying past the landing area.

Once you leave the training hill to begin making "high flights" you will need a new set of skills, and new levels of knowledge and judgment. Of course your first high flights will be made under the direct supervision of your instructor, and you will be relying a great deal on your instructor's knowledge and judgment. You will make your first high flights in ideal conditions; light winds, smooth, non-turbulent air, a relatively easy launch, and a short glide to a large, unobstructed landing area. This will give you the opportunity to develop the special skills and knowledge required for making more challenging high flights in a relatively unpressured and safe learning environment.

Perhaps the most important of the new skills you will need for high flights is the ability to set up an approach to your desired landing area.

On the training hill you can typically launch and fly straight ahead until you descend to ground level and you will be at a suitable spot for landing. You may, while on the training hill, choose a different spot (perhaps closer in to your launch spot) on which to try to land, and making a landing on this closer spot will then require some turns to bring you down at the right place. If you do the turns improperly, or at the wrong places, you will land short of, or beyond, or to one side of your intended target. This is the beginning of your work on the concept of a landing approach.

A landing approach on a high flight, however, is a different and more complex matter. At many intermediate or advanced flying sites, if you take off and fly to the landing area, you will arrive with somewhere between a few hundred and perhaps as much as a few thousand feet of altitude. Further, for any given site, your altitude on arrival at the landing area will probably be different on each flight, as you encounter different amounts of lift, sink, and wind on your way to the landing area. You may even arrive from a slightly different direction on each flight, making your view of the landing area different as you approach. You will not necessarily know the direction or speed of the wind in the landing area at the time you launch, and will have to obtain that information while in the air, and adjust your landing approach appropriately. You may find yourself arriving at the landing area at the same time as other pilots, and may have to sequence yourself safely into the traffic flow. One thing you will not be able to do with any consistent level of success is to just "wing it," wandering around aimlessly in the vicinity of the landing area until you reach the ground hoping that you make your landing in about the right place.

The first step in any landing approach on a high flight is to thoroughly examine the landing area from the ground. There are several reasons for this. One is that power lines, or other cables, ropes or wires strung above the ground are nearly invisible from the air. You will rarely see them if you don't already know where they are. If you know exactly where they are, especially in reference to other objects you can see, you have some hope of not flying into them. This is no joke, and it is not an exaggeration. It applies to other hazards besides power lines as well. Ditches, holes, rocks, small trees, barbed wire fences, and other obstacles that can injure you must be identified and located in reference to landmarks you are sure you will be able to recognize from the air.

The other thing that is often impossible to find from the air is the wind indicator. As big and as obvious as it looks from the ground, you will often find it next to impossible to see from the air unless you know exactly where to look. So know exactly where to look.

Evaluate any large obstacles, such as trees or structures that exist around the landing area. Determine how they will affect or restrict your ability to approach the landing area, and whether they may create turbulence in an area you may need to fly through on approach.

At this time it is a good idea to plan your intended approach path. Keep in mind, though, that circumstances may require you to change your plan in the air. And remember that the landing area will look much smaller from the air than it does on the ground.

6

Judging Glide Angle

In order to make consistent landing approaches you must first learn to interpret your glide angle. If you hold a consistent vector (speed and direction) in a constant airmass you will maintain a constant angular relationship (declination) to the point on the ground that you will eventually intercept. For instance, assume you are flying directly into a light wind and achieving a glide path across the ground of 5 to 1. Your point of constant declination will be twelve degrees below you. A point closer than your intercept point will continue to drop steeper beneath you as you approach and a point farther away than the intercept point (shallower angle) will continue to decrease in angle as you descend.

If you want to learn to make consistent spot landings then you must learn to recognize this point of constant declination and be able to regulate your glide so that the point of intercept coincides with your desired aim point.

The easiest way to recognize your glide path is to have a visible "yardstick" in the foreground to compare against the distant aim point. Look past your harness or extended legs and recognize the point on the ground that is remaining stationary with respect to some point on you or your harness. If this intercept point is beyond your target then you are above the required glide path and must either steepen your glide angle or maneuver laterally to use up altitude. If the intercept point is prior to your desired aim point then you must either increase your glide ratio (if possible), find lift, or pick a new landing spot.

Being able to evaluate glide angle is also valuable when judging if you will clear an obstacle. If the obstacle is falling in your field-of-view (or eclipsing less background behind it) then your glide angle will clear it. If the obstacle is rising in your view or increasingly blocking the terrain behind it then you will not clear it.

If you hold your feet still they can make an excellent yardstick for which to judge your glide path.

The Aircraft Landing Pattern

The classic landing approach used by most aircraft is called, appropriately enough, the aircraft approach. It is a very good approach to use in a paraglider, because it starts upwind of the landing area which helps to insure that you will not be caught too far downwind of your intended target unable to penetrate through the headwind to reach your target area. One of the biggest limitations a paraglider has as an aircraft is its absolutely abysmal ability to move forward against a headwind. Any time you are downwind of the landing area, you run the risk of not being able to reach it if the wind speed picks up to the point where it equals your maximum forward flying speed.

The aircraft approach starts at an "initial point." This point is upwind, and to one side of your landing target, and should be at an altitude of 300 to 500 feet. Its specific location is chosen so as to allow you to start from that point and proceed with all of the remaining steps of the aircraft approach sequence, and, in any conditions of wind, lift and sink that you would choose to fly in, be able to execute all of the steps of the approach. The altitude of the initial point is a

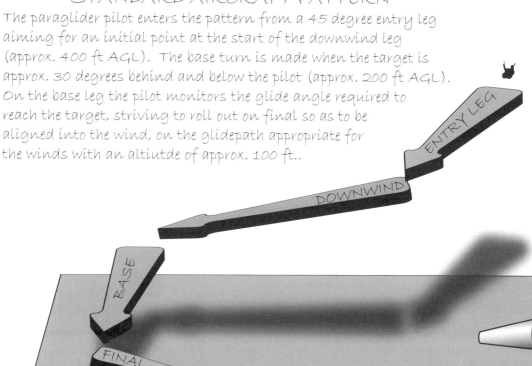

STANDARD AIRCRAFT PATTERN
The paraglider pilot enters the pattern from a 45 degree entry leg aiming for an initial point at the start of the downwind leg (approx. 400 ft AGL). The base turn is made when the target is approx. 30 degrees behind and below the pilot (approx. 200 ft AGL). On the base leg the pilot monitors the glide angle required to reach the target, striving to roll out on final so as to be aligned into the wind, on the glidepath appropriate for the winds with an altiutde of approx. 100 ft..

ENTRY LEG

DOWNWIND

BASE

FINAL

6

function of its distance from your final landing target; it should lie at a constant angle of descent or declination to the target.

> **NOTE:** There will be times when you can't get to the initial point at the specific altitude you have set. In fact there will be times when you can't get to the initial point at all; you may have just enough altitude to reach the landing area flying straight towards it. In many of these situations, you can still use the aircraft approach; you will merely enter the approach pattern part way along the normal flight path. Such abbreviated patterns will be discussed below.

As you approach the landing area, you will want to check all around for other traffic, noting the altitude and location of each other aircraft in the vicinity. You need to keep track of every one of these other aircraft which are anywhere near your altitude, to make sure that you don't put yourself in conflict with another aircraft while executing your approach.

Next, you will want to locate the windsock (or wind streamers) and determine the direction and strength of the wind. You will want to check them again as you proceed with your approach because wind speed and direction may change.

Now proceed towards your initial point. Remember your initial point is not a point on the ground but a point in space, at some specific predetermined altitude above a specific point on the ground. When you arrive in the vicinity of the initial point, you may fly circles, rectangles, or figure 8's centered over the initial point until you arrive at the specific point in space at the proper altitude. This is when your approach pattern begins, and when you become irreversibly committed to your landing.

> **NOTE:** Until you arrive at the pattern entry altitude at the initial point, you may still choose to climb up and away if you encounter an especially good thermal. Of course you won't do this on any of your first high flights, but later when you have mastered your soaring skills, you may. But once you pass through the initial point at the pattern entry altitude, you should consider yourself committed to completing the landing approach.

The chosen location of your initial point relative to your landing target will depend on many things; the performance of your canopy, the locations of obstructions around the landing field, the expected presence of lift, sink, turbulence and wind. We will describe a pattern suitable for a high performance entry-level canopy such as the Airwave Wave or Swing Arcus. Since your early high altitude flights will hopefully be in relatively mild conditions to a relatively large and unobstructed landing field, we will describe first a typical aircraft approach pattern for such a field in light wind conditions without significant turbulence.

In this case we will fly a left hand pattern, meaning that each of our final two turns in the pattern will be left turns. (You should learn how to do patterns equally well in either direction; with left hand turns or with right hand turns. Some landing areas will work better with a right pattern because of the shape of the terrain or the location of trees, power lines, or other obstacles.) Let us say that we have chosen an altitude for the initial point of 500 feet above the ground. The point on the ground directly below our initial point we locate upwind and to one side of our intended target, at 45 degrees off the wind direction line from the target. The distance of this point from the target is about 400 to 500 yards, which puts the target on about a 2.5:1 to 3:1 glide slope from the target. We arrive at this point at 500 feet, and begin our pattern by flying directly towards the target. This is the "pattern entry leg", sometimes referred to by pilots as "the forty-five."

Since our glide ratio is much higher than our relative elevation angle to the target, we will find the target moving below our glide slope, and we will soon have the target at about a two to one glide (30 degree declination). At this point we make a 45 degree right turn, to fly directly downwind, with the target on our left. This is our "downwind" leg.

As we pass by the target, we monitor our altitude, the angle back towards the target in the horizontal plane, and the ratio of our glide slope to the target (the angle in the vertical plane).

When we are about 30 degrees downwind of the target in the horizontal plane, and we have descended so that the target is again on about a 2.5:1 glide below us (25 degrees), we make a 90 degree left turn from our downwind leg to our "base leg." We are now flying directly across the wind direction, and are generally downwind of the target.

6

As we approach the point which is directly downwind of the target, we will have descended further until the target is now at about a four to one glide from us (15 degrees). At this time, we turn 90 degrees left again, so as to exactly intercept a flight path that is both directly into the wind, and directly towards the target. If we have chosen the proper pattern, and flown the pattern correctly, the target is now exactly upwind of us and exactly on our descending glide slope. We fly straight to the target, execute our landing flare, and plant both feet square on the bull's-eye!

Now reading through this description, you will have noticed several things. One is that it probably seems to be a hopelessly complicated process, with far too much detail to remember. Another is that it may seem to be much too mathematical in nature, with all this talk about angles and glide ratios and all the implied reference to what may seem like excessive precision. And finally, you may feel that this method cannot work in anything but perfect conditions, since it leaves no room for spontaneous pilot decisions that may be required by changing or unanticipated conditions.

And you are partly right. It is a complex process, it does rely on the ability to judge angles and execute maneuvers with a degree of precision, and it will not work exactly as stated in most conditions. However, the ability to judge angles and to judge your glide to anticipate where you will land, and the ability to fly a chosen ground track and execute turns at specific points with precision are fundamental to your skills as a pilot, and will be required in every phase of advanced flying that you pursue. And finally, in the real world, your ability to make the necessary adjustments to the standard aircraft approach that will make it work in changing conditions will depend on your acquiring the same abilities in judgment and precision flying that are needed to execute the basic pattern.

And once again, this description of the aircraft approach pattern applies to an approach in light or calm winds. As we have said before, your glide ratio over the ground becomes less when flying into a headwind. Therefore, when making your approach in wind you will have to make your last turn to your final glide either at a higher altitude or closer in to the target (or both) than you would in light or no wind. This suggests that you would want to move your entire base leg upwind closer to the target, by making your turn from downwind to base earlier. We'll discuss this in more detail later.

We mentioned that sometimes you will not be able to reach an initial point that is upwind of the target. You can enter the normal aircraft pattern at any point, so long as you have a picture of the pattern in your mind. If you can make it to a point adjacent to the target, but cannot reach the initial point, you will simply enter the pattern on the downwind leg. If you reach the landing area downwind and to one side of the target, you can make a "base entry," entering on the base leg. If you have really cut it close and have to fly straight upwind to the target in order to reach it, you are making what is called by pilots a "straight in" approach. If you cut it this close, you have probably made a mistake somewhere; either in flight planning or perhaps even in your decision to fly in the first place.

Upwind, Downwind and Crosswind Flying
- Flight Path Versus Ground Track

There are other considerations that apply to making an approach in wind. One of these is also one of the other fundamental skills you need for intermediate and advanced level flying, which is the general ability to fly in wind, including the ability to follow a specific chosen path over the ground when flying in some significant amount of wind.

Your first exposure to the complexities of flying in wind may come in the following scenario: You are flying from the top of a small (two to three hundred feet) hill. Your instructor has had you making turns after launch, to practice your techniques for turning and to begin work on the basic skills of a landing approach. Today, the wind is blowing across the hill somewhat from the left, perhaps 30 degrees or so from straight up. Your flight plan calls for a left turn after launch, and then a right turn to fly back across the face of the hill. Turning left after launch, you are turning into the direction the wind is coming from. Everything seems pretty normal; your groundspeed (speed over the ground) into the wind is slow, and you feel relaxed. As you make your turn to the right to fly back across the face of the hill, things suddenly begin to happen very quickly. You seem to accelerate, and soon the ground is flying by underneath you. You will probably feel an urge to pull on some brakes and "slow things down."

But to do so would be a mistake. Your airspeed is normal, and this is what is important to the flying behavior of the canopy. It is only your groundspeed that is high, and that is only because you are being carried downwind in the moving parcel of air in which you are flying, so that your speed over the ground is the sum of your airspeed and the speed of the wind. (Since you are not flying directly downwind, your groundspeed is not quite as high as your airspeed plus the wind speed, but we are illustrating a general principle here, not making a specific calculation).

The proper procedure in this situation is simply to recognize and understand your increased groundspeed, know that you will have to make decisions sooner because every obstacle or terrain feature in front of you will approach much more quickly, and fly the canopy normally with respect to airspeed and use of the brakes. Confusing groundspeed with airspeed, and trying to slow your groundspeed to what feels normal when flying downwind, will result in your stalling and collapsing the canopy, and hitting the ground very hard.

Crabbing

One of the most important skills for flying in wind is the ability to follow a chosen path over the ground when you are flying at an angle to the wind direction. If you are flying pointed (or "heading") towards the north, and the wind is from the west, your actual path over the ground will be angled to the east of straight north. Non pilots, and sometimes even pilots, often think of this incorrectly. They think that somehow the wind is pushing on the side of the aircraft, and as a result the aircraft is being pushed off course. But this is not what is happening.

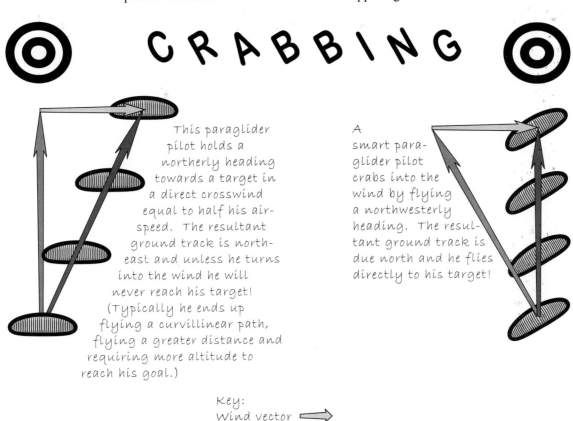

CRABBING

This paraglider pilot holds a northerly heading towards a target in a direct crosswind equal to half his airspeed. The resultant ground track is northeast and unless he turns into the wind he will never reach his target! (Typically he ends up flying a curvilinear path, flying a greater distance and requiring more altitude to reach his goal.)

A smart paraglider pilot crabs into the wind by flying a northwesterly heading. The resultant ground track is due north and he flies directly to his target!

Key:
Wind vector ⇨
Glider's heading vector ➡
Resultant ground track vector ➡

Think of it this way. Imagine yourself in a boat on a wide, smooth river. You point the boat directly across the river towards a landing on the opposite shore. You start the motor and cast off, driving the boat across the river towards the landing. Relative to the water, you are driving the boat straight across the river. But you will not end up at the landing you set out for, because in the meantime the whole river is moving downstream. The water is not something pushing on the side of the boat; it is the entire medium in which the boat's motion takes place.

Another example: Imagine a train with a flatcar moving slowly through a station with an elevated platform. You wish to cross the train to a phone booth that is directly across from where you are standing. You step onto the surface of the moving flatcar, and walk directly across towards the phone booth. But you arrive at the other side of the platform "downstream" of the phone booth, because the motion of the car has carried you there while you walked across it. To an observer on the car, your "flight path" was directly across the car. But to an observer on the station platform, your "ground track" was an angled combination of your motion across the car and the train's motion down the track.

It is exactly the same in flight. The wind is not a force pushing you sideways when you fly at an angle to the wind direction, the wind is instead simply the large scale motion of the entire medium in which your flight takes place. Your motion over the ground is simply the combination of your motion through the air and the air's motion over the ground.

A constant rate turn which describes a circle in the air...

...becomes an elongated oval over the ground when flown in wind. Dangers include drifting downwind into the side of the hill, or out of range of a safe landing area.

Multiple circling turns result in a looping oval track over the ground.

Circling Turns in Wind

The wind has a similar effect on your path over the ground when you fly continuous circling turns in wind. A single constant rate turn, which makes a circular path in the air, becomes an elongated oval over the ground. Multiple circling turns (sometimes called "360's") become linked looping ovals, as you drift with the wind. The danger of continuous circling turns in wind is that you may drift downwind into the side of the hill you launched from, behind a large obstruction which may be creating rotor turbulence, or out of gliding range from your intended landing area.

Vectors - Quantities with Size and Direction

Things that we measure (quantities) that have both size (or magnitude) and direction are called "vectors." Things that we measure that have only size are called "scalars." Speed is a scalar; we say we are going 20 mph. But if we say we are going at 20 mph and moving due north, we have stated the vector quantity of velocity. Speed and velocity are not two words for the same thing; speed is the scalar magnitude of the vector quantity of velocity.

Understanding exactly how a crosswind affects your motion over the ground when you fly is a matter of understanding how vector quantities add together. If you add the speed of 3 mph to the speed of 4 mph you get 7 mph. So if a man standing on a rolling freight car which is moving at 3 mph, walks forward (in the direction the car is moving) at 4 mph, then the man has a speed of 7 mph relative to the ground.

But what if the man walks across the car, in a direction perpendicular to the car's motion? We can't simply add 3 mph and 4 mph. What we do is add the vector quantity of 3 mph north (the car's velocity) to the vector quantity of 4 mph east, (the man's velocity relative to the car). The easy way to do this is to draw an arrow, three units long to represent the car's velocity; and another arrow 4 units long to represent the man's velocity relative to the car. We then slide one vector along the other, maintaining it's directional orientation, until it's tail is at the head of the other vector. Finally, we complete the triangle by drawing the "resultant" vector from the origin to the head of the translated vector. The vector sum of the two velocities is the diagonal arrow which connects the starting point with the head of the translated vector. (Note: It doesn't matter which vector we move, the result is the same). If you measure this arrow, its length in units will be exactly the magnitude of the man's velocity relative to the ground, and the direction of this arrow will be exactly the direction the man is moving relative to the ground.

Vector Representation of the Combination of Two Separate Motions

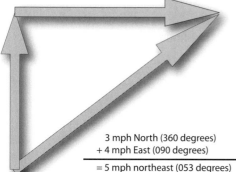

3 mph North (360 degrees)
+ 4 mph East (090 degrees)
= 5 mph northeast (053 degrees)

This is easy to understand if you simply realize that under the conditions stated, the man moves 3 miles north in each hour that passes, and he also moves 4 miles east in the same hour. Thus his total movement in that hour must be both 3 miles to the north, and 4 miles to the east, which is what is described by the "resultant" velocity vector shown of 5 miles in the direction shown.

This is not the first time we have seen vector quantities. The forces of lift, drag and gravity were all vector quantities; they have both magnitude and direction. In our look at aerodynamics, we saw how for a glider flying along a downhill sloping glide path, the two forces of lift and drag could combine to balance the force of gravity and each other, even though no two forces pointed in exactly opposite directions.

None of this discussion is to suggest that you have to plot out arrows drawn to scale on a piece of paper in order to fly a chosen path over the ground in a crosswind. (Although this is exactly the way student pilots working towards their airplane license will plot the headings for their first cross country flight). The purpose of this discussion is rather to make you understand correctly the reason why you have to fly in a direction through the air which is different from the direction you want to go over the ground when you are flying at some angle to the wind.

So let's get back to our pilot who wants to fly north in a west wind. Let's say the pilot is flying at a speed of 20 mph through the airmass in which he is flying. (That is how aircraft fly, remember, relative to the air in which they are flying.) Let's say the entire airmass is moving at 10 mph towards the east. (In other words, there is a wind from the west of 10 mph). As we have already seen, flying straight north isn't going to cut it; the pilot will drift to the east in the moving airmass. Obviously, the pilot will have to fly at an angle, heading partly into the wind; he will have to fly generally towards the northwest.

How much of an angle west of north does his flight heading need to be? There are two ways of answering this. For the pilot, there is one simple and direct way; he simply watches his flight track over the ground while he angles his heading more and more west of straight north. When his heading is correct, his ground track will be due north.

For those of us that want to see how it works, we can go back to our vector diagrams again. First we draw an arrow 10 units long pointed east (representing the wind). Next, we draw a line due north, that crosses the wind vector at the head of the arrow.

This represents the alignment of the vector which will be our ground velocity; the speed and direction of our resultant path over the ground. If we then mark off on a ruler 20 units of length, (the speed of the paraglider), we can slide and angle the ruler until one end of our 20 unit section is at the tail of the wind vector, and the other end is on our vertical line representing the resultant vector. Now we have a completed vector sum diagram and we can see the exact angle that the flight heading vector has to point, and the exact size of the resultant ground track vector.

Using a Vector Diagram to Compute the Required Heading for a Given Ground Track

Desired ground track is due north

10 mph west wind

20 mph airspeed

Resulting ground track is due north and the ground speed is 17.3 mph

Heading required is 30 degrees west of north

Required flight heading and resulting ground speed are measured from the completed vector diagram

Notice something here: The size of our ground track vector is quite a bit smaller than the vector which represents our motion through the air. We are making progress over the ground at a good deal less than our 20 mph flying speed, even though we are not flying into a headwind!

This process of angling your heading towards the wind to obtain a desired ground track is called "crabbing" or "setting up a crab." (This is in reference to the sideways walking motion of a crab, where they don't go where they are pointing. A crabbing aircraft points one direction, but moves another direction over the ground.) Please note that crabbing is not "side slipping." A side slip is something else entirely; it is the act of flying the aircraft partially sideways through the air. In a side slip, the flow of air over the aircraft is not in alignment with the direction the aircraft is pointing, while in a crab, the airflow is exactly aligned with the direction the aircraft is pointing. In a crab, only the motion of the aircraft over the ground does not line up with the direction the aircraft is pointing. Side slipping is a technique used in sailplanes and airplanes for various purposes. Paragliders (and hang gliders) are not really capable of side slipping.

We have worked these examples out using situations where the wind happened to be at right angles to our flight heading, or at right angles to our intended ground track. This is not at all necessary for the analysis to work, however. The method of drawing vector arrows at the proper angles and with the proper lengths, and using the methods for adding them that we have described, will give the correct results no matter what relative angles are involved. The inflight intuitive method of simply adjusting your flight heading until you obtain the desired ground track will also work regardless of the relative angles involved.

Now let's look at a simpler case of flying in wind; where your flight path is directly into, or directly with the wind direction. As before, realize that the only effect on your flying will be that which results from combining your motion through the air with the motion of the air itself.

Let's look at flying directly into the wind. Obviously the wind will have no effect on the direction of your flight path over the ground. However, it will affect something, and that effect is very important. As we mentioned before, what it affects is your glide ratio relative to the ground.

Let's say you have a 7:1 L/D (an average L/D of a DHV-1 canopy). That means your wing produces seven times as much lift as drag, and in still air you will move forward seven feet for every foot of altitude you lose. From 100 feet of altitude you will glide forward 700 feet. And let's say you obtain this 7:1 L/D at a flying speed of 20 mph. (Your L/D will vary some at different speeds because the wing is not equally efficient at all angles of attack).

Now let's imagine you are flying into a 10 mph headwind. Even though you are moving forward through the air at 20 mph, your actual forward progress over the ground is only 10 mph, because the air itself – the medium in which you are flying – is moving 10 mph in the opposite direction. However, your sink rate is unchanged by the wind; you are still descending at your normal rate of 2.86 mph down. Therefore, your flight path relative to the ground looks like this: 10 mph forward and 2.86 mph down, yielding a glide ratio over the ground of only 3.5 to 1.

This is really important. It's important in any type of glider, but it's especially important in a paraglider for two reasons. One is that the paraglider is such a slow flying aircraft, and because of that it only takes a very little bit of wind to drastically effect your glide ratio. A ten mile per hour breeze isn't very much wind, and yet in this example it cuts your glide ratio into the wind in half. Now, all of a sudden, that landing area you reached easily in no wind is beyond your gliding range! The other reason that all this is more important in a paraglider is because the paraglider's speed range is so limited. Let's consider a headwind, which is equal to the flying speed of your canopy. You are flying at 20 mph into a 20 mph headwind. Your canopy is getting a nice 7:1 L/D, but your forward speed is zero! Your glide ratio is zero! You are descending straight down.

The Effect of Headwind on Glide

This paraglider has a forward horizontal speed through the air of 20 mph and with a lift to drag ratio of 7 : 1, the vertical descent speed is 2.86 mph (251 fpm).

2.86 mph descent speed

The same glider in a 10 mph headwind. The resulting forward speed over the ground is cut in half to 10 mph.

20 mph airspeed

10 mph wind

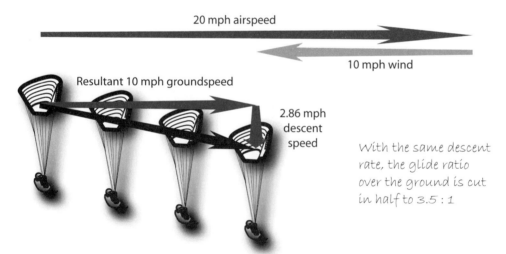

Resultant 10 mph groundspeed

2.86 mph descent speed

With the same descent rate, the glide ratio over the ground is cut in half to 3.5 : 1

In a hang glider or sailplane, you would simply speed up to "penetrate" this headwind. (The use of the term "penetrate" is unfortunate and misleading here, since it takes us back again to the idea that the wind is some kind of opposing force that we have to "power through," when in fact wind is, once again, nothing more or less than the large scale motion of our flying medium.) Here's how it would work for a hang glider, for example: The glider obtains an L/D of 12:1 at 30 mph. The wind is blowing 30 mph, reducing the glide ratio to zero. The pilot increases his flying speed to perhaps 48 mph. Now, as we have said, the glider is not as efficient at this higher speed, so the L/D drops to perhaps 6:1. Therefore the sink rate is 8 mph. The forward speed is 15 mph. So the glide ratio relative to the ground is 2:1; not great, but at least the pilot has the ability to move forward, and to land someplace other than directly below where he is.

The paraglider pilot has no similar ability to increase his flying speed to move forward into a strong headwind. He can speed up slightly, but he has nowhere near the same range of speed to utilize. The lesson here is this: As a paraglider pilot you must be very concerned with the speed and direction the wind is blowing, because even a small amount of wind will severely limit your options. Because of this, you need to pay attention to weather patterns in general, and to wind and weather forecasts. Under certain weather conditions, such as when a frontal system is moving through, the wind speed and direction can change drastically and very quickly. If you are in the air when this happens, the consequences can be disastrous.

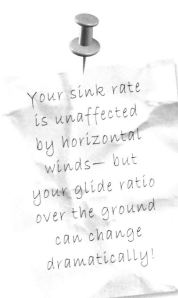

Your sink rate is unaffected by horizontal winds— but your glide ratio over the ground can change dramatically!

Of course the opposite effect exists when flying downwind. Your speed over the ground is increased, your sink rate remains the same, and your glide ratio increases. Flying at 20 mph downwind in a wind of 10 mph will increase your glide ratio to 50% above your L/D ratio.

Now let's go back to flying across the wind for a minute, because this also affects your glide ratio. In the example we used earlier, the pilot had to fly a heading angled towards the west to maintain a northbound ground track in the presence of a wind from the west. His groundspeed in the direction he was moving over the ground was reduced below his flying speed by the need to "crab" into the wind. Now here's the thing; since his sink rate stays the same, the reduction in his speed of motion over the ground has the affect of reducing his glide ratio, the same way it does when flying into a headwind.

In fact with a little trigonometry and a little algebra, we can look at exactly how this relationship works. We won't bore you with the details of the calculations (they are all based on the vector addition methods we have already talked about), but it turns out that in a crosswind you need between 10 degrees and 30 degrees, depending on the wind speed, of tailwind component to get back to your still air L/D. Also, when the wind equals your flying speed, you have no glide ratio at all until the wind passes through 90 degrees.

Up until then, you have to point directly into the wind to keep from being pushed off course, and since your flying speed equals the wind speed you have no forward progress. Flying in wind that equals your flying speed therefore constrains you to flying only in that half of all possible flight directions which has at least some tailwind component.

The Landing Approach in Wind

Based on the foregoing discussion, you can see the implications of wind for flying the aircraft landing pattern.

First, you will have to angle your flight heading towards the wind on your 45 entry leg and on your crosswind leg in order to achieve the ground track you desire. The amount you need to angle towards the wind depends on the wind speed.

Second, your glide ratio will be reduced on the crosswind leg and on the final leg, so you will need to set up higher; which essentially means turning from downwind to base earlier, when you are at a steeper angle of declination to the target. Of course your glide angle will be increased when flying downwind, so you will be higher and therefore at a steeper angle to the target at each point along your downwind leg than you would be in no wind. **Even so, you will have to turn at an earlier point, because the effect of the increase in your downwind glide ratio is much less than the combined effect of the decrease in your cross wind and upwind glide ratio.**

Also, your ground speed will increase when on the downwind leg, so everything will be happening faster, and your reactions need to be faster. The changes in your "sight picture" or the perspective view you have of the target and the landing area will be considerable in even a fairly light wind, again because of the very slow flying speed of a paraglider. You almost cannot set up too high when making an approach in wind in a paraglider.

Figure Eight Approach

In winds of more than 10-12 mph, you may find that a figure eight approach works better than an aircraft approach. In the figure eight approach you don't use any downwind leg. You approach the target from downwind, at an altitude that would cause you to overshoot if you flew straight to the target. You then use a series of reversing turns to fly repeated "base legs" until you are low enough to turn directly towards the target and fly straight in to your landing.

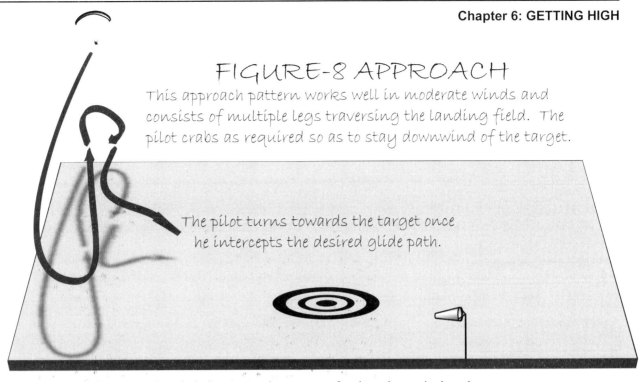

FIGURE-8 APPROACH

This approach pattern works well in moderate winds and consists of multiple legs traversing the landing field. The pilot crabs as required so as to stay downwind of the target.

The pilot turns towards the target once he intercepts the desired glide path.

Note that the stronger the wind, the greater the amount of crab angle required on the "base legs" and the less the degrees of turn required at the end of each leg. (In calm winds you would actually have to turn greater than 180 degrees to keep from steadily moving forward towards the landing spot during each reversal).

Dealing with Lift and Sink During Your Approach

As if all this were not enough to deal with, you will also have to deal with the effects of lift (rising airmass) and sink (sinking airmass) when making your approach. Just as horizontal motion of the airmass (wind) affects your glide ratio, so does vertical motion of the airmass (lift and sink). The effect is exactly the same; because the medium in which you are flying is moving, its motion combines with your motion through it to determine your motion relative to the ground.

In the case of vertical air movement, it is your sink rate that is affected, not your forward speed. If you fly into a parcel of air that is rising at 250 feet per minute (about 3 mph, and not at all uncommon) your sink rate relative to the ground goes to zero, and your glide ratio goes to infinity! By the same token, if there is air moving upwards at 250 feet per minute in one place, then somewhere else there is air moving downwards at 250 feet per minute. If you fly into that sinking parcel of air your sink rate will double, so your glide ratio will then be cut in half.

Since the presence of lift and sink is random and unpredictable, you cannot pre-plan your approach pattern to take its effects into account. You must therefore learn how to adjust your pattern "on the fly" to correct for the effects of lift and sink. **The general rule is: Turn towards the target in sink, turn away from the target in lift.** Let's take each segment of the pattern in sequence and see how this applies.

The 45 Entry Leg

If you fly into sinking air on the 45, do nothing. You are already flying directly toward the target, that is the best you can do. If you fly into lift on the 45 and it is strong enough that you actually start to climb, simply turn around and go back to the initial point. Lose altitude back to your pattern entry altitude and then start over. If you find yourself in weak lift on the 45, just continue the pattern.

The Downwind Leg

If you hit sink on the downwind leg, get ready to turn your base leg early. Remember that your base leg turn should be triggered by when you are at an appropriate angle of descent to the target so that you can fly your base and final legs and arrive at the target with zero altitude. If you hit lift on your downwind leg, do not extend your downwind leg. The reason is that you don't want to get too far downwind of the target, even if you have a proper angle of descent to the target, because if the wind picks up or you

LOW ON DOWNWIND
In this instance, the paraglider pilot finds himself lower than standard on downwind and compensates by turning an early base and angling in towards the target for a shortened and slightly angling final.

HIGH ON DOWNWIND

In this instance the paraglider pilot finds himself high on downwind. He should never extend downwind to work off the extra altitude (he might hit sink or a headwind and not be able to make the LZ). The pilot chooses to work off the extra altitude by angling his base leg slightly away from the target as well as by flying past the target so as to have a slightly longer and angling final in which to work off the rest of his altitude.

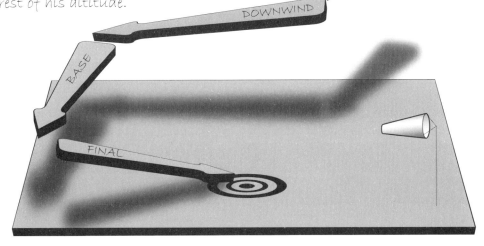

hit sinking air, the greater distance from the target will result in a greater margin by which you could come up short, which could be dangerous if there are power lines, trees, or other obstructions at the downwind end of the landing area. Instead, turn to your base leg at or near the normal point, but make the turn less than 90 degrees and thus angle the turn away from the target slightly.

The Base Leg

If you hit sink on the base leg, again, turn toward the target. If you hit lift, extend your base leg past the point exactly downwind of the target, fading slightly downwind, and double it back so that you arrive back at the entry point for your final leg at the proper point.

The Final Leg

By the time you turn final, you should be close to the target and fairly low (75 – 100 feet). If you hit lift or sink at this point, prepare to ride it out and land where you land. You may come up a little long or short, but you should be close. Once you are on final and close to the ground, you should not turn out of the wind to try to correct your altitude. To do so involves too much risk of getting turned downwind without adequate time for recovery, and thus landing downwind with a high groundspeed.

The Good News

If all this makes it sound like executing a landing approach in a paraglider is an impossibly difficult task, take heart. A paraglider is probably the easiest aircraft to shoot an approach and landing in, so long as you understand the limitations of the aircraft. As long as you make sure you stay high enough relative to the target to be able to reach it, things will generally work out OK. It's true that you don't have the glide path control of a sailplane, or the speed range of a sailplane or hang glider, but you do have one big advantage. Because your glide ratio is so much smaller, and the glide slope of your approach therefore so much steeper, the landing pattern is much more forgiving of error.

In a 12:1 hang glider landing in a 10 mph breeze, for example, if the pilot turns from base to final 25 feet too high, he will land about 200 feet beyond the target. In a 7:1 paraglider landing in a 10 mph breeze, the same 25 foot altitude error on the turn to final will only result in about an 80 foot error in landing distance.

Flight Planning

One other thing you need to know for making high flights is how to make a flight plan. In actuality, all of your flights should involve a flight plan, but as a beginning student your flight plans will be pretty simple, your instructor will be directly involved, and the lack of a flight plan on the training hill is less likely to have serious consequences. When making a high flight, you will need to carefully take into account the wind speed and direction, how it will affect the flight heading you will need to fly to the landing area, and how it will affect your approach. You should have alternate "emergency" landing areas picked out if there is any chance you won't be able to reach the normal landing area. You need to be aware of the likely presence of lift, sink or turbulence in certain areas, and which route of flight will be most likely to take advantage of lift and avoid sink and turbulence.

Enjoying the smooth calm air of an early morning winter Alpine day — Swing photo

NOTES

ADVANCED FLYING TECHNIQUES

ACTIVE PILOTING, CANOPY COLLAPSES, & ADVANCED MANEUVERS

Failure to keep the wingtip loaded properly during a wingover will result in a collapse — Andy Stocker photo compilation of a Dave Stank video

Chapter 7
— ADVANCED FLYING TECHNIQUES

ACTIVE PILOTING, CANOPY COLLAPSES, & ADVANCED
MANEUVERS

Active Piloting

Flying a paraglider in anything but smooth air will eventually lead to a partial canopy collapse. Flying a paraglider at the bottom edge of its speed range, as is common when attempting to soar, greatly increases the chance of a stall or spin of the canopy. Flying a canopy at the upper end of the speed range, (especially using a speed stirrup or trimmer system) will increase the chance of a front collapse. Before you ever fly a paraglider in any significant thermal lift or turbulence, and before you attempt to deliberately soar in conditions requiring flight at minimum sink airspeed, you must thoroughly master, through simulator and inflight training and practice, the control of surges, pitch oscillations, and asymmetric collapses.

Active piloting involves taking a proactive approach by sensing small changes in the pressure in the brake lines and risers and making corrections prior to a significant surge or collapse. In potentially turbulent conditions you should fly with a small amount of brake pressure (this is mandatory if at low altitude – see the section titled Getting Low). By having pressure in the brake lines you can be more sensitive to small changes in the internal pressure of the wing. Active flying involves continuously controlling the brakes to maintain constant and symmetrical pressure in the handles.

As an example, a gust of downwards air will decrease the angle of attack of the wing, reducing pressure within the canopy and lightening the pressure in the brake lines. Failure to respond quickly could lead to a forward surge or even frontal collapse. Correcting from this situation could require aggressive braking which could lead to over-controlling into a stall or pitch oscillation.

In the same situation, an active pilot would use a timely increase in brake travel to regain the proper pressure and correct the wing prior to it moving too far forward or starting to collapse. Once the correction was made the active pilot would release the increased brake travel prior to the pressure increasing and the canopy starting to move too far back.

It is important to note that active piloting involves maintaining symmetrical brake pressure not symmetrical brake position. When thermalling it is common for one side of the canopy to start to "get light" as it encounters sinking flow at the thermal's edge. Again, pull the individual brake handle to maintain the pressure in that side and apply some opposite weight shift to maintain the desired turn rate.

Controlling the Canopy in Turbulence
(Active Piloting)

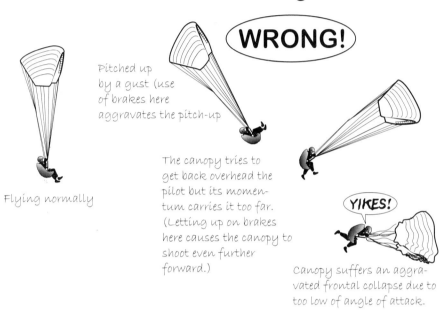

WRONG!

Flying normally

Pitched up by a gust (use of brakes here aggravates the pitch-up

The canopy tries to get back overhead the pilot but its momentum carries it too far. (Letting up on brakes here causes the canopy to shoot even further forward.)

YIKES!

Canopy suffers an aggravated frontal collapse due to too low of angle of attack.

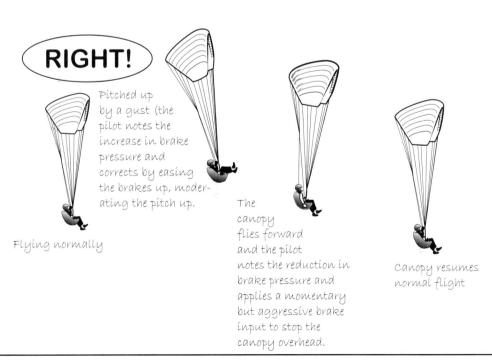

RIGHT!

Flying normally

Pitched up by a gust (the pilot notes the increase in brake pressure and corrects by easing the brakes up, moderating the pitch up.

The canopy flies forward and the pilot notes the reduction in brake pressure and applies a momentary but aggressive brake input to stop the canopy overhead.

Canopy resumes normal flight

Similarly, differences in riser pressure should be countered by weight shift. If a wing starts to lose pressure and lift, it will support less weight on that side and you will feel a slight tilt in that direction. You should oppose the tilt by weight shifting towards the high side while increasing the brake pressure on the lower side. It is important to point out that weight shift towards the higher pressure will help maintain a constant heading with minimum altitude loss. In theory, weight shifting towards the lighter side may lead to a quicker reinflation but likely with a large change in heading, greater altitude loss, and a more dynamic recovery.

QUIZ:

Active piloting entails making repeated corrections to maintain a constant brake handle

☐ position

☐ pressure

At higher altitude your active flying should be geared towards prevention of canopy collapses, surges, and stalls. At low altitudes (below your ability to recover from a severe collapse, stall, or spin) it is vital that you always keep the canopy overhead. The farther off center the canopy gets, the greater the amount of the pendulum arc your body will cover during the recovery. Contact with the terrain during a downward swing is extremely dangerous. If you combine a downward swing with a downwind turn and rising terrain then you have one of the most severe impact situations possible. It is likely preferable to land in a stall (B-line, parachutage, or full stall) than to hit during the downward swing of a stall recovery.

Lastly, just because you are adept at active piloting does not mean you should fly in conditions that warrant it. The slower an aircraft flies and the lighter the wing loading, the more susceptible it is to turbulence. To put it simply, the slower an aircraft flies, the greater the amount of judgment and respect for conditions required for safe operations. Each year conventional gliders encounter gusts severe enough to cause an unusual attitude and each year a small number of hang gliders tumble in rough air. A paraglider pilot that thinks he can handle similar turbulence with active piloting skills is naïve.

Using the Speed Stirrup

Unlike the beginning days of the sport, manufacturers now certify their gliders for recovery from collapses with the speed bar engaged. Using the speed system doesn't have to be saved for last-ditch efforts to avoid being blown over the back of the ridge, it should become a part of your daily soaring. The speed stirrup can be used to increase your penetration over the ground when countering headwinds or sinking air. It should never be relied on as a means to fly in winds that approach or exceed the trim speed of the glider. Flying in stronger wind increases the likelihood of encountering turbulence and use of the speed system reduces the glider's resistance to turbulence-induced frontal tucks and asymmetric collapses.

Inputs to the speed stirrup should be done smoothly to avoid surges caused by sudden changes in the canopy's speed in relation to the pilot's body. These surges can dramatically increase the likelihood of a collapse. A progressive input will allow the pilot's mass to match the change in canopy speed, eliminating surges and pendulum oscillations.

Use of the speed bar in potentially turbulent conditions increases the tendency towards collapses but active, judicious use is possible if you are not at low altitude. Actively react to changes in canopy position or pressure by moving your feet in the opposite direction. A gust that slows the canopy can be countered with increased stirrup travel while a forward surge should be countered by reducing stirrup travel.

Not only is the glider more prone to deflations while accelerated, the higher airspeed will mean a more dramatic response and recovery. Remember to release the stirrup pressure entirely and use the brakes if you cannot control the surges easily and quickly with speed bar alone. If a collapse occurs it must be quickly countered before it turns into a dangerous diving spiral.

In anything other than perfectly smooth conditions you should never use the speed bar at an altitude lower than you can safely recover from a major collapse. See *Chapter Eleven – Safety and How to Practice It* for additional thoughts and recommendations on flying safety and use of the speed system.

Canopy Collapses and Canopy Control Maneuvers

After you master pitch control of the canopy, you should then undergo supervised training in canopy collapses, re-inflations, stall and spin avoidance, and other advanced canopy control maneuvers. What follows is a general description of some of these maneuvers. It is provided for general information purposes. Consult your Owner's Manual for any specific instructions or precautions concerning advanced maneuvers and recoveries.

None of these maneuvers should be attempted for the first time without the direct supervision of a qualified instructor, experienced in the maneuvers being taught on the canopy being used.

You should use a canopy with known, predictable and docile responses in all planned maneuvers. Remember, modern canopies will likely recover from most situations without pilot input. Excessive or panicked inputs can cause larger oscillations, cascading problems, and a greater loss of altitude. Initial attempts at intentional asymmetric collapses and B-line stalls should not be initiated below 1000 feet AGL. Full stall and spin training should not be attempted below 2000 feet.

Tip Fold / Asymmetric Collapse

A practice accelerated tip collapse

A common turbulence-induced collapse is a partial collapse of the outer wing panel of one side of the canopy. You can train for dealing with such a collapse by intentionally causing a tip fold. You should be able to recover from such a collapse with only minor altitude loss and change in heading. The severity of the tip fold / collapse depends on how many A-lines are pulled and how far they are pulled. For your initial attempts you should pull just an outer A-line (or the outer split A-riser, if so equipped). With experience you may induce much larger collapses (up to 50% of the wing) by pulling the A-risers on an entire side.

An unintentional large collapse requires a quick response to avoid an excessive change of heading which could point you towards the terrain. Even with a quick recovery, the resulting pendulum action could be hazardous. Left uncorrected, a large asymmetric collapse will result in a diving spiral that can be disorienting. The resulting high centrifugal forces and g-loading will require high brake forces to correct and/or great effort to deploy a reserve parachute.

How To Enter: For smaller collapses you can retain both brake handles in their respective hands. If you are going to induce a large collapse then you may need to release the brake handle on that side so that you do not inadvertently pull on it while you are pulling down the A-riser. Reach up with one hand and grasp the desired amount of A-riser just below the rapid links, or as high as you can reach. Pull down at a moderate rate until the outer wing collapses.

What The Canopy Will Do: One side of the leading edge will fold under, for some distance along the leading edge, depending on how severe a collapse you create. The canopy will enter a descending turn towards the collapsed side; with the speed of the rotation and the descent rate dependent on the amount of collapse and the speed at entry.

Recovery Is Made: First maintain directional control and stop any turn by using opposite weight shift (roll your hips away from the turn) and applying opposite brake as necessary. Next, to develop a feel for the canopy's behavior in this mode, allow a turn towards the collapsed side to develop and then stop it. Then use weight shift and opposite brake to turn away from the collapsed side. Finally release the A-riser and watch the wing reinflate. If it does not reinflate by itself, either:

1. Apply the brake at a moderate rate on the side of the collapse until it opens, or if this is ineffective or the canopy appears caught or tangled,

2. Pump the brake sharply on the side of the collapse.

If part of the canopy is caught in the lines (cravat) then do the appropriate cravat recovery procedure described later in this chapter.

Do not apply excessive opposite brake during the maneuver – this could cause a stall or spin. An indication of using too much opposite brake (and an imprending stall) is a sudden softening of brake pressure.

In any large asymmetric collapse where you cannot completely control direction with weight shift and moderate opposite brake, you may have to allow the glider to turn slowly towards the collapse as you work to re-inflate the wing. This is preferable to a full stall or spin from over application of the opposite brake. If efforts to correct a large collapse are unsuccessful and you are above 500 feet AGL, then you should consider performing a full stall (both brakes symmetrically to full arm extension) and full stall recovery (see later in this chapter). If less than 500 ft. or a tightening spiral is encountered then an immediate reserve deployment is recommended.

Big Ears

By collapsing both wing tips you decrease the wing area and increase the drag. Depending upon how much you pull in the wing tips, the rate of descent can increase from gentle to moderate (up to 1000

Big Ears

fpm) with a minor change in forward speed. This is normally a very benign maneuver, and is a good way to introduce yourself to the characteristics of the canopy when partially collapsed. It is also a good method for producing a mild increase in sink rate, and a significant reduction in glide ratio as an aid to landing approach. By pulling large big ears you can decrease your glide angle dramatically. In turbulent landing zones the use of big ears will increase the canopy loading and reduce the span, both of which may increase the resistance to collapses.

Consult your Owner's Manual to ensure there are no specific warnings against using big ears, or any precautions regarding the use of the speed bar with big ears, or any unique recommendations for entry and exit (some manuals recommend entry and exit be done one tip at a time).

How To Enter: Collapse the outward portions on both sides of the canopy by pulling down symmetrically on the outer A-riser (if split A-risers) or the outboard most one, two or three A-lines on each side until the canopy on each tip folds under. Hold the brakes normally, reach as high as you can and grasp the outer A-riser or line(s) with your fingers. Pull down symmetrically to collapse the ears. (Depending on the length of your arms, and the adjustment of the brake lines, and your harness, you may not be able to collapse the ears without releasing the brakes.) Try using weight shift control to steer the canopy while holding the tips collapsed. You may also use differential big ears (pull more on one A-riser group while letting up on the other side) to increase your turning control.

What The Canopy Will Do: The outboard portions will fold under from the leading edges. The center of the canopy will remain inflated, and you can fly the canopy indefinitely in this mode. The further you pull the A-line down, the larger the amount of collapse. This maneuver will increase the sink rate and may slightly increase the

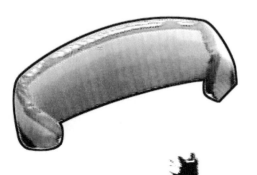

forward speed of the canopy. The larger the area of collapse the greater is the reduction in canopy area and greater the increase in descent rate. There is a small possibility in this maneuver that the canopy may become partially entangled in the lines, and will not recover to normal shape (a cravat). Dealing with a cravat is covered later in this chapter. A small canopy deformation, however, will not prevent you from flying the canopy to a safe landing.

Recovery Is Made: Release the A-line(s) symmetrically on both sides. Recovery from big ears is glider dependent. Most beginner wings will smoothly and spontaneously recover when released (which can make it difficult to use big ears and brakes at the same time). Some intermediate and advanced wings may remain in big ears when the A-lines are released (which can be handy if you want to use the brakes for mild turning). These gliders will require either weight shifting away from the stuck tip and/or a pump on the brake handles to re-inflate the tips.

Big ears is a safe and gentle maneuver when performed with limited turning. You should never, however, combine big ears with higher g-loading maneuvers such as spiral descents because you could exceed the design loads on the individual lines and canopy attach points. You should be especially wary of entering a big ears induced parachutage if your canopy is wet.

> **QUIZ:**
>
> "Big Ears" are used to increase:
>
> ☐ forward speed
> ☐ descent speed

The steeper descent angle and reduced wing area of big ears means the canopy is flying at a higher angle of attack. On some models this may be close to a parachutage stall. You can increase the forward speed slightly and the safety margin in smooth conditions by applying speed bar with the big ears. Note, however, that although the overall averaged angle of attack for the wing is still relatively high, with the use of the speedbar the angle of attack at the center section is reduced enough so that it may still be susceptible to a frontal collapse in turbulence. An accelerated frontal collapse with big ears can be very dramatic (see the section on Frontal Collapse, this chapter).

Because of the small chance of a parachutage stall or surge on recovery, you should either recover at a sufficient altitude to correct for these problems (above 100 feet) or at a low enough altitude that it will not really matter. It is perfectly acceptable to wait to release the A-risers until you are pulling the brakes in the landing flare below fifteen feet. Lastly, remember that big ears gives an increased rate of descent, not an extreme rate of descent. There have been numerous landing accidents caused by pilots trying to aggressively recover from big ears only to induce a low altitude stall or collapse. Remember that even if your glider somehow remains in big ears and you do not even flare, your impact will be similar to that of landing under a round parachute – certainly something that does not warrant extreme measures (and possible loss of control) to avoid!

7

Frontal Collapse

Frontal Collapse and Front Horseshoe

A frontal collapse occurs when the angle of attack is reduced below the critical value required to maintain the wing shape and the leading edge tucks under. A "frontal" can occur due to turbulence or can be induced by pulling on A-lines. Susceptibility to frontal collapses as well as the resulting severity of the collapse is increased with the use of a speed bar. It is common for a complete reversal in heading to occur during a massive frontal collapse.

If you pull on only the innermost A-lines then only the center section of the wing will collapse and the wing tips will fly forward forming a "front horseshoe." In the front horseshoe configuration, the canopy comes down at a steep angle and slow airspeed. It is not a normal rapid descent method because other techniques (big ears, B-line stalls, and spirals) offer faster rates of descent with better flying qualities and more consistent recoveries.

How To Enter: Pull down on the A-risers slowly and evenly until the leading edge collapses. As you pull the risers you will initially feel an increase in pressure and then a decrease as you near the critical minimum angle of attack.

What The Canopy Will Do: The forward portion of the canopy will tuck under and collapse against the lines. If you pull further the entire canopy will collapse and rapidly fall behind you.

Recovery Is Made: You can increase the angle of attack with a rapid brake application, however, many turbulence-induced collapses are momentary in nature and an aggressive brake application may retard the canopy excessively and cause the resulting forward surge to be more severe than it would have been if left alone.

If the frontal was induced by use of the A-risers, then wait for the canopy to momentarily stabilize overhead and let the risers up smoothly and quickly. The canopy will normally reinflate immediately. Be prepared to apply brake input to correct for any resulting forward surge.

In an accelerated collapse the canopy will rapidly move aft. Ensure the speed bar is fully released and be ready to provide judicious use of brakes to control the resulting surge.

B-Line Stall

A B-line stall occurs when the B-lines are pulled downwards sufficiently to destroy the airfoil shape. The loss of lift and increase in drag results in a vertical descent of nearly 2,000 fpm. A B-line stall can be useful for losing altitude rapidly in an emergency, such as if you were being sucked up into a cloud, and in some situations may be preferential to a spiral descent (easier to maintain orientation and recovery). The B-line stall is safe when performed on modern canopies and is easy to recover from although a remote chance exists to enter a parachutage stall or spin when exiting.

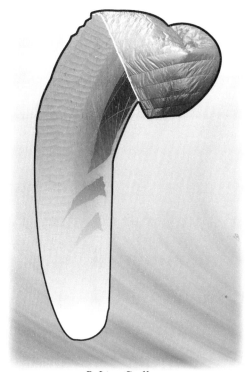

B-Line Stall

How To Enter: Pull down on the B-risers slowly and evenly until the chord collapses down at the B-lines. As you pull the risers you will initially feel an increase in pressure and then a decrease as the stall occurs. Most canopies retain a significant amount of pressure on the B-risers during the stall. If you plan on holding the stall for an extended period you may find it less fatiguing to initially grasp the risers with your palms facing forward and your thumbs downward, and rotate your wrists forward and downward as you pull you arms down and tuck your elbows at your sides.

What The Canopy Will Do: The canopy will lose forward speed and pick up a greatly increased descent rate. The internal pressure will drop, and the canopy will bow upwards between the lines and take on a slack appearance. It is difficult to use the brakes while holding the B-risers down (and is not recommended anyway). Minor changes in heading can be done by using weight shift and a small amount of asymmetric pull on the B-risers (pull more in the direction you wish to turn). Avoid large asymmetric pulls which could result in a spin entry.

Recovery Is Made: Release the B-risers gently and evenly at a moderately quick rate and the canopy will likely recover by itself. If it does not, grasp and pull down evenly on all the A-risers until the canopy accelerates out of the stall. (You may instead push forward on the speed stirrup if it is immediately available.) If this does not work, perform parachutage stall recovery by pulling the brakes sharply down to your seat and then releasing them quickly, making the canopy shoot forward. Be ready to control the surge with an

QUIZ:

B-line stalls are used to increase
☐ forward speed
☐ descent speed

additional brake application. If the B-risers are not released at the same rate then a spin may result. See the following section on spin recovery.

Recovery from a B-line stall should be completed by 200 feet AGL to ensure sufficient altitude exists to take corrective action.

Steep Turns and Spiral Dives

• The term "positive spin" has been used to describe a steeply banked, prolonged spiral diving turn. This is a misnomer since the maneuver is not a true spin, as there is no stall of any part of the canopy. The maneuver is produced by normal turning control inputs, and recovered from by normal turning control methods. The transition from a steep turn to a true spiral dive occurs when the leading edge of the canopy rotates forward and downward. The glider will rapidly pick up speed and descent rate as it enters a stable leading edge downward attitude and high turn rate spiral.

• A steep turn / spiral dive is an advanced maneuver and achieves the greatest rate of descent of any of the controlled maneuvers (greater than 2000 fpm). Unlike the B-line stall, however, a spiral can be disorienting due to the high turn rates and elevated g-loading.

• There have been instances of paragliders maintaining extended high speed spirals until ground impact. It is possible to achieve g-forces strong enough to make it extremely difficult to apply opposite brake or even deploy a reserve parachute. An untrained person will typically start to lose consciousness after several seconds above 4-g's. Military pilots learn to withstand elevated g-forces by tensing muscles (especially abdominal and chest muscles), inhaling quickly and then exhaling slowly in a straining, grunting manner over several seconds.

How To Enter: Apply weight shift and brake just as you would enter a normal turn. Do not apply any opposite brake.

What The Canopy Will Do: The glider will increase its turn rate, bank angle, and descent rate. You will feel an elevated g-loading due to the centrifugal (centripetal) force. Watch for any tendencies for the spiral to tighten up more than desired or to enter an extreme nose low attitude.

Be aware of the danger of some canopies accelerating into the spiral when banked more than 35 degrees, or when held continuously in a steep turn. The high speeds which can be attained in a steep banked or prolonged spiral can be dangerous, because they can lead to severe oscillations during a rapid exit from the spiral, or, in a worst case, to overloading the structure of the canopy. DHV certification only requires spirals with descent rates of up to 14 meters per second (2750 fpm) which may be less than the maximum attainable rate of descent.

Recovery Is Made: Slowly release the inside brake and apply opposite weight shift. In some cases opposite brake may be necessary. As the bank angle lessens the excess airspeed can cause the glider to want to climb sharply. Be prepared to reapply inside brake momentarily to slow the rate of recovery so as to use up some of the excess airspeed to prevent a steep climb and possible severe surge.

One technique to avoid bank angles tightening up more than desired is to weight shift towards the high side for a portion of each revolution. The glider will lessen its bank angle for a few moments during the weight shift. Such an oscillatory spiral achieves a high average rate of descent but with less tendency to over bank. Note that some pilots mistakenly refer to an oscillatory spiral as an "asymmetric spiral" which others may mistakenly envision as entailing a partial wing collapse.

Do not ever combine the elevated g-loading of a spiral with a canopy reduction (such as big ears). The combination can overstress the fewer number of load bearing lines and canopy attach points.

Do not combine a spiral with use of an accelerator system – a collapse at high speeds would be extremely violent.

In a mature spiral dive the leading edge is pointed nearly straight down. The glider and pilot are undergoing significant g-forces.

Full Stalls

If you habitually fly with the brakes on to almost the point of stall, you are always on the edge of entering a full stall or spin. The following discussion of full stalls and spins is for information purposes only. We do not recommend that you ever deliberately attempt to enter either a full stall or a spin except under the radio guidance of an experienced instructor. Even then you should be intimately familiar with possible canopy motions and recovery techniques. A stall/spin recovery can be so dynamic that an instructor may be unable to interpret the canopy motions and tell you what to do in a timely enough manner.

Even after you have received proper training a full stall should be reserved for recovery from a severe cravat or a last-ditch effort to recover from an extreme collapse (while still at altitude) prior to deployment of your reserve parachute.

A full stall is caused by a symmetric and complete stall of the entire wing from operating at too high an angle of attack. This is caused either by the application of too much brake, or as the result of a severe forward pendulum motion on the part of the pilot. If the canopy undergoes a full stall, it will collapse rapidly and fall behind the pilot. The pilot will be swung forward and onto his back, and will feel himself going weightless and falling as the lines go slack. Shortly after, the canopy will re-inflate violently and surge rapidly forward. The full stall is an extremely dangerous situation and requires timely, proper, and large brake inputs to correctly control the surges. In an extreme case it is possible for the canopy to fly all the way around the pilot in front, ending up below the pilot. In this scenario it is possible for the pilot to fall into the canopy and become enveloped in it.

It is unlikely you will be able to execute the proper procedure to recover from a full stall if you have not practiced it and there are pilots who have demonstrated recovery from a full stall during a maneuvers clinic but failed to properly recover from an inadvertent stall at a later date. The practice of it is probably more dangerous than the chance of experiencing one, so what is important is kowing

Time sequence photography of a full stall entry (characterized by the wingtips falling back and the canopy taking on a reverse horseshoe appearance). Heading control is erratic at best.

how to avoid one and the situations that might warrant its use. For your information only, here is the generally recommended recovery procedure for a full stall.

1. Do not let up quickly on the brakes after the canopy has fallen behind you and you have gone weightless. By this time a rapid surge is inevitable, and raising the brakes will only make the surge more extreme. Instead, pull the brakes as far as you can and jam your hands together under your seat and hold them tightly. The forces on the brake lines will be quite strong, lock your arms and hold the brakes tightly to ensure they do not get pulled up prematurely.

2. Hold this position until the canopy has stabilized over your head and you are descending vertically. The canopy will normally be in a reverse horseshoe shape with the tips to the rear. Then let up on the brakes at a moderate rate to about the 1/3 (shoulder level) position. Be prepared for the canopy to surge forward.

3. As the canopy surges forward, be prepared to apply brakes aggressively to limit the surge to no more than 30 degrees forward of vertical. Some forward surge is necessary for recovery, but you don't want to allow any chance of the canopy passing below you.

4. If you let the brakes up too slowly, the glider may enter a parachutage stall. If you let them up asymmetrically, you may enter a spin.

Note: if the glider is oscillatory during the full stall then it is not quite stalled enough and recovery should be started as soon as the glider is most symmetrical and oriented in the direction of forward flight. If it was a practice full-stall (not recommended) then next time you should take a wrap or two of the brake lines prior to initiation of the maneuver.

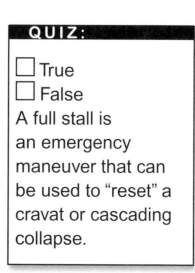

QUIZ:

☐ True
☐ False
A full stall is an emergency maneuver that can be used to "reset" a cravat or cascading collapse.

Recovery from a full stall is characterized by a sudden pitch over. If the brakes are released too fast the pitch over could end in the pilot falling into the canopy!

Parachutage (Constant) Stall

A parachutage stall is a French term for a deep constant stall that may occur after recovery from a collapse, other stall or spin, turbulence, or flying in the rain. An intentional parachutage is difficult to practice on a modern paraglider.

Warning — A glider in parachutage is in a pitch stable condition and may not recover without pilot intervention.

How To Enter: Practice intentional parachutage stalls are typically most easily entered by exiting a B-line stall with a very slow release of the B-risers. Most modern paragliders are extremely resistant to parachutage entry when dry.

What The Canopy Will Do: The canopy will pick up a moderate rate of descent (typically less than that of a B-line stall). The canopy will lose most of its internal pressurization and the brakes may feel disconnected. A parachutage stall is much less dynamic than a full stall and may not be immediately recognized.

How To Recover: First attempt to momentarily increase the drag and angle of attack by a quick full brake application. Immediately bring the brakes back up to eye level and the canopy should accelerate forward. Be ready to control the surge with additional brake input. Another recovery technique is to accelerate out of the stable high angle of attack region by decreasing the angle of attack. You can either pull down on the A-risers (or push them forward) or apply speed bar if it is already on your feet. The first recovery method is normally preferred because it is quicker to initiate.

You should normally deploy your reserve parachute prior to hitting the ground in a parachutage stall, however, if in a stable parachutage descent at less than 200 feet you may elect to land in the stall instead of risking pendulum oscillations from a low altitude recovery or chute deployment. This should not be construed as a recommendation to do so, depending upon the terrain and descent rates either method could result in anything ranging from no injury to a fracture or much worse.

7

Spins

Although spins are not practiced by recreational pilots because of the possibilities of complications, knowledge of spin avoidance and proper recovery technique is important for the advancing pilot.

A spin is caused by an asymmetric stall of the canopy which causes one wing to rotate backwards while the other rotates forward about a point within the span of the wing. One scenario which is highly likely to cause a spin is flying at the edge of stall, with both brakes near 100%, and then rapidly letting up on one brake, or rapidly applying the other brake beyond the stall point, or both. Another way is to apply one brake on exit from a B-line stall, or to let the B-risers up asymmetrically when recovering from a B-line stall. If you fly a glider that is too large for your size then you will need more brake application to generate a turn – use caution to avoid an inadvertent spin entry.

Spin entry is characterized by one wing stalling and flying backward along with a simultaneously softening of the brake pressure on the stalled side.

There are two types of spins, those that remain at a relatively flat attitude (helicopter spin) and those that are banked. A flat spin is often caused by slowing the glider down to near stall with symmetrical brake application and then using an asymmetrical amount of brake as the glider stalls. The glider descends vertically during a flat spin with little centrifugal force on the pilot. It is common for the canopy to spin faster than the pilot and the risers to wrap up. A banked spin is more likely to occur when using too much inside brake during a steep turn. During a banked spin it is possible for the canopy and the pilot to be on opposite sides of the axis of rotation. You will not only feel centrifugal force in a banked spin but also the sensation of flying backwards!

Canopies typically rotate very rapidly in a spin, and it is not uncommon for a significant collapse to result during the spin as well as during the recovery. Recovery from a spin requires unstalling the wing. Bring both brakes up rapidly to your shoulders and prepare for a severe surge as the canopy recovers. If you are in a banked spin and the canopy is behind you then you should wait for it to swing overhead prior to initiating the recovery or else the resulting surge may be too severe to control.

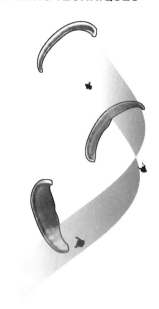
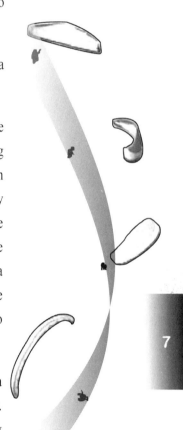

A test pilot demonstrates a banked spin entry and immediate exit. Notice how far the glider pitches down to recover.

If bringing both brakes up does not unstall the wing and start the recovery from the spin, then bring the opposite brake down against the rotation, and apply both brakes all the way to induce a full stall. Follow the full stall recovery procedure from there.

A spin is not a coordinated turn. It is important to note the signs of an incipient spin. If things get quiet and a wing starts to backup you should immediately let up on the brake on the slow wing – do not wait for the spin to develop. The use of opposite brake in a spin should only be used as described above to stop the rotation prior to a full stall recovery attempt. Excessive application of opposite brake can cause the canopy to enter a spin in the other direction. Do not delay recovery from a spin since there is significant danger that the canopy will spin at a different rate than the pilot, causing the risers to twist up and binding up the brake lines thus rendering the brakes ineffective. This can be very dangerous and the best course of action could well be an immediate reserve parachute deployment. If you have the altitude and the wherewithal then you can also consider two alternate courses of action. The first is to try to untwist the risers by grasping them as high as you can and applying force opposite to the direction of twist. We do not recommend this because you will likely be unable to untwist the risers while the canopy spins. Instead, reach above the twists, grab both B-risers and perform a B-line stall. The canopy should stop its rotation and you should now be able to perform a B-line stall recovery using just the risers. After you have recovered, it should now be a simple matter to let the risers untwist themselves or to help them along with your hands and/or by kicking your feet.

Hopefully it is clear that full stalls and spins are extremely dangerous situations that should be avoided. There is no reason to fly in such a way as to expose yourself to these dangers. Leave yourself an adequate margin above stall when flying, and stay away from full stalls and spins.

Cravats

A cravat is another French-derived term given to the canopy when a wingtip becomes entangled in the lines. Cravats are not intentionally practiced but can occur after a collapse or a botched aerobatic maneuver (especially on high aspect ratio canopies). Some cravats could be so minor such that flying qualities are barely affected. More severe cravats must be corrected immediately prior to a loss of control and possible unrecoverable spiral dive. The severity of a cravat is more dependent upon the manner the canopy is entangled than the size of the collapse. Relatively minor appearing cravats can render the canopy unflyable.

If you suffer a cravat, then your first action should be to apply opposite brake to stop the turn. If the cravat occurred during a recovery from a full stall, spin, or aerobatics then the first indication you may notice may be the start of an increasingly severe spiral. Recovery requires immediate application of outside brake to correct and the force required can be significant. Do not accept a tightening spiral, if you cannot stop it then immediately deploy your reserve parachute.

Stopping a turn can take a lot of opposite brake and too much brake could cause a spin. So how much brake is too much? If you ever feel the brake pressure start to decrease then immediately back out a couple of inches. Softening of brake pressure is an indication of approaching tip stall.

If you are able to stop the turn then you may be able to pump out a minor cravat by using the brake on the affected side. Since a cravat is normally a caught wingtip you may be able to pull it free by reaching up and pulling on the stabilizer line (you should know where that line is and which riser it attaches to *prior* to ever trying advanced maneuvers). If that does not work then you must release the tension on the lines that are restraining the cravat. This is done by pulling on the A-riser(s) (if possible, try the outer A-riser first). Pull only as much as required to release the tip. If the tip is still constrained then consider a full stall and recovery to clear it. If your rate of descent is excessive or control is in doubt and recovery not completed by 500 feet AGL then you should deploy your reserve parachute.

A major cravat may only be recoverable by releasing all outer line tension. This is best done with a full stall initiated by pulling the opposite brake as required. This force on the brake can be so extreme that it requires the use of both hands on the single handle. Once the canopy stalls, wait until it shoots back overhead and then bring the brake back up to shoulder level. A quick full stall to clear a major cravat can recover the glider in less than 200 feet. Other techniques may require significantly more time and a correspondingly greater loss of altitude.

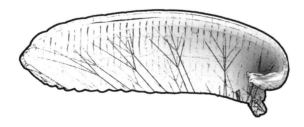

A relatively minor cravat can cause major handling problems!

Advanced Landing Approach Considerations
The Landing Approach in High Winds

If there is any question of your ability to penetrate forward then setup on the upwind side of the LZ while paying attention to your distance to upwind obstructions to avoid rotor turbulence. When penetration is assured, you can crab backwards as you descend or in some situations you may choose to regulate your backwards track by using brakes to slow down towards minimum sink speed. Always strive to fly your final 75 feet of altitude in a wings level attitude with forward motion.

The Super-adiabatic Layer – Handling Low Altitude Lift

During mid-day conditions the ground may absorb more solar energy than it can release through convection. In these conditions the ground will radiate this energy back into the lower atmosphere, heating up the atmosphere closest to it. This results in a "super-adiabatic" lapse rate in the lowest few hundred feet of atmosphere. Such layers of unstable air close to the ground may try to wreak havoc on landing approaches. Often a pilot may be setting up for a landing only to be bounced about by small pockets of buoyant air. These thermals are often too little and too late to take advantage of but serve to disrupt an otherwise perfect landing pattern. Exploiting the super-adiabatic layer for soaring is discussed in *Chapter Eight – Principles and Skills of Soaring Flight*, and *Chapter Ten – Cross Country Flying*.

Using Big Ears During Approach and Landing

As you gain experience you will find that using big ears is a handy technique for dealing with lift during your downwind or base legs. Often you only have to maintain the big ears for a few seconds to get back on the desired glide path. Alternatively, you may find you achieve your greatest spot landing precision by maintaining big ears throughout the approach and modulating them as required to fly a steep glide path to a point just prior of your desired touchdown spot.

There is a danger zone during every approach when you have descended below your minimum altitude for dealing with a major canopy collapse, surge, or stall yet are still high enough to get hurt. This threat is best dealt with by proper preflight planning and having the good judgment to not fly in such potentially turbulent conditions. Regardless, you should have a mitigating procedure for dealing with an elevated risk of hazardous turbulence during your landing approach.

You can reduce the risk of turbulence problems by taking measures to reduce the chance of collapses, by taking measures to reduce the severity of a collapse, and by taking measures to reduce the amount of time you are vulnerable to a collapse. One technique that addresses all three areas is the use of big ears during the approach. Remember, collapses may occur due to wind shear across the wingspan, loss of internal pressurization, or insufficient angle of attack. The big ear configuration reduces wingspan, decreasing the chance of encountering shear within the remaining span. The reduced span translates into reduced volume, a higher wing loading, and greater internal pressure within the inflated center section. The angle of attack is increased and the increased rate of descent significantly reduces the amount of time in the danger zone. Big ears, however, is not a panacea or cure all for potential turbulence. The glider is less controllable and more susceptible to stall while in big ears. If you use big ears in turbulent low altitude conditions then maintain the configuration until you are ready to flare for landing.

Restricted Landing Fields

As you advance in skill and before you consider doing cross country flying, you must first become adept at landing in small landing zones. Such restricted landing fields may also be lined with obstructions such as trees, buildings, power lines, and fences that further reduce the usable approach and landing area. The approach pattern should be adjusted to mitigate the potential hazards due to the smaller field size and any obstructions to the approach. Remember the approach pattern must be flown so that the landing zone can always be reached in the event of unexpected headwinds or sink. Honoring this precept at small obstruction-lined landing fields will preclude flying the normal aircraft style approach.

There is no single technique that is guaranteed to be the best technique for all landing fields in all conditions. You should be adept at performing steep approaches using spirals, B-line stalls, and big ears. Remember to exit spirals and B-line stalls by 200 feet AGL.

If the winds are moderate or stronger then you need to pay particular attention to upwind obstructions and possible mechanical turbulence, particularly if the winds are strong enough to force you to set up your approach on the upwind side of the field. If you feel you must transition through a potential rotor area then you should minimize your time spent doing so. Obviously it is best to avoid such landing conditions.

The Overhead Key Approach

One tight pattern technique that works well in light winds is an overhead key approach. This approach is based on the patterns flown by other low L/D aircraft such as flamed-out military fighters, lifting bodies, and winged spacecraft. The pattern uses checkpoints called "keys" that are windows of altitude and horizontal ground position along a descending 360° spiral approach. The high key and low key positions serve as a means to gauge the approach so as to ensure a consistent base key and final approach.

The overhead key approach starts at the high key window on an upwind heading with a lateral offset from the target. The goal is to maintain a steep 20-45° vertical angular relationship (declination angle) to the target as you fly around it in a downward spiral to a close base key position.

To setup for the approach use any appropriate technique so that you are roughly overhead the landing target at 300 feet AGL. Aim to enter high key facing into the wind at 250 feet AGL. The high key window is laterally offset approximately 150 feet from the target (you may decide to start even closer as you gain experience). Fly upwind and maintain a constant horizontal distance from the target by starting a gentle crosswind turn. Aim to cross the extended upwind center line of the target perpendicular to the wind. This first ninety degrees of turn should give you a good idea of the pattern winds and your penetration capability. Maintain the constant radius ground track and aim to cross the low key window directly abeam the target on a downwind heading at 150 feet AGL.

The approach from high key to low key is designed to enable you to evaluate conditions and performance. From low key you now transition to a steeper approach with a tighter radius to cross the base key position at 100 feet AGL, playing your turn as required to roll out on final directly downwind of the target at 50-75 feet AGL. In light winds you will need to increase your rate of descent from the low key position to avoid being high at the base key. Pulling big ears is recommended instead of extending your downwind or base legs because it allows you to turn more directly to final without excessive low altitude maneuvering. Use a combination of weight shift or differential big ears to hold the desired turn radius. In light winds you will have to use some degree of big ears on final to maintain the steep glide path.

OVERHEAD KEY APPROACH

If the LZ is small and the winds light, then this spiral approach pattern can work well. Aim so as to be wings level on final no lower than 50 ft. AGL.

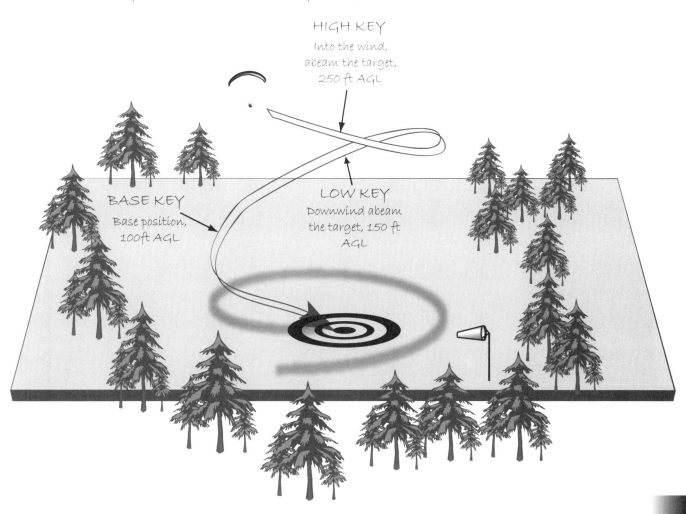

HIGH KEY
Into the wind,
abeam the target,
250 ft AGL

BASE KEY
Base position,
100ft AGL

LOW KEY
Downwind abeam
the target, 150 ft
AGL

Overhead Key Approach Contingencies

If you have any problems penetrating to the crosswind key position then you should not fly a high groundspeed downwind leg but instead abort the overhead pattern and follow the "Landing Approach in High Winds" procedures.

Unlike the downwind entry from the conventional aircraft pattern, the initial upwind leg from high key should automatically compensate for winds so if you find yourself high at the low key position then you either encountered lift or flew an excessively tight pattern. Avoid the temptation to extend downwind from the low key position, instead use big ears to arrive at the proper base key position.

If you find yourself low at any point prior to low key then tighten up your turn as appropriate to cut across the circle so as to intercept the arc at the appropriate height. With practice you will find the overhead key approach is a versatile pattern.

The Last-Ditch "Land at all Costs" Helicopter Spin Landing

There is one last technique that is successfully used by some advanced pilots to side hill land in strong conditions or in minuscule landing areas. Side hill landing using normal techniques can be impossible when the upward velocity of the wind (the ridge lift) exceeds your sinking velocity. You may be able to lose altitude and get in close to the hill but each time you slow and turn into the wind in preparation for touching down, you gain altitude or start moving downhill. If you are an advanced pilot with a thorough knowledge of your canopy then there is a technique that you may consider – a controlled spin for landing. When performed correctly at a very low altitude, it is possible to land on your feet, facing uphill and with the canopy in position for a subsequent reverse inflation!

To setup the maneuver, work your way down as close to the terrain as possible. Ideally you would like to be within a few feet, in some situations over smooth terrain you may accept a few feet higher. You should be upright in your harness with your feet reaching for the ground as you increase brake pressure towards the stall point. Your sink rate should increase and it may be enough to touchdown. If not, DO NOT STALL YOUR WING! Just prior to the stall point (where the canopy falls behind you and you swing forward), pull one brake to the limit while letting up the other one and weight shifting fully towards the high side (away from the buried brake handle). The wing will immediately spin towards the brake application.

Normally, it will feel as if you are being pulled up and back from the side of the flying (unstalled) wing. You will rotate towards the stalled wing but at a slower rate than the canopy. The wing will be diving behind you and you will essentially be free falling a few feet to touchdown. The canopy will continue its quick revolution and likely complete a full 360°, impacting on the trailing edge as you touchdown. You must be prepared to touchdown at any time (even before you face the hill) and be ready to take a couple quick steps towards the canopy while you regain normal control of it.

The exact timing of the maneuver depends upon your height above the ground, the slope, and the wind speed and gradient. In higher winds or less gradient (stronger winds close to the hill), you can pick up some downwind movement. If you recognize such conditions you can compensate by starting the maneuver a few feet further forward.

If you full stall the wing prior to the spin, your body will pendulum forward and you will land hard on your backside. Aside from the possibility of injury you will also not be in position to control the canopy. If you are too timid with the brake application then the glider will turn downwind with all of the hazards normally associated with a low altitude downwind turn.

Prior to ever using this technique on the side of a hill, you should have practiced it extensively over a large, flat and forgiving LZ or coastal sand dune.

Para Ski - Launching With Snow Skis

A ski launch is recommended if you are launching on snow in calm or light winds and are either encumbered with bulky footwear or deep powdery snow. Lay out your wing as you normally would for the slope and wind conditions. If you are on a moderate or steeper slope and do not have a launch assistant or some clothespin tethers then you may want to put some snow on the trailing edge to keep the wing from lifting up or sliding downhill.

Once you are hooked to the canopy you will need to hold your position while you prepare for a forward launch. You may choose to set your edges and face across the fall line or in deep snow you may face downhill with the tail of one ski jammed downward into the snow. Commence your forward inflation by releasing the edges and turning downhill or popping the tail out as appropriate.

On groomed snow you may choose to set up for a reverse launch, holding your position with a backward snowplow. Release the edges as you pull up the canopy, verify a good inflation and, as you feel yourself get light on your feet, do a slip turn to face downhill and proceed with the launch.

With adequate equipment paragliding can be a year-round sport

Emergency Procedures
Control of Direction Without Brake Lines

You may control the direction of the canopy without the use of brakes (in the event of a brake line failure, for example) in the following ways:

a. Shift your weight in the seat in the direction you wish to turn. (Lift your opposite leg off of the seat and lean towards the intended turn). This will be more effective if the chest strap is loose.

b. Pull down on a stabilizer line on the side towards which you wish to turn.

c. Pull down on the rear riser on the side to which you wish to turn.

d. The brake line itself could conceivably get caught up in the pulley. In that case simply reach above it, grasp the brake line and pull it down.

Power Line Landings

The first rule of power lines is to avoid them at all costs. Before you can avoid them, however, you have to be able to see them. Power lines are often nearly impossible to see from the air so preflight knowledge and planning is paramount. When flying over unfamiliar terrain you must continuously scan the terrain for telltale signs of power lines, looking for their support structures, patterns through the vegetation, and so forth.

Tip:
Avoid an encounter with live power lines at all costs!

Do not ever accept a power line landing as inevitable because the outcome is too unpredictable and the potential risks too great. In light winds a downwind landing and in stronger winds a B-line or even full stall landing is generally preferable to the possibility of severe burns or death.

If despite your best efforts you find impact with power lines imminent then you should stand up in your harness with your feet and knees together and try to descend as vertically as possible. Keep you arms and elbows tucked in close as best you can. If you get hung up in the lines do NOT allow anyone to approach you to help as they may complete the ground circuit and electrocute both of you. Stay calm and wait until the power company arrives. There are some inventive techniques possible for unhooking from your harness and climbing down until you are low enough to let go and drop to the ground. We will not recommend any technique, but as a general rule you should ensure that no part of your body or anything you are touching will ever either contact the ground or touch anything that is not insulated from the ground.

Water Landings

Landing in fresh water should only be attempted in controlled conditions. Maneuvers clinics and some aerobatic competitions are conducted over water with the pilot wearing proper flotation gear. Without flotation gear modern foam and airbag harnesses will likely float a pilot face down in the water.

You should never consider landing in any moving water. Landing in surf is likely as dangerous as a power line landing. If the canopy lands in the water it will rapidly fill and become a sea anchor that will pull you under regardless of the number of people trying to assist you. Even if you can unhook from your harness you still have the risk of line entanglement.

If you find yourself faced with an imminent unplanned water landing, you should consider unhooking your harness leg straps when below 100 feet. In smooth conditions you should also consider unfastening your chest strap a few seconds prior to landing. Land directly into the wind and pull the brakes fully at touchdown to ensure the canopy stops and falls behind you. Immediately complete the unhooking process, exit the harness and separate from it with a slow backward sculling motion in the water. Do not try to retrieve any gear until you are safe in a rescue boat.

Tip: Avoid a landing in the surf at all costs!

If the canopy falls on top of you after landing then after unhooking you should locate one of the chord (fore and aft) seams and slowly pull it hand over hand from behind you to the front. Do this while slowly treading water as you back away from the glider. Gently pull any lines around you up and over your head as you continue your backward movement. You should be clear of the canopy within a few seconds but you should continue your slow backwards movement until you are sure you are clear of all the lines. Do not panic or do any rapid kicks or swim movements as this increases your chances of having an entangled line tighten around you.

Tree Landings

Tree landings are usually less dangerous than power line or water landings but are still best reserved for the birds. Depending on the conditions (winds, slope, type and height of trees) it may be preferable to land in the trees instead of taking drastic measures to avoid them. It is usually better to accept a controlled tree landing instead of making a valiant but unsuccessful attempt to avoid them.

Tip:
An intentional tree landing is usually safer than an unintentional tree encounter!

Once you decide that a tree landing is probable then you should set up the approach so as to ensure a controlled flare and landing in the thicker foliage near the top of the tree. Probably the greatest danger is an unsuccessful landing or bouncing off a tall tree and falling to the ground below. Make your approach into the wind and flare so as to stop your forward movement. Let go of the brakes immediately after you contact the tree and make every effort to grab the largest branch you can get a hold of.

Remember that most injuries in tree landings occur after the landing so maintain a firm hold until the canopy is deflated. Secure yourself as best you can and then release the canopy to avoid a wind gust pulling you from your roost. In areas where tree landings are a real possibility you should fly with a small kit for lowering yourself to the ground. A couple of carabiners, a couple of webbing slings, some 7-mm line and a bit of prior planning are all that is required to secure yourself and rappel down. Be sure to include a small rope saw (if dry wood) or a folding blade saw (for moist, resinous lumber) to cut branches if required. A small wench to unscrew the quicklinks is invaluable for pulling hopelessly snagged lines from the branches. It normally works better to grasp the canopy and pull it up and away from the tree instead of trying to pull the canopy down by the risers or lines.

If you are landing in the trees from an out of control situation (stall, spin, etc.) you should make an effort to protect your major arteries and veins. This procedure is contained in the Parachute Landing Fall section.

Reserve Parachute Systems

Reserve parachutes may be deployed by hand, or using a rocket deployment system. The rocket deployment is much faster, and thus can save you at a lower altitude. On the other hand, rockets usually cannot be aimed during deployment, they are more expensive, they impose a higher burden of care and safety precautions because of the danger to anyone in the vicinity in an accidental deployment, and they may not be as reliable because they are more complex. In fact, rocket deployment systems are getting harder and harder to find.

The bridle length on the reserve should be as short as possible to enhance rapid deployment and reduce the chance of the canopy falling to a position directly below you before it deploys, which can result in your descending into the inflating reserve. The bridle must not be so short, however, that you pull the lines out of the rubber band stows when you wind up to throw it.

The attachment to the harness should be to structural support straps in the harness at the top center of the back. The reason is that this attachment will allow the pilot to land on both feet. The older practice of attaching the reserve to one or both carabiners results in the pilot falling on his side (one carabiner) or possible on his back or the base of his spine (both carabiners) and also requires that the reserve connection be verified each time the harness is attached to the paraglider. In all cases, follow the recommendations of the harness and parachute manufacturer.

Accidental deployments are a hazard. You should ensure your parachute is attached to your harness in accordance with the manufacturers' recommendations. Ensure the deployment pin is securely in place prior to flight. Lastly use caution when making harness adjustments or grabbing equipment from harness pockets to avoid inadvertently hooking the deployment handle. You should also have a hook knife in easy reach to cut the reserve bridle if required once you are on the ground.

Use of Your Backup Emergency Reserve Parachute

Emergency parachutes have been in common use by paraglider pilots for over a decade and have been successfully deployed hundreds of times. You should never deploy a reserve parachute unless you have a genuine emergency; an unrecoverable equipment malfunction, perhaps as the result of a midair, a major collapse, stall or spin at too low an altitude to allow time for recovery, or a medical emergency. The deployment of a reserve parachute will normally result in a rapid descent, with little or no directional control and with the possibility of dangerous oscillations or down planing.

Down planing is when the paraglider reinflates while traveling downwards, and then flies to a slightly inverted attitude so that it is "lifting" in a negative direction against the drag of the reserve canopy and thus increasing your sink rate. If your paraglider re-inflates and begins down planing following a reserve deployment, you may attempt to pull on one brake line to turn the canopy and fly it back up over you. If you are at low altitude, it is probably safer to simply pull in enough of the B-risers or C-risers on your main canopy to collapse it approximately 50%. This will enable the main canopy to help dampen any oscillations, while preventing it from re-inflating, which can result in down planing.

A paraglider that is downplaning opposite of a reserve parachute will result in a fast rate of descent. Use your risers or brakes to deflate the paraglider.

If you ever need to deploy your reserve, you will have a much greater chance of success if you have practiced the proper procedures in a simulator. The correct deployment procedure is as follows:

LOOK   To find your deployment handle.

GRASP   The deployment handle.

PULL   The deployment handle, opening the container and pulling the parachute and deployment bag free of the container.

LOOK   To find a clear airspace into which to throw the parachute.

THROW   The parachute as hard as you can into clear air. (If you are spinning, use whatever centrifugal force exists to throw the parachute to the outside of the spin into the direction of the spin.)

FIND   The parachute bridle and start reeling it in. This will help to pull the lines from the deployment bag, speeding deployment, and if the canopy does not begin to inflate you will eventually have it in your hands again for another attempt to deploy it.

DISABLE   The main canopy by pulling in on the "B" or C-risers.

In parachute re-packing and deployment seminars that we have conducted over the years, pilots who attend each year see a steady decrease in their deployment times and a marked increase in their percentage of successful simulated deployments.

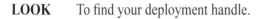

WARNING

The decision to deploy a parachute must be based on altitude and not a visual interpretation of your altitude and rate of descent. Waiting to deploy until you sense the urgency of the situation (ground rush) is too late and will likely result in death or serious injury.

7

The Parachute Landing Fall

All sport parachutists get trained on the proper technique for doing a parachute landing fall (PLF). The idea of a PLF is to use a controlled technique to reduce the impact forces by spreading them out over time. To do a proper PLF you should start by facing into the wind with your feet and knees together and your eyes on the horizon (fight the urge to look down which can cause you to stiffen up just prior to impact). Upon impact you should twist your hips so you sequentially fall on the side of your calves, thighs, and hips before rolling onto your back. By having multiple impact points you reduce the stress on your feet and legs.

Many instructors and instructional manuals espouse the virtue of a good PLF for dealing with any hard impact. In fact, if you ever see someone hit hard and walk away uninjured it will usually be attributed to a good PLF and good back protection. If you ever see someone hit hard and not walk away uninjured then you will likely hear someone voice the opinion that injury could have been avoided with a proper PLF.

In reality, PLFs provide additional protection up to a certain vertical velocity. Above this velocity you will be unable to control your body orientation during the impact sequence and landing on your feet will probably no longer be the best course of action. As a case in point, Hollywood stunt men stop trying to land on their feet after falls of more than several meters. They, like pole vaulters, find it more comfortable to land on minimal padding as flat on their backs as possible.

Another problem with a PLF is it is designed to be a controlled maneuver and most hard impacts in our sport tend to be uncontrolled. If we are landing under a reserve canopy then we have no directional control and likely will not have the luxury of landing into the wind in the planned LZ. Instead, it is much more likely that we are drifting downwind into a slope with no control of our drift or even body orientation. If we are hitting hard and are not under a reserve canopy then we are also unlikely to be coming down vertically into the wind. In these situations, worrying about a proper PLF will likely be as useful to you as being given a set of the emperor's new clothes.

Therefore, emphasis should not be on what to do but on what *not* to do. You should not try to stay on your feet. You should try not to hit vertically on your butt. (Even modern back protection is inadequate for prevention of a spinal compression injury caused by impact in the sitting position.) Back protection does, however, offer significant protection for prone impacts on your back. If you have any choice in the matter then you should either strive to land feet-first facing upwind or semi-reclined, letting the flat of your back absorb as much impact as possible. If you land with forward momentum then you should try to twist at impact so that your back protection can take as much of the subsequent impact as possible.

In the case of a blown launch, low altitude collapse, stall, or spin; then you likely will have even less control of your body position. If possible you should protect your face, neck, and chest as best you can.

With an unsteerable reserve, the possibility exists for landing in an inopportune spot such as water, trees, or power lines. Generally follow the same advice previously given for landing a paraglider in such hazards. If you are descending into trees then you should ensure your feet and knees are together, your elbows are tucked into your sides, your head tilted down, and your palms cupped around the sides of your neck with your thumbs and fingers together (to protect your major arteries and veins from puncture).

Once on the ground you should immediately collapse your reserve to avoid from being drug. If you cannot run downwind or alongside the chute then do not waste your time trying to pull on the bridle – it will not stop you. You must either immediately release from your harness or cut the reserve bridle with your hook knife. Even if the winds are light and you are not in any danger of being drug, you should immediately collapse your reserve and ball up your wing as a signal to others that you are not badly injured.

7

NOTES

_____

_____

_____

_____

_____

_____

_____

_____

_____

_____

_____

_____

_____

_____

_____

_____

Chapter Eight:
STAYING ALOFT

THE PRINCIPLES & SKILLS OF SOARING FLIGHT

8

Ridge soaring at "the Dumps", Pacifica, California

Chapter 8 — STAYING ALOFT
THE PRINCIPLES AND SKILLS OF SOARING FLIGHT

Soaring is the act of extending the duration of your flight by flying in rising parcels of air. It is the goal of virtually all pilots who fly unpowered aircraft. Think of other sports that require the use of gravity for enjoyment such as skiing or surfing. Soaring flight for a pilot is the equivalent of a mountain that miraculously grows as a skier skis down it or an endless wave for the surfer. Luckily, soaring requires more thought and skill than simply riding a bicycle down an up escalator (it is also more scenic), therefore it can be one of the most profoundly enjoyable and satisfying recreational experiences you can have. In this chapter we will take a look at what makes soaring possible and how to do it.

Staying Up - What Makes it Possible

An unpowered aircraft must always be descending through the air in which it is flying. (Technically this isn't quite true, a glider can, after building up speed in a dive, climb upwards through the air mass for a brief period of time, trading energy of motion for altitude. However, after the whole cycle of dive and climb is over, the glider will be lower than when it started.) We looked at the reasons why we must always descend in a glider when we looked at aerodynamics and the need to tilt the flight path downwards in order to make lift, drag, and gravity all balance each other.

If the air mass is still, then our descent through it also results in a descent towards the ground. If we want to arrest our descent towards the ground, we need to find some upward moving air.

Let's dispel a misconception here. Upward moving air does not "push" the glider upward in the sense of an extra or increased force acting to lift the glider. The lift force on a glider which is at equilibrium (subject to balanced forces of lift, drag and gravity) but rising relative to the ground by virtue of flying in a rising parcel of air is the same as the lift force on a glider which is at equilibrium and descending relative to the ground in a parcel of still air. A glider which is "climbing" in "lift" is simply responding once again to the motion of the medium in which it is flying. The glider is descending inside a parcel of air which is rising at a rate faster than the descent rate of the glider. It is as if you were to go to the department store, and walk slowly downwards on the up escalator. You would move continuously downwards in the "medium" of the escalator on which you were walking, yet at the same time rise continuously upwards within the store itself.

So soaring is made possible by the existence of parcels or regions of rising air. Where do they come from?

Thermals

One source of rising air, or "lift" is thermals. A thermal is a region of rising air which has been warmed to a temperature greater than that of the surrounding air. As a result, the air has expanded, become less dense and therefore lighter, and has begun to rise. Normally thermals are created when an area on the ground becomes hotter than the surrounding area, and in turn heats the air above it to a warmer temperature. Initially the warmer air has a tendency to adhere to the surface, but given enough of a temperature differential, or perhaps a little wind to disturb it, the thermal eventually breaks free and begins to rise.

Whether or not the thermal continues to rise depends on the stability of the air, as we discuss in the chapter on weather. As the thermal rises, it cools due to expansion. (It expands because it is rising to a higher altitude where the surrounding air pressure is less.) If the thermal cools below the temperature of the surrounding air, it stops rising. If, at some altitude, the air suddenly becomes warmer than the rising thermal, this is called an inversion, and the thermals usually stop dead at that altitude. If you stand on the top of a 5000 foot mountain in the Los Angeles basin on a summer morning, you often can clearly see the inversion as a flat topped layer of hazy brown air about 1500 feet below you.

If the air is just slightly unstable, thermals rise weakly. If it is strongly unstable, then as the thermal rises, the air around it cools faster with altitude than the thermal cools from expansion, and the thermal accelerates upwards.

Air flowing into the thermal along the ground to replace the rising air often picks up a rotational flow, and a thermal's location over a dusty field is sometimes marked by a miniature cyclone of rising dust. "Dust devils," as these are called, often mark thermals which are extremely turbulent, especially close to the ground, and it is not recommended that a paraglider pilot deliberately fly into a dust devil.

In fact all thermals represent some degree of turbulence, or chaotic motion of the air. Violent turbulence can lead to the loss of control of any aircraft, and turbulence is therefore potentially dangerous for any pilot. However, paragliders, because of their completely flexible wing structure, are particularly sensitive to the effects of turbulence. Turbulence can affect the paraglider in several ways which are dangerous

8

for the pilot; it can cause oscillations, it can lead to constant (parachutage) stall or spins, and it can cause canopy collapses. This is why we have emphasized so strongly that in order to fly safely in soaring conditions, the pilot must first master the control of the canopy, including canopy collapses and recovery, that we discussed in the last chapter.

Thermals require local differences in temperature and places that heat up with respect to their surroundings will serve as thermal trigger spots. Trigger spots can take many forms and examples include a ridge that directly faces the overhead sun, an asphalt parking lot surrounded by grassy fields, a rock outcropping on a ridge line, etc.

Once a sufficient temperature differential exists, the thermal releases from its trigger spot and begins rising (the hotter it is with respect to its surroundings, the faster it rises). How long before another thermal is generated depends on the trigger spot, atmospheric, and solar conditions. Some trigger spots will appear to function almost continuously during the heat of the day and are often referred to as "house" thermals.

More often there will be a time delay between successive thermals while the trigger spot absorbs additional solar energy and begins to radiantly heat the surrounding air. This "cycle time" is often consistent during a given part of the day and typically ranges from five to twenty minutes. On the ground you may sometimes note a passing thermal by a slight increase in temperature but more likely you will notice the slight change in wind velocity as the thermal passes by and draws in the surrounding air to fill in the void left behind as it rises. When waiting to launch you should observe the movement of the wind in the bushes and trees below for signs of approaching thermals or gusts. Small streamers placed below launch level are valuable for observing the subtle changes. In light to moderate winds, streamers placed 75 feet upwind will give you five to ten seconds of "heads-up" prior to the thermal's arrival.

In light winds a strong thermal can actually cause a reversal in surface wind direction as it approaches. Obviously, launching into a switching tailwind is something that is best avoided. Conversely, if you note the arrival of a thermal and wait too long before launching then you may find yourself starting out below the thermal and unable to climb to it. To make a more educated decision on when to launch you should try to estimate the cycle time by noting the time of each passing thermal and mentally logging the length of the gusts and the number of minutes between them. You should then try to launch several seconds after the next gust has stabilized.

Thermals are like fingerprints and no two are identical. You will find thermals that form a rising column of air stretching from the ground upwards thousands of feet with dozens of gliders dispersed throughout. You will also find thermals that break loose from their trigger source and form a small bubble capable of supporting only one or two lucky gliders. A third thermal model involves a vortex ring, the thermal rising like a horizontally oriented smoke ring. This third model is, however, one based on myth and not reality; thermals do not trigger with the same mechanism as a vortex ring nor have the strength to sustain the toroidal flow.

The atmosphere maintains a state of overall equilibrium so air that rises in one spot must descend in another. Thus, on the local scale, thermals are usually surrounded with areas of sinking air. Because the area of the sinking air is greater than the area of the rising air, the velocity of the sinking air tends to be significantly less, normally in the range of 25-50% of the lift velocity.

Thermals generally start out small in diameter, increasing in size as they rise. They often appear to follow the fall line of a slope, winding upward following the path of least vertical resistance as they snake their way towards the summit. A good visualization technique is to mentally invert the terrain and picture the natural drainage that would occur if water were dripping from the base towards the summit. The water would follow the gullies to the spines and the spines towards the summit, stopping and dripping off any rock outcroppings along the way. Experience has shown thermals to respond similarly to terrain.

In the presence of wind, thermals are decelerated by rising terrain and thus will stack up at a higher density than in the flat lands. Winds also serve to channel the thermals into the gullies and bowl shaped ridges that face the flow. The multiple cores may combine into a single upper-level thermal.

Even over flat terrain, thermals are rarely randomly spaced, instead lining up in parallel lines of lift and sink stretching downwind. If there is sufficient moisture to form clouds these lines of thermals will be capped by cumulus clouds and are referred to as "cloud streets". On good days, it is possible to follow a cloud street for extended distances, sometimes without having to circle to stay in the lift.

8

For a given location, thermals will tend to be smaller and with greater lateral shearing action on high pressure days as compared to low pressure days. Thermals generated on the leeward side of a ridge are similarly characterized as smaller and "punchier" than those on the windward side.

If you were to read and take completely to heart all of the above, you would probably conclude that thermals exist only on sunny days and only over land. In reality, however, the main requirement for thermal activity is unstable air. Even along the shore of the ocean, and even on overcast days, if the air is unstable enough you will encounter discrete rising parcels of air. In fact the thermals on a cloudy but unstable day will be much more abundant and stronger than the thermals on a hot and sunny but stable day.

Recent advances in sensors have lead to a greater understanding of the low altitude structure of thermals. Thermals can be broken up into two distinct layers, the surface layer and the mixing layer. The surface layer extends from the base of the thermal upward to a height varying from tens of feet to a maximum of perhaps ten percent of the total thermal height. This layer is characterized by a super-adiabatic layer (high lapse rate) and wind gradient due to surface roughness. Thermals start out as irregular plumes, often rising slowly and branching out in seemingly random directions (to include horizontally). Many of these plumes never reach above the surface layer, others coalesce with nearby plumes combining into what we recognize as a thermal. Rising thermals cause hexagonal circulation patterns and in the presence of moderate winds these patterns will line up to create streets. Circulation patterns due to the sinking air between the rising plumes of the surface layer will cause small areas of convergence lift. These small ridges of lift can vary in size, strength, and duration. Land soaring birds such as hawks and buzzards are adept at working these small seams of lift. For most paraglider pilots the super-adiabatic layer only forestalls landing but in some locations it may be possible to significantly extend your flight by knowing how to work such "microlift". For additional information on soaring within the surface layer read the section at the end of this chapter titled Microlift Soaring.

The mixing layer extends above the surface wind gradient and is characterized by lesser lapse rates and more uniform winds. Cloud streets are encouraged to form when the mixing layer winds are "stacked" (increasing strength with altitude and without a change in direction). If the increase in winds with altitude is strong or the winds change direction rapidly then the shear effects of the wind can break down the structure of the thermal. A shear of more than four mph of wind per thousand feet of altitude denotes a high amount of shear and may signify tough thermalling.

The top of the surface layer is the top of that lower area of our atmosphere characterized by the vertical mixing of air of different densities (temperature) and commonly referred to by meteorologists as the boundary layer.

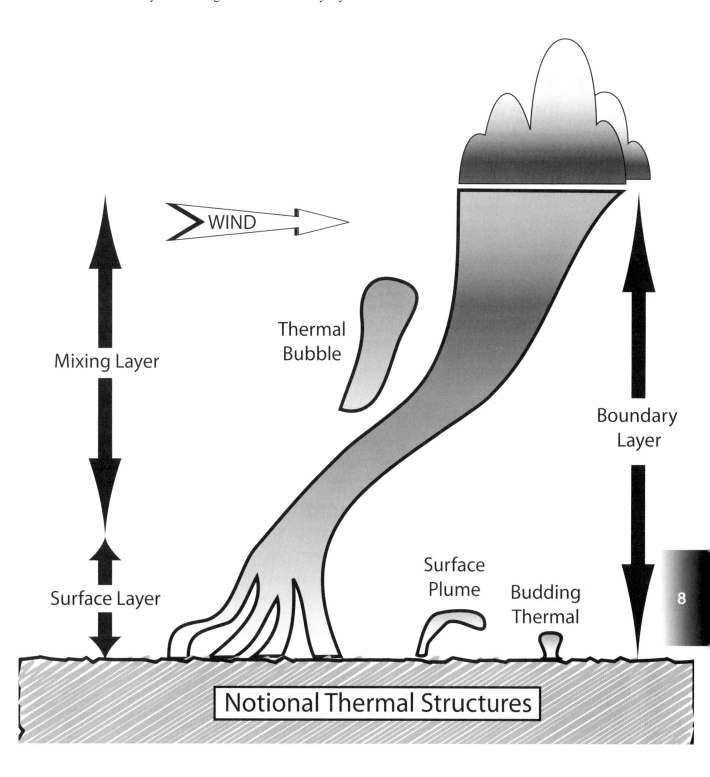

Notional Thermal Structures

Wind blowing against a ridge line is deflected upwards, creating a band of lift where the upward component of the wind velocity is enough to cancel the sink rate of the glider. A glider flying in this lift band can maintain altitude indefinitely.

A steeper slope deflects the air upwards more effectively, creating a larger lift band that is angled more forward of the cliff edge.

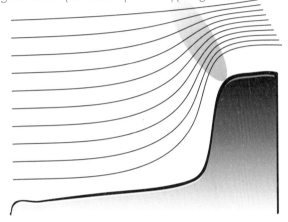

A shallower slope has less of a vertical lift component and a smaller lift band that is closer to and over the face of the ridge. The wind speed required for soarable lift is higher.

Ridge Lift

Another source of rising air is known as "ridge lift." This occurs when wind meets a large obstacle of terrain, such as a ridge, cliff, or hill, and is forced to flow upwards to get over the object. Often a hill does not support ridge lift very well, because it is too easy for the wind to go around instead of going over. If the hill is extended, however, into a long ridge, the wind is to some degree forced up over the top, and a band of rising air is created in front of and above the ridge. Since ridge lift depends on wind, it also implies the presence of turbulence in those areas downwind of the ridge top where rotors are likely to exist.

As a general rule of thumb, the stronger the wind, the more perpendicular it is to the ridge face, and the steeper the slope, the stronger the lift. The vertical orientation of the lift band is also a function of wind speed and slope angle. In higher winds and steeper slopes the lift band will be oriented further in front of the apex of the hill.

The stability of the atmosphere also has an effect on ridge soaring. In cases of strong winds and neutral static stability, you can expect increased turbulence and rotors without greater height. Normally the lift will be stronger and reach higher altitudes on unstable days, however, there are special cases where unusually good ridge soaring conditions can occur in stable air that is capped with an inversion layer. This effect often occurs during late afternoon or evening and is characterized by an unusually smooth and large lift band. Pilots refer to these conditions as "glass off" because the lift is glassy smooth. Glass off conditions are often attributed to convergence lift caused by the change from anabatic to catabatic flow as the now-cooler air close to the higher elevations runs downhill causing an uplifting of the warmer valley air. The true lifting mechanism may sometimes actually be due to small-scale wave action but the important point is to realize the potential for great ridge soaring can occur at the end of the flying day.

Convergence Lift

As the name implies, convergence lift can occur when differing flows come together. Convergence lift can often be found due to frontal passage, solar heating on the leeward slopes, and obstructions to the wind. When two air masses of different temperatures and densities meet, the heavier colder air pushes the lighter warmer air upward. A passing cold front can be lead by convergence lift reaching upwards above ten thousand feet. Soaring this large-scale convergence is best left to sailplanes with their extended speed range and capacity to handle turbulence.

One type of convergence that can be exploited by a paraglider is convergence due to solar heating on the leeward (downwind) side of a large ridge. Flying sites that face the morning sun and are protected from the prevailing winds are prime candidates for this type of convergence lift. Examples include the Lake Elsinore site in southern California; Walt's Point in the eastern Sierras, Owens Valley, CA, and Mount Zion (Lookout Mountain) on the eastern slopes of the Rockies, Golden, CO. In all cases the launch site faces east on a mountain range with prevailing afternoon westerly winds. With adequate solar heating the morning upslope thermals can overpower the early prevailing flow (setting up what is commonly referred to as a thermal block). With sufficient levels of instability, the rising air can be pushed even higher by the convergence set up by the interaction of the prevailing winds and the anabatic upslope winds.

The ability of solar heating to overpower the prevailing winds is site dependent and includes factors such as the strength of the prevailing winds, the height of the blocking ridge, solar intensity, and lapse rate. It is important not to confuse safe anabatic upslope flow with dangerous leeside rotor turbulence (that may appear to be upslope flow). Dangerous leeside conditions can often be detected by observing rapid cloud movement from the backside of the hill or hearing strong winds blowing through the trees at higher elevations despite only feeling light winds at launch. Experienced local pilots often have established rules-of-thumb that help predict the potential for a given day. Another source of valuable information is the winds aloft forecast.

Convergence lift can cause thermals and thermals can cause convergence lift. A strong thermal causes enough lifting action to cause the surrounding air to flow inwards towards it. Similarly, on a larger scale there can be enough lifting air over a mountain or high plateau that the surrounding air on all sides is drawn inwards towards it and

8

the resulting convergence can feed the thermal intensity. This is one reason large cloud buildups often occur over isolated peaks.

The Sea Breeze Front

Another type of convergence lift that can be exploited regularly is convergence due to the passing of a sea breeze front. As the name implies, sea breeze fronts occur within close proximity to large bodies of water. The daily anabatic heating of the land mass results in lifting air that is replaced by cooler marine air and convergence lift will occur at the boundary of the two masses. A typical sea breeze front will penetrate tens of miles inland (more or less depending on blocking terrain and the strength of the inland heating).

The sea breeze flows inland during the day and ebbs back to sea at night, the cycles being longer in distance (and duration) during the summer months when the inland heats up to its maximum. Sites that are renowned for sea breeze convergence are located at the distance from the coast where the frontal passage does not occur until sufficient solar heating has enabled the soaring aircraft to be prepositioned in thermals well above the terrain. In summer months the sea breeze may move inland so early that sites closer to the coast will not have had sufficient time to heat up and provide upslope thermals. These sites may provide soarable convergence during spring and summer month when the passage occurs later in the day.

Sea breeze convergence has been flown on both coasts as well as the western shore of Lake Michigan. A special sea breeze convergence can occur on peninsulas where you can have onshore flows from both shores. A long line of lift may form along the long axis of the land mass where the dueling flows meet. This has been observed along Cape Cod, Long Island, the DELMARVA peninsula, and central Florida. In the latter example, the colliding air masses provide for plentiful opportunities for long distance cross country flight. Use caution however, since the convergence of the warm moist air masses often occurs with an unstable upper air mass causing rapid overdevelopment, thunderstorms, and tornadoes.

Convergence lift is also possible with air of similar densities. Even in stable atmospheric conditions, air that deflects around both sides of a large object may cause a line of lift where the air converges together on the downwind side (visualize water in a shallow stream flowing around a rock and rising on the down-flow side). By definition, convergence involves a mixing of airflow which means the presence of turbulence in these boundary areas. Mechanical convergence is often difficult to exploit due to the expanded turbulence areas and the localized nature of the lift.

Techniques for Thermal Soaring

To soar in a thermal you first have to find one. Since thermals need to be heated, you can try looking for thermals over areas of bare ground or rock faces which you would expect to heat up faster than surrounding areas of vegetation. You can also look over high ground, where the ground tends to heat to the same temperature as the lower ground, but the air is cooler so the temperature differential is greater. And you can look in the regions above lee side faces that are shadowed from the wind but in full sun, where the air has a better chance to heat up before being blown away. Don't be surprised or disappointed, however, if you don't find thermals where you expect them. In the real world, thermals are often not where they ought to be, and sometimes are where you wouldn't expect them to be.

The best way to find a thermal is to steal one. Watch the soaring birds; if you see a hawk circling, and you can glide to where he is, at near the same altitude or above, fly over there. (Note: If he is a she, and she is within 1500 feet of the ground, and it is middle to late spring, you may want to reconsider. Hawks have been known to chase and even physically attack hang gliders during nesting time, and although a hang glider is pretty impervious to hawk attack, we shudder to think of what a hawk's talons would do to a paraglider.) Watch also other pilots, for clues to thermal location. Watch the clouds; cumulus clouds tend to form at the tops of thermal updrafts. (Do not enter a thermal directly under or climb to anywhere near cloudbase of a cloud with greater than 5000 feet vertical development. The experience of being upside down, weightless and blind while totally whited out in the middle of a violently turbulent and ice filled cloud with your canopy collapsed in a ball and your lines draped around your face is not one you want to have. You cannot see the level of vertical development of a cloud from below, and you don't know how big it is. The lift under a large cloud will often become suddenly much stronger in the vicinity of the base of the cloud, and a paraglider does not offer much in the way of options for escaping from a cloud.)

And finally, just fly around. The fact of the matter is that even among the expert pilots, most thermals are found simply by blundering into them.

8

How to Work a Thermal

A variometer (an instrument that measures rate of climb or descent) is a big help here when you are learning to thermal. After awhile you won't need it, although it will always help you, but in the beginning it's really nice to have. It is best if it has an audio output, so you can look around while you're flying and listen for the indications of lift.

To work a thermal, you generally fly circles within it. Sometimes you fly ovals. Sometimes you fly squares or rectangles. Sometimes figure-eights. It depends on the presence of terrain, or other gliders, and it depends on the shape of the thermal, and they're all different. Thousands of words have been written about thermalling technique, but basically it all boils down to this:

Go where the lift is.

In a little more detail, here's what you do. When you fly into a thermal, you will somehow detect the presence of lift, and the fact that you are rising. It will either be a beeping on your vario or you will visually notice the nearby terrain on your horizon dropping in your view. You may also feel an upward tug as you initially accelerate upwards, although once you establish a constant climb rate this upward pull disappears. If you are flying at faster than minimum sink speed, pull on some brakes and slow down to minimum sink.

At this point you wait. If the thermal is not big enough for you to stay in the lift for at least a few seconds, there's no point in turning in it.

If, after a few seconds you are still in lift, start a turn keeping your speed slow, but not too slow. (If you try to maximize your climb rate by all the time flying around on the edge of stall while doing turns in thermals, you will eventually go too far and enter a spin. If you're high enough, and react properly and quickly enough, this may not be a big problem, but you'll definitely lose a bunch of altitude. If you're close to the ground, or you don't react correctly, it could be a much more serious matter.)

Which way you turn (if you're well clear of the terrain) doesn't matter unless you turn the wrong way. The wrong way is away from the center of the thermal. The right way is towards the center of the thermal. You may not have any indication of where the center is, in which case one way is as good a guess as the other, and you'll be wrong half the time. However, most thermals have stronger lift near

8

the center, so if you feel the glider being turned in one direction as you enter the thermal, then you want to turn the other direction; towards the stronger core which is lifting more strongly on one wing.

Now, if you've done it right, and the thermal is big enough and strong enough, you are circling in the thermal and going up. As you fly around you are feeling and hearing on your vario that some areas of the thermal have stronger lift and some areas have weaker lift. Watch your circles and your flight direction in relation to the terrain, and try to map the lift distribution in the thermal. If you find you are always climbing faster when you're flying upwind towards the landing area, and climbing slower when headed back towards launch, the stronger center of the thermal is upwind of you. Flatten out your turn as you come around into the wind, and then tighten your circle on the backside to move your turn out towards the thermal center. In fact the general rule of flattening your bank angle when flying into increasing lift, and steepening (and thus tightening) your turn when flying into decreasing lift will usually help you to center your circle in the strongest lift. This process of mapping the thermal and centering your turn in the strongest lift is not something you do once but something you do continuously because the thermal is always changing. Also, not all thermals are circular, with concentric bands of stronger lift towards the center. (In fact, very few are that simple or that symmetrical). Some thermals have multiple areas of strong lift, and you may find that a triangular, or oval, or rectangular path gives you the most time spent in the strongest rising air.

How small a radius of turn you fly in a thermal depends also on the distribution of lift. You need a steeper bank angle to turn in a smaller radius, and the steeper your bank angle the higher your sink rate. If the thermal strength increases very rapidly towards the center, you may achieve a faster climb rate with a steep banked small radius turn. If the thermal strength is more gradually distributed, you will climb better with a shallower, larger radius turn.

QUIZ:

Even though they have a higher sink rate, paragliders may be able to outclimb sailplanes in a thermal because they fly

_____

and can stay within the strong core.

Controlling the Canopy in Thermals

Thermal gusts and other turbulence may cause the canopy to enter pitch oscillations, with the pilot swinging forward ahead of the canopy and then back behind the canopy as the canopy flies over him. Such oscillations must be controlled by the aggressive and properly timed application of brakes – brakes applied as the canopy is shooting forward – in order to stop the oscillation and re-stabilize the canopy over the pilot's head. Failure to do so can result in the canopy collapsing from too high or too low an angle of attack. Flying with some brakes applied in the presence of strong thermals will tend to reduce the tendency of the canopy to enter pitch oscillations, and will reduce the tendency of the canopy to collapse due to gust induced changes in angle of attack.

Read the entire chapter on advanced maneuvers for further important information on oscillations and active piloting.

Thermalling Etiquette

How you behave in a thermal with other gliders present is called thermalling etiquette. It's really more than good manners though, it can mean life or death. So, a few rules:

1. The first glider in a thermal sets the direction of circling. All gliders entering the thermal afterward circle in the same direction.

2. Lower glider has the right of way. The reason is that he can't see you and you can see him. If he is climbing into you, get out of the way and let him go by.

3. Fly circles of a size appropriate to accommodate the number of gliders at or near your altitude. You can't go around flying rectangles, triangles and ovals in a thermal with other pilots, because that's not what they expect. You also can't fly a tight circle in the middle of the core if there are two other paragliders at your altitude, because there won't be room for them. By the same token, in a large thermal you should not fly your circles in

such a way as they would conflict with others (in fact same-direction circles with different centers can cause more potential near-misses than opposite direction circles!).

4. Weaker thermals may drift horizontally faster than they climb and even though gliders may be circling in the same direction, if they are at different altitudes the circles will not be concentric. In some cases you may need to adjust your turn radius to avoid conflicts, in extreme cases it may work best to circle the opposite direction.

5. Bearing all this in mind, it is imperative to look around and make eye contact. Let other pilots know that you see them. Make your moves deliberate, so that they can see what you intend to do. Telegraph your intentions by crossing your legs to set the weight shift.

6. If you're uncomfortable, get out. Flying in a crowded thermal is an advanced skill. If you're not up to it, go find another thermal.

Following the Thermal Drift

Thermals tend to drift with the wind. Some books on thermalling emphasize the need to follow the thermal drift, and give techniques for how you do that. Our recommendation is that you not worry about it. If you are using the techniques above for mapping the thermal and centering in the lift, and if you follow the basic rule of thermalling (Go Where The Lift Is), you will automatically follow the drift of the thermal. On the other hand if you try to fly the thermal with some preconceived notion about which way it is going to drift, you'll probably fly out of it, because it will probably do something different from what you expected. If you're thermalling along happily in good lift and all of a sudden you're not in good lift anymore, one of three things has happened; you have flown out the side of the thermal, you have fallen out the bottom of the thermal, or the thermal has reached the inversion level and just quit. The last two of these you can't do anything about, but on the chance that it is the first, make a 180 degree heading change from your flight direction when you lost the lift, and fly straight for several seconds trying to re-enter the thermal.

There are two useful things to remember about thermal drift. One is that since thermals do drift, if you are looking for a thermal on the basis of a thermal indicator like a bird, other pilot, or a cloud, you should search upwind of the indicator if below it, and downwind of the indicator if above it.

8

The other is that thermal drift can get you into trouble if you don't pay attention. If the wind is relatively strong, and the lift relatively weak, you may drift farther downwind following the thermal than your gain in altitude will allow you to glide back from. In other words, you may enter the thermal with a safe landing area within your glide angle, and yet even though you gain altitude in the thermal, you may end up so far downwind that you cannot glide back to where you first entered the thermal, or to the landing area. In fact, if you are following the thermal over the back of a ridge, you may not be able to glide back to the ridge top, and you could end up behind and below the ridge in the rotor.

Again because of the slow flying speed of paragliders, this is a very significant concern. Be especially cautious of this when flying in wind, because when you are first learning to thermal, your attention will be focused on technique, and you may lose track of where you are. Finally, it's a good idea to remember that wind speed often increases with increasing altitude.

Advanced Thermalling Techniques and Theory

Maximize your climb rate while thermalling by using maximum weight shift with judicious brake application. Your overall left and right brake applications should average around the minimum sink position with your inside brake applied slightly deeper and your outside brake slightly less. A sudden decrease in your turn rate is usually an indication of approaching stall. Do not apply more inside brake (you may cause a spin), instead let up some on the outside brake.

Small, strong thermals are often characterized as being punchy due to the more abrupt shear between the rising core and the descending air on the periphery. There may be occasions when you encounter such a thermal at low altitude and may be inclined to leave it for smoother air. Remember, if you had a collapse on the way into it then you may well have a collapse during the exit. It may be preferable to stay within the thermal and climb to a higher altitude where the shear will be gentler and you will have more altitude for dealing with a collapse.

When it is time to leave a thermal then maximize your altitude on your last pass by flying wings level through the core. For added resistance to asymmetric collapses, it is best to exit the thermal the same way you want to enter it – as perpendicular to it as possible.

Low Altitude Thermal Theory

Thermals create a low pressure area at their base which surrounding air rushes in to fill. The incoming air will assume an accelerating rate of rotation, due to the principle of conservation of angular momentum. Unlike large low pressure systems like storm systems, which will always rotate counter clockwise in the northern hemisphere due to the Coriolus effect, a thermal may rotate in either direction, as it is too small to have the direction of rotation determined exclusively by the Coriolus force.

The fact that thermals may rotate near their bases begs the question of what is the proper direction to turn to thermal most efficiently? There is one school of thought that says you should turn opposite the thermal rotation so that you will encounter a headwind and extra lift on entry. Others dismiss this since a paraglider has a relatively low amount of inertia and will reach a steady-state velocity within a few seconds. This is true if you stay in the thermal but what if you inadvertently fly out of the thermal? In the case where you are flying against the circulation, your inertial speed will be reduced and anytime you leave the thermal core you will not only find sink but you will also find yourself slow. Having to gain airspeed in sink requires an even greater loss of altitude. If, on the other hand, you were rotating with the circulation, your inertial speed would be greater and any encounter with the slower moving air would cause an apparent headwind. Thus, an inadvertent encounter with sinking air at the edge of the thermal would have less penalty because it would be countered by a short increase in lift due to the airspeed change.

We suggest that you do not get overly concerned with turn direction based on a preconceived rotational flow but instead turn as best you can to center in the lift (e.g. turning towards a rising wing).

The influx of air near the base of a thermal is relatively low velocity (a few mph) and is usually unnoticed in other soaring aircraft. Because paragliders fly so slowly an alert pilot can sense the corresponding change in ground speed at low altitudes. In fact, a strong thermal will often visibly draw a paraglider towards it. This influence usually extends outwards for only several seconds of flying time. If you recognize a thermal draw you should turn directly with it (downwind) so that you will encounter the thermal head on.

Winds will affect thermals more than just the obvious effects of thermal tilt and drift. Thermals will elongate along the direction of the wind and the lift distribution within the core will be stronger at the upwind edge. In these conditions an astute

8

thermalling pilot will recognize that classic centering techniques may give the highest instantaneous climb rates but not give the maximum overall rate. This is because trying to center in the strongest lift can result in the glider spilling out of the thermal during a portion of each circle, decreasing the average climb rate. Instead of centering in the strongest lift, you should elongate the circle towards the upwind side to maximize the time spent in the strongest lift. In these situations a variometer that can also display averaged climb rate is a very valuable training aid.

Ridge Soaring Techniques

Most pilots perceive ridge soaring as being easier than thermal soaring, because the location of the lift is more readily identifiable in relation to the terrain. As we have said, when the prevailing wind meets a ridge at near right angles to the face of the ridge, the air is forced up over the top creating a band of rising air in front of and above the ridge. If the ridge is large enough, and long enough (so the wind can't go around more easily than over) and the wind is strong enough, the upward component of the wind in the lift band will be enough to cancel the glider's sink rate, and keep the glider aloft.

A higher, longer, or steeper ridge is soarable in lighter winds. A more shallow, or lower, or shorter ridge requires stronger wind. A ridge is most soarable when the wind blows straight in at right angles to the ridge line. As the wind direction becomes more cross, the lift decreases markedly.

On days when the lift is just strong enough to allow soaring flight, you will want to maximize the lift by minimizing your rate of descent. This speed is slower than the speed for maximum glide angle and for most paragliders requires braking to around the shoulder level. If the wind is not perfectly straight into the ridge then your initial turn after launching should be towards the wind so that you can minimize your ground speed while you are closer to the terrain.

There are many reasons why ridge soaring can be more difficult and more dangerous than thermal soaring for the beginning soaring pilot. The presence of wind implies the presence of turbulence, especially rotors behind the top of a steep faced ridge with a flat top. In cross winds on a ridge, the likelihood of turbulence along the ridge increases. Another concern on a ridge is the presence of gaps or low spots in the ridge which can result in increased wind with decreased lift. Any flying that takes place in stronger conditions; strong wind or strong turbulence, is more dangerous for the paraglider pilot, and especially so for the less experienced pilot. Stronger conditions, aside from being more dangerous in themselves, are also indicators that the conditions can be more subject to rapid change. While thermalling can take place, and often does take place in strong conditions, it is often possible to select conditions for thermalling late in the day when the lift and turbulence are mild, and the winds are light. Ridge soaring usually requires stronger winds than are required for thermal soaring, and wind is always a safety concern for the paraglider pilot.

Ridge soaring also usually requires flying in close proximity to the terrain, while flying slowly, which is potentially dangerous. Thermalling need not take place near the terrain. When ridge soaring, you are normally flying in more crowded conditions, since everyone is constrained to the same lift band. The ridge soaring pilot needs to be intimately familiar with the rules for flying in traffic, and needs to be able to control his glider without thinking about what he is doing, so that he can concentrate on working cooperatively in the traffic and staying in the lift band.

There are a number of special skills involved in ridge soaring, which are not necessarily required for thermalling. One is the ability to launch from a steep faced ridge or cliff in significant wind. Another is the ability to crab in order to fly a specific ground track very precisely in a crosswind. You must stay in the lift band, which follows the ridge line, so your ground track is perpendicular to the wind direction and your flight heading needs to be angled into the wind. As we saw in our previous discussion of crosswind flying, the actual angle of the flight heading required depends on the speed of the wind. You must also stay in the lift band when turning to reverse your direction along the ridge, which may require you to drift back slightly towards the ridge before you turn, if the radius of your ground track during the turn would otherwise carry you out far enough in front of the ridge to be out of the lift band.

The above is not meant to suggest that thermal soaring is always easier or less dangerous than ridge soaring, but rather only to counter the common assumption that the opposite is true. The fact is that both ridge soaring and thermal soaring can vary from being relatively easy, simple, and safe, to being extremely complicated, challenging and potentially dangerous, depending on the nature of the site and the conditions.

8

Rules of the Ridge

The equivalent to thermal etiquette in ridge soaring is knowing and following the rules of the ridge. These are a variation of standard aircraft right of way rules adapted to the special concerns of flying along a ridge.

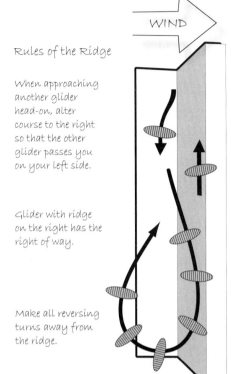

Rules of the Ridge

When approaching another glider head-on, alter course to the right so that the other glider passes you on your left side.

Glider with ridge on the right has the right of way.

Make all reversing turns away from the ridge.

1. When approaching another glider head on, give way to the right. This means that the pilot with the ridge on his left passes to the outside of an oncoming pilot. (*Note the exception to this rule as explained below.) This also means that the pilot with the ridge on his right has the right of way, since he may not be able to alter course to his right.

2. Make all turns away from the ridge.

3. Visually clear all turns prior to starting the turn.

4. Look around, make eye contact, and show your intentions by making your moves deliberate.

5. When overtaking another glider on the ridge, ... don't. (This rule is usually written either "pass to the inside," on the assumption that the other glider, if he turns, will turn away from the ridge and not hit you; or else it is written, "pass to the outside," on the assumption that the other glider, if he plans to turn, will look to the outside, and see you, while he is drifting to the inside in preparation for his turn. The problem is that if you go inside, and he looks outside while drifting in, you're in trouble. If you go outside, and he turns out without looking, you're in trouble again. Technically, the proper method is to pass inside, but we never do it.)

*The exception to rule number 1 involves a conflict between it and rule number two. If you are following behind another glider, each of you with the ridge on your left, and he begins his reversing turn, what do you do? After he has turned, he will be coming back towards you, and rule number one says you should alter course to your right and pass outside him. But if you are close behind him (within say 200'), you will need to pass him just after he makes his turn, when he is farthest out in front of the ridge, which will put you outside the lift band. In addition, when he begins his turn, you are already in a position to be drifting in against the ridge in preparation for your own turn. The proper move in this case is to follow his flight path, and therefore "violate" the rule by passing inside him as he passes through the 180 degree portion of his turn and begins to come back towards you.

If, on the other hand, you are well behind him, he will have completed his turn and come back in against the ridge before you reach him. In this case you should obey the rule and alter course to your right passing outside of him. Then you go in against the ridge in preparation for your turn. The correct procedure in each of these two cases is fairly obvious. The problem arises when you are in the region of critical separation, where you could go either way. In this case, it is important that you and the other pilot communicate with each other.

One of you has to decide how the exchange will go, and tell the other pilot. The best way to communicate is to establish and maintain eye contact, and make crisp, deliberate maneuvers during the critical decision period. If you are the following glider, plan ahead as you near the end of the ridge, and decide ahead of time how you want the exchange to go; whether you will pass inside or outside of the reversing glider.

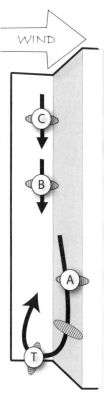

Rules of the Ridge
-- the EXCEPTION

Glider "A" is close behind the turning glider "T", and should follow the turning glider's path and violate the rule.

Glider "B" is in the region of critical separation and must decide whether to pass inside or outside of turning glider "T" and communicate his intentions to "T".

Glider "C" is far enough behind the turning glider "T" that "T" will have time to come back to the ridge by the time "C" is reached. "C" should alter course to the right and pass "T" on the outside, in compliance with the ridge rules.

When he makes his turn and comes around to where he can see you, you should already be pointed slightly in the direction you wish to go. When you first establish eye contact, make a sharp deliberate turn in the direction you want to go, telling him clearly what you intend. If you are the leading pilot, watch your fellow pilot over your shoulder as you approach the turn point and prepare to make your turn. Look for clues about his intentions. Decide before you make your turn how you want the exchange to go. If you intend to complete the turn and pass inside of him (in compliance with the rule) initiate a sharp, rapid turn, and hold it for a full 225 degrees, until you are pointing back inside his flight path by 45 degrees and are flying towards the cliff. If you intend to pass outside, (in violation of the rule) make a slow, shallow turn, stopping at a heading of 45 degrees short of reversing your direction, and allow yourself to drift out away from the cliff.

Whichever pilot you are, the safest choice is to try to pass outside. Even if both pilots choose this, and stick to it, the impasse will end with both pilots flying side by side harmlessly away from the ridge. If both pilots choose the inside route, and stick to it, you will each end up flying downwind towards the ridge and the rotor or attempting a dangerous downwind 180 into a traffic region you have not cleared.

Getting Low

As a by-product of soaring flight, you will undoubtedly find yourself in the position where you are "scratching" for lift. Perhaps you are between thermal cycles or the winds are light and you find yourself searching for lift close to the terrain. Regardless the cause, you must remember that safe flying involves continuously assessing the potential risks versus the potential rewards and low altitude flying requires extra considerations.

In the early days of hang gliding, when gliders were constructed of bamboo and plastic sheeting, there was the adage, "do not fly any higher than you care to fall." In time, construction standards improved and pilots learned what skydivers already knew – reaching high altitudes rarely hurts you but sudden impact with terrain likely will.

The same is true with paragliding. If you have done your homework and are flying in safe weather conditions then about the only real threat at altitude is running into another aircraft. But low altitude flying can expose you to multiple risks. When close to the terrain you are more susceptible to turbulence and may have insufficient altitude to counter a canopy collapse or to deploy your reserve parachute. For added protection when ridge soaring at low altitude you should apply a constant weight shift on the side away from the ridge. This will help keep the glider from turning into the hill in the event of a sudden collapse or turbulence.

Remember, thermals grow in size as they rise and may often be unusable at extremely low altitudes. Smaller thermals also mean the distance between the strongest lift and the bordering sink is smaller and thus the horizontal shearing gradient is stronger, increasing the chances of having part of your wing in lift and part in sink, potentially causing a tip collapse. In the absence of sustaining ridge lift, it is often better to ensure a minimum of a couple hundred feet AGL to be able to adequately work a thermal.

Perhaps the best indicator of whether scratching is OK would be an honest appraisal of "what is the worst that could happen to me right now?" If you are scratching on a smooth coastal sand dune then the greatest risk from a sudden loss of lift might be a laugh or two at your expense from your flying buddies. If you are scratching over a bushy hillside then perhaps your greatest risk will be the hassle of untangling your glider and gear and climbing back to launch. At many sites, however, the terrain is less forgiving and the potential risk much more severe. You must have the good judgment and common sense to make the right decision.

For more thoughts on safety and minimum altitudes, read *Chapter Eleven – Surviving a Career in Aviation.*

The Dreaded Downwind Turn

In the early days of aviation there were a number of low altitude turns downwind which resulted in stalls and crashes. Pilots learned to fear turning downwind because they felt their aircraft reacted differently and were prone to stall and crash. The early days of hang gliding were no different and pilots were injured and killed when they crashed downwind. Chapter Six addressed the issue of not confusing increased groundspeed as increased airspeed and most instructors go to great lengths to explain that neither the glider or the pilot can feel any difference between a downwind and upwind turn. Sometimes, however, you may hear stories to the contrary.

Many soaring books discuss supposed effects the wind gradient can have on a banked glider. They explain that if you do a steep banked turn at low altitude, the upper wing tip will be in faster moving air and the lower tip will be in slower moving air. Some hang gliding and paragliding manuals claim this gradient will cause stronger winds to push against the high wing which will make a turn towards downwind tend to get steeper and a turn upwind tend to shallow out. Some conventional soaring books make the opposite statement – the higher wing sees a higher airspeed and thus the wing will try to raise higher regardless of the direction of turn. We suggest you not worry too much about wind gradient effects when turning but simply have a healthy appreciation for the hazards of turning downwind into rising terrain.

In Chapter Three we discussed the importance of a smooth brake application for turning. Take the scenario of a pilot who decides he is ready for soaring flight and decides to do a 360° turn close to the hill. He is trying to soar and is already flying with both brakes at the minimum sink position. He may be unsure just how much room it will take to do a complete circle and decides it would be best to do a quick, relatively steep turn. In this scenario he starts the turn with an abrupt brake application, the glider banks up quickly and turns downwind. As the glider starts to point towards the hill, the pilot – who initially was swung outwards due to the centrifugal force of the quick turn – now swings back under the canopy. This causes a decrease in the bank angle and a decrease in the rate of turn. Our pilot may now be surprised by how quick the terrain is coming towards him and may be tempted to rapidly increase the brake application to "keep the turn coming". This second abrupt application with the glider already at a slow airspeed could be enough to cause a low altitude stall and spin with probable disastrous results.

Another very real danger of a low altitude downwind turn is the possibility of encountering sinking air. Many accidents occur when pilots start a low altitude 360° turn in light lift only to find a loss of lift or sink on the backside. When you are judging the altitude required to complete a turn you must include the additional altitude required for possible contingencies. It is rare to be flying perpendicular to a ridge in winds that are blowing exactly straight in. In crosswind conditions you should turn in the direction that results in your greatest groundspeed or most direct vector towards the terrain initially, when you have the greatest altitude and are most likely to remain in the same airmass that you started your turn in. This way after 180° of turn you will likely be turning towards a headwind and downward sloping terrain.

You should not attempt low altitude downwind turns until you are very familiar with the turning performance of your glider and understand the concepts involved.

Tip:
Flying low can have greater risks than flying at higher altitudes!

Microlift Soaring

You may be able to work the weak lift of surface layer plumes and small convergence seams by using the microlift techniques used by land soaring birds. Hawks and buzzards can often be seen with their wings outstretched, maintaining altitudes of a couple of hundred feet for long distances. Instead of circling, their flight paths are characterized by sudden changes in heading. These soaring birds can likely sense small changes in lift and wind velocity and are thus able to follow the buoyant air. The key point to soaring microlift is to sense the changes in lift within the wingspan of your glider and make a quick heading change to center in it. Microlift seams may stretch for short distances or meander for miles. If you are over terrain that allows you the freedom of meandering about then you may want to investigate microlift soaring.

Dynamic Soaring

The term dynamic soaring refers to some theoretical techniques for soaring due to wind shears. These shears may be vertical lifting and sinking air or even horizontal shears of different velocities. Although dynamic soaring was predicted well before WW II, it has commonly been thought of as a practical impossibility similar to alchemy, perpetual motion, or cold fusion.

In actuality it is common knowledge that albatrosses can fly for thousands of miles at low altitude over the ocean without flapping. They do this, not by soaring the ridge lift from waves, but by dynamically soaring the low altitude wind gradient. In recent years remote control model sailplanes have demonstrated dynamic soaring in high winds by doing quick transitions to and from the high velocity flow above a sharp ridge line to the sheltered lee side air on the backside. In these conditions the model sailplanes can gain energy at an amazing rate and sustain speeds in excess of 200 mph.

Doing extreme maneuvers in piloted aircraft at low altitudes in rotor conditions is a likely recipe for disaster. There are, however, certain dynamic soaring techniques that a paraglider pilot can use to momentarily gain energy or at least minimize energy loss.

The basic principle in dynamic soaring is to use the glider's momentum to oppose the motion of the shear prior to reaching an equilibrium state. Compared to other aircraft a paraglider does not have much inertia or velocity and thus only a very short time to exploit any shear.

Anyone with a basic knowledge of physics learns that energy is usually absorbed by changes in momentum. It takes more energy to do a lap on a bicycle on a hilly course than on flat terrain even though the average altitude remains the same. If you drop a ball on a trampoline it rebounds in successively smaller amounts until it comes to rest.

Yet gaining energy by opposing sudden impulses to momentum is common in everyday life. When you jump on a trampoline you seemingly gain energy because you instinctively time your jump so that it occurs just as the trampoline is rebounding against your feet. To stop from reaching an unnerving height you subconsciously mistime your jumps so as to absorb some of the rebound. Similarly an advanced skateboarder can gain speed across a series of bumps and dips without having to put a

8

foot on the ground and kick off. He has simply learned the proper timing to bend and extend his knees to gain energy from the changes in slope. Even more dramatically, the skateboarder can seemingly gain energy in a circular swimming pool, increasing his speed and height by well-timed thrusts and dips with his legs.

You can gain energy from a vertical shear (entering a band of lift) by applying a short brake application. In theory, aircraft can even gain energy from a downward shear by performing a negative g maneuver – an impossibility on a paraglider. In fact, active flying techniques likely preclude taking advantage of any sinking air in a paraglider.

While we tend to think of our best soaring as being due to lift, the best dynamic soaring possibilities are due to horizontal shears. You can gain a bit of energy from a sudden gust of headwind by once again pulling on the brakes momentarily. The problem with pitch maneuvers is the glider's attitude changes rapidly and in short order is no longer oriented to properly oppose the gust. But what about a quick horizontal maneuver? If you encounter the same headwind shear you could rapidly bank up in a steep angle of bank (maximizing the surface of the wing exposed to the flow) and once again do a quick application of brakes. In theory, the glider will gain energy (as well as turn downwind). The interesting point is with the increased groundspeed when you fly back across the shear into the slower moving air you will once again feel a "headwind" gust. With proper timing in a theoretically "ideal" glider you could continuously bounce back and forth between the boundary of a horizontal shear, gaining energy with each reversal. This example is not to encourage you to do radical maneuvers but to help you understand the theoretical application. Dynamic soaring in the wind gradient over flat terrain is also likely best left for the birds.

One dynamic soaring method you may find usable is to exploit the wind gradient in sloping terrain. When you fly away from the hill you fly into faster moving horizontal air. In some situations the gradient may be sufficient that you could do a hard turn to extract energy from it and then ease off your brakes as you turn back towards the hill (you don't need to turn directly downwind, just aim generally towards it). As you approach the hillside you will once again encounter decreasing wind speed. As an added bonus this slower flow has a more vertical component to it because of the slope effect. A hard reversal in this slower moving air can gain additional energy. In fact, one of the authors of this book has repeatedly demonstrated the use of this technique so as to gain a quick fifty feet of altitude and make a top landing possible in conditions that would have precluded top landing with the use of standard ridge soaring techniques.

It is unlikely that paragliders will ever by able to soar using only dynamic soaring techniques over flat terrain, however, by combining dynamic soaring and microlift techniques we have the capability to substantially extend a low altitude glide, thereby increasing our chances of finding the elusive thermal.

Advanced Launching Techniques - The Cliff Launch

During your beginning and intermediate flying, you will have had the opportunity to launch from a variety of slopes, some shallower, and some steeper. The skills for slope launches are pretty much the same, regardless of the degree of the slope. You will have learned that the steeper the slope, the more easily you are lifted off the ground, and therefore the more quickly things can happen during the launch. Shallower slopes require a more aggressive driving run, but give you more opportunity to check the canopy and correct any problems.

Gentle slope leading to a rounded cliff edge makes for a relatively easy launch

The cliff launch combines the most challenging aspects of the flat slope launch and the steep slope launch. A true cliff launch is relatively flat on top, with restricted room to run, and then drops off precipitously. To launch safely from a cliff, your skills at pulling up the canopy squarely and controlling it as it comes up overhead must be extremely well developed. You must be able to inflate the canopy, stop it over your head, check it, and then drive forward keeping the canopy flying square and precisely oriented in relation to you without the help of gravity pulling you down the slope. In wind, you must deal with the additional complications of turbulent air behind the edge of the cliff where you will be inflating the canopy, and with the need to use assistants to help stabilize you on launch and keep you from being pulled off before you are sure you are ready to go.

A level top leading to a sharp cliff edge makes for a sudden transition to vertical flow

The cliff launch is not something to teach yourself. You should have competent instruction and direct supervision when you first attempt it. You can practice the technique for pulling up and driving on flat ground, and you can practice the launch itself on a flat topped hill with a fairly steep slope. You should not attempt to launch from a true cliff until you have full confidence in your mastery of all of the skills required.

An overhanging cliff can have rotors that can cause dangerous and erratic canopy response!

Advanced Landing Techniques – Top Landing

One of the more rewarding aspects of soaring flight is at some sites you can have the ability to land where you took off from. Top landings can be done safely as long as the landing area is suitably sized and you can avoid leeside or rotor turbulence. Your landing approach will likely depend on the type of soaring. If you are ridge soaring then you may choose to fly a downwind, base, and final leg or you may simply crab back far enough to leave the lift band and land. Your decision should be based on your altitude and knowledge of the site (potential rotor locations and protocol). At sites where the rotor is closer to the cliff you may want to turn directly downwind to quickly fly past it. At smoother sites you may simply angle over the flat part of the hill sufficiently enough to leave the lift band and land. If the winds are strong then you may find yourself descending nearly vertically once you leave the lift and are in the horizontal wind flow. In this situation you may find yourself almost hovering as you work your way down. Use caution for the tendency to over-control laterally (due to pendular action) when attempting to spot land in such conditions.

Flying with Hang Gliders - General Flying Etiquette and Site Protocol

Paragliding in the U.S. is still relatively new, while hang gliding has been around for more than thirty years. As a result, you will often find yourself flying with and among hang gliders, at sites which were first flown by hang glider pilots, and which often will be maintained, regulated, insured and administered by the local hang gliding club. As a paraglider pilot, it is important for you to have some perspective on the sport of hang gliding, on the history of the efforts which have been required to open and secure flying sites, on the attitudes hang glider pilots are likely to have, and on the different performance characteristics of hang gliders and how that will affect flying with them in the same airspace.

On the Ground

Understand first that it is completely natural for people to initially mistrust that which they don't understand. While a fair number of hang glider pilots have taken up paragliding in the last five years, many hang glider pilots still know very little about, and therefore do not very well understand paragliders. Hang gliders, which started out as largely flexible wings, have over the years evolved into much stiffer and more rigid structures. Very early in the history of hang gliding, one of the earliest equipment related safety problems had to do with hang glider sails deflating in steep dives. As a result, hang glider pilots tend to look on the concept of completely flexible wings which are expected to deflate and collapse in flight as being confusing at best and highly suspect at worst. Try not to be overly sensitive if you run into some initial disapproval from hang glider pilots. Maintain your good humor, and explain patiently how the wing is designed to recover from collapses under the safe control of the pilot. Show them a complete set up and launch in the time it takes them to get their battens sorted out, and show them a few effortless, feather soft landings right on target and they'll begin to come around. (Of course what you don't want to do is show up at an advanced site with weak, beginner level skills, get dragged around on launch trying to control your canopy in gusty winds, and stumble off the hill out of control with a riser twist. That won't make a favorable impression at all. Stay on the training hill until you have solid canopy handling and launch skills.)

In the Air

All the normal rules of thermal and ridge etiquette are important, but there are other considerations in addition when you are flying with hang gliders. Your fastest speed in a paraglider is not much faster than a hang glider's slowest speed. This gives you the ability to do things in thermals that hang glider pilots simply can't do, like stop in the middle of a small thermal core pointing into the wind and do hovering figure-eights back and forth while going up. This is no problem if you're by yourself in the thermal, but it causes big problems if there is a hang glider pilot trying to work that same thermal with you. The other thing to realize is that you consume about three times the vertical space that a hang glider does. Put a couple of 20-foot tall paragliders waffling in random directions in a thermal with a hang glider pilot and he's going to feel like a sports car with a stuck throttle and no brakes on the Hollywood Freeway at 5 PM.

There are several things you can do to make it easier for hang glider pilots to fly safely with you in the same thermal. First, fly circles. It's the convention, and it's what people expect. Second, fly a little faster. In most thermals you will still be able to climb just fine flying at best L/D speed instead of minimum sink. Third, avoid sudden use of the brakes to slow down in stronger lift. That hang glider behind you doesn't have brakes, and if you stop suddenly right in front of it, the pilot may have no option but to hit you.

Torrey Pines Gliderport in La Jolla, California is famous for its 350 ft. cliffs that face the prevailing winds. Here paragliders share the air with hang gliders, remote control sailplanes, and occasionally full-size sailplanes. Knowledge of and adherence to the rules of the ridge is extremely important.

Site Protocol

Thirty years ago, most hang glider pilots were "outlaws," flying wherever they could find a convenient hill facing into the prevailing breeze and without regard for land ownership, or other legal complexities. Over the years, as sites have continuously been lost to development, to liability concerns and to the aggressive enforcement of landowner's rights, hang glider pilots have been forced to organize, to deal in a business-like manner with landowners and government agencies, to obtain and provide insurance coverage, and to regulate themselves. Most sites are flown today only under a use permit or ongoing agreement with a government agency or landowner, and the continued availability of many such sites is tenuous at best. These sites are only available for flying as a result of long, hard, and continuing work by local hang gliding clubs. When you fly a hang gliding site, learn and respect the local site regulations. Join the club, and support the efforts to maintain the site and keep it open.

Realize also that some sites suffer from overcrowding, and that the addition of a large group of new pilots to a site will make any such problem worse and naturally cause some resentment among the pilots who think of the site as "theirs."

If paraglider pilots and hang glider pilots think of themselves as members of one flying community, and treat each other with mutual respect, both sports will be strengthened and benefit. There will be a larger pool of energy, talent and resources to secure and maintain flying sites, and share information. The hang gliding community possesses a vast reservoir of practical knowledge and experience regarding micro weather as it effects site use and safe flying practices, and paraglider pilots should avail themselves of that knowledge. Paraglider pilots can bring to the sport of foot launched flying a renewed sense of excitement and enthusiasm for personal flight in its simplest, most elegant and most accessible form.

Pioneering New Sites

There are many benefits to flying established flying sites – the corporate knowledge already exists and aside from having permission to fly, the best launch spots, soaring techniques, landing approaches, and hazards have already been identified. But just as scaling an unclimbed peak has special rewards so does pioneering a new flying site. Who knows, maybe that one spot you have been considering will turn up to be the best soaring site around! Perhaps the best advice for pioneering a new site is to use common sense and good judgment. To ensure you have both of these, you should at least have intermediate-level skills and experience.

You should make initial flights in mild conditions and keep good records regarding the wind speed, direction, and other applicable factors such as lapse rate, maximum altitude reached, etc.

Probably the worst thing you could do after you discover a promising flying location is to fly it without first getting permission. Doing so risks alienating the appropriate authorities into never allowing paragliding operations in the future. Find out who the landowners are and respectfully approach them with your request. Having a copy of the USHPA waiver and liability insurance coverage is an asset. For further information on securing site permission and site preservation you should contact the USHPA.

NOTES

CROSS-COUNTRY (XC) FLYING

HEADING FOR THE HORIZON

Thousands of feet above the flatlands, a pilot heads downwind for his next ticket to cloudbase

Chapter 9
— CROSS COUNTRY (XC) FLYING
HEADING FOR THE HORIZON

After you've refined your soaring skills to where you can consistently stay in the air whenever soarable conditions exist, you may get the urge to "go cross country." Cross country flying is basically anytime you fly to a landing area that is outside of the gliding range of your launch point. In a practical sense, cross country flying means taking off, gaining altitude, turning downwind, and flying from one lift source (thermal) to the next to extend the distance you can fly. Paragliders have already made cross country flights of more than 200 miles, and even 300 miles seems possible.

Paragliders don't have enough glide ratio performance to consistently glide from one thermal to the next without landing when thermals are distributed in their normal density. Therefore, cross country flying in paragliders depends on flying when and where thermal density is enhanced above normal. One way to do this is to fly along a range of mountains, which will tend to be a collector of thermals. Another is to fly on days when the air is particularly unstable, when thermals will be abundant, strong, and carry to high altitudes.

Obviously, both of these methods have serious safety implications for paragliders. Mountain ranges typically include fingers and canyons extending out from the main ridge. These tend to produce turbulence, sink and accelerated winds, which can trap a paraglider and force a dangerous landing or lead to a canopy collapse and crash. Unstable days tend to be associated with strong weather, often with storm systems, and thus with higher winds and turbulence.

The safest way to fly cross country in a paraglider is probably to utilize a site where the terrain downwind of launch is mostly flat, and to fly in weather that is unstable enough to produce a higher than normal thermal density, but not so unstable so as to produce high winds or strong turbulence.

Another safety concern for flying cross country is where you are going to land. It is imperative that you always keep a safe landing area within easy glide, and that your landing areas are near enough to a road that you don't get stranded out in the middle of nowhere. If you are injured on landing, your life could depend on it. Landing in an area that you have only seen from the air can be extremely hazardous. As we talked about in the chapter on landing approaches, obstacles like power lines can be truly invisible from the air.

You can look for power poles as an indicator, but even they can be hard to see, or hidden by trees. Other obstacles like fences may also be hard to see, especially if there is tall grass in the field. Things that look like small bushes from high in the air may turn out to be fairly good sized shrubs or small trees. Finally, you may have a lot of difficulty in determining from the air what the wind direction is. If there are no wind indicators like flags or blowing smoke, you can do constant radius 360's over the middle of the landing area and note your drift direction.

The best procedure is to plan your cross country flight ahead of time and look at potential landing areas along your route from the ground. It is also a good idea to make your first flights along routes that have been flown before, and to fly with a more experienced pilot who has made the flight before.

With few exceptions, great cross country flying is the product of great preflight preparation. You should have food and water to handle not only the expected flight duration but also the amount of time possibly spent "away from civilization." A radio for in-flight communication with your chase vehicle as well as other pilots is almost

Great XC flights require proper preflight planning and preparation

always mandatory as is a map for both you and your driver that shows terrain data, major highways, and potential retrieval routes. Even with radio communication a cellular telephone will often allow chase and emergency coordination in places where radio reception is impossible or cumbersome. You should also pack a first-aid and emergency supply kit to contain supplies commensurate with your planned route. At a minimum you should include basic first-aid supplies and signaling devices such as a whistle and rescue mirror. Lastly, a sign or T-shirt emblazoned with "PILOT NEEDS RIDE" may come in handy.

Prior to setting out to fly XC, you should first study the weather for the planned route of flight (see the section titled "Forecasting Soaring" in Chapter Five). You should have a good knowledge of the lapse rate and forecast winds for the possible flight altitudes along the planned flight path.

Tip:
Record-setting XC flights are set in moderate winds at sites where the lift extends directly downwind.

You can increase your chances of consistently finding a thermal by practicing "buddy flying." Fly with another pilot (hopefully a mentor) but instead of following each other, strike out abeam each other in search for the next thermal. By flying alongside each other, you double the chances of one of you flying into a thermal. When a thermal is found the other glider heads over and joins up. After topping out in the thermal then once again head on course with a lateral offset. The distance between the two gliders should be commensurate with the AGL altitude, at low altitudes it may just be a couple of hundred feet, at higher altitudes it could be hundreds of yards.

The two greatest opponents of XC flying are headwinds and sinking air. To the maximum extent possible, you should limit your exposure to either. At all costs you should avoid flying upwind in sinking air as you can lose thousands of feet in the space of a few short minutes. You should only consider upwind XC flying if you can do so in lift.

Just as lift tends to form in streets parallel to the wind, so does sink. If you find yourself in extended sink there is little to be gained by continuing downwind (or worse, upwind). Consider a ninety degree course change in an attempt to fly perpendicular to the streets to hopefully encounter a lift street.

You may not have the luxury in many locales to fly XC by simply heading downwind beneath a cloud street over flat terrain. To be successful you often need to follow ridge lines and make educated decisions on when and how to make the jumps to fly

Smart "buddy flying" increases your chances of finding the next thermal

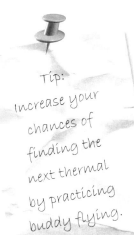

Tip:
Increase your chances of finding the next thermal by practicing buddy flying.

the best route. To make the most out of the slow flying speed of a paraglider you should know the wind forecasts at the various altitudes as well as have a general knowledge and understanding of the local flows around your route. In many cases the winds in the lower foothills may be at a significantly different strength and direction than the winds over the spine of the main mountain ridge. In light wind conditions it is often best to stay high over the main ridge and use the stronger thermals, higher wind velocities and higher true airspeeds to make the most distance. If the winds are stronger it may be best to stay lower and further forward over the foothills to avoid getting trapped by the venturi effect in a back bowl or canyon. You may also discover you can make upwind progress by staying in the lighter winds down low.

If the predominant flow is adverse, you may make the best progress by searching for thermals on the lee side of the fingers of land that feed into the main spine. Searching for thermals in the lee should always be done with caution. Always leave yourself enough altitude to get back to the front side in case you encounter sink. Use caution due to the shear turbulence associated with punchy lee side thermals and the mixing air at the transition to the windward flow.

9

Speed-to-Fly Theory

There are sailplane books dedicated entirely to the application of speed to fly theory. We will not cover the theory in great detail because, in this day and age, if you are that serious about cross country flying then you should purchase a modern instrumentation package (variometer, altimeter, airspeed indicator, and GPS) integrated with a flight computer that continuously computes and displays the optimum speed for the current conditions.

To know what speed to fly in varying conditions you must first know the performance of your glider throughout its speed range (its glide polar). Once you know the glide polar and know the vertical (lift/sink) and horizontal (wind speed and direction) movement of the airmass, you can then compute the best speed to fly to optimize your glide in the desired direction across the ground.

You may be able to get your glide polar from your manufacturer or from internet sources. You should always take published performance figures with a grain of salt because glide polars are difficult to attain with the accuracy and precision required to be able to directly compare different gliders.

Even if you do not have an exact polar, you can achieve suitable results by using a generic set of data for a typical beginner to intermediate paraglider. The minimum sink rate is 225 fpm at an indicated airspeed of 18 mph. The maximum glide ratio of 8/1 occurs at 21 mph with a sink rate of 240 fpm. With full speed bar application the glider will reach a maximum speed of 30 mph with a sink rate of 600 fpm.

We learned in *Chapter Eight – Principles and Skills of Soaring Flight*, that you maximize your time aloft by minimizing your rate of descent (flying at minimum sink speed). If you are more concerned with covering the greatest distance through the air then you should fly at the speed that gives you your maximum lift to drag ratio (usually hands-off trim speed). This occurs at the point on the polar curve that is tangent to the origin of the two axis.

Maximum L/D speed is your most efficient glide speed if you are trying to maximize your performance within a given parcel of air but it is not necessarily the proper speed if you are trying to maximize your performance with respect to the ground (which is really the goal of XC flying). The obvious example is when flying in winds that exceed the glider's trim flying speed. If you want to make progress against these

- Vertical axis: Sink rate (fpm)
- Horizontal axis: airspeed (mph)
- Min-sink speed
- Best glide speed

Paraglider polar diagram showing best glide and minimum sink speeds

winds then you need to fly at a faster speed than your still-air maximum L/D speed. In fact, if you are trying to maximize your glide across the ground then you should speed up by some amount when flying in any headwind.

Knowing just how much to speed up is the problem. It would be a cumbersome process to do in flight (that is what speed to fly computers are for) but a glide polar can be adjusted to correct for the movement of the air mass. The easiest way to visualize the correction process would be to move the polar along the axis to reflect the moving airmass (if there is a ten mph headwind then you would move the polar to the left that amount). In practice, instead of redrawing the polar it is easier to compensate for airmass movement by changing the origin of the "zero point" for the tangent line. So instead of drawing the tangent line originating at the center of the graph (zero horizontal speed), start at the velocity required to oppose the air movement. A headwind is a negative influence so you would move the origin to the right. For example, to compute the most efficient speed to fly in a ten mph headwind, start the tangent line from the positive ten mph point. The proper speed to fly in this example is 23 mph.

The converse is also true, you should slow down in tailwinds because the slight decrease in glide angle through the air is more than offset by the slower descent rate and greater time aloft.

9

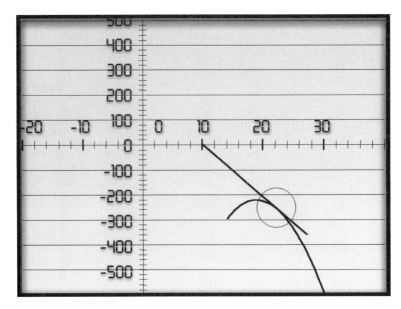

Speed to fly in a ten-mile per hour headwind

The effects of lifting and sinking air are similar. You should slow down toward minimum sink speed to maximize the time spent in lifting air and speed up to minimize the time spent in sinking air. For maximum efficiency, do not slow down to

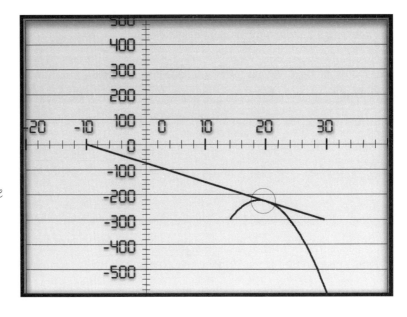

Speed to fly in a ten-mile per hour tailwind

your minimum sink speed until the amount of lift is equal to your minimum sink rate (i.e. your vario indicates zero rate of climb).

Correct for sinking air by drawing the tangent origin from the upper axis corresponding to the sink rate of the air. Be sure to subtract the sink rate of the glider from the total sink rate. So if your variometer indicates 750 fpm rate of descent and you are flying at 22 mph then the air is sinking at 500 fpm, if you are flying at 30 mph then the air is only sinking at 150 fpm.

In mixed conditions start at the vertical and horizontal velocities required to oppose the air movement. For example, to compute the most efficient speed to fly in a ten mph headwind with 300 fpm of sink, start the tangent line at the point formed by the intersection of a line extending upward from the positive ten mph point and the line extending horizontally from the positive 300 fpm point.

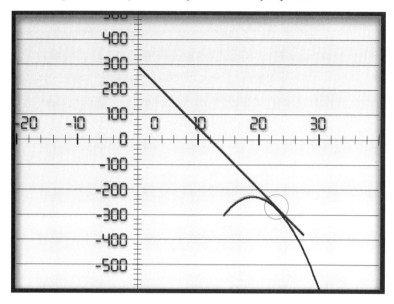

Speed to fly in 300-fpm sink

You can also optimize your speed to fly between thermals by making adjustments based on the expected strength of the next thermal. An adjustment is made similar to that made if flying in sink, that is if you expect to average 400 fpm of climb in the next thermal then you would fly at the same speed between thermals as if you were in air that was sinking at 400 fpm.

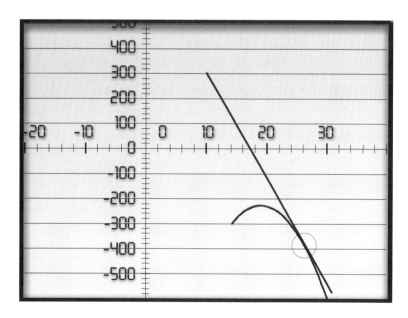

Speed to fly in a ten-mph headwind with 300-fpm sink

Speed To Fly Rules-of-Thumb

If you do not have a speed to fly computer then you may make an educated guess in flight by using the following rules-of-thumb devised for our generic paraglider.

The rule-of-thumb for speed adjustment is to change your indicated airspeed by one-third of the wind value. If a tailwind exceeds ten mph then you should fly at min sink speed. A similar rule-of-thumb for sinking air is to increase your speed by 1 mph for every 150 fpm increase in the variometer's displayed sink rate. To make things even simpler, if your variometer indicates in excess of 1000 fpm down, then you should be using at least one-half speedbar (turbulence and altitude permitting). In cases of both wind and vertically moving air, you can sum the individual adjustments together to arrive at the final speed to fly.

It pays to have a general understanding of speed-to-fly theory but we recommend you do not get overly obsessed with trying to compute exact speeds because there are too many unknowns and too many causes of errors. For instance, just how strong will your next thermal really be and what if you cannot even find another thermal?

Dolphin Flying

On great soaring days it is possible to find streets of lift where dolphin flight is possible. Dolphin flight consists of soaring without bothering to turn in the lift, merely slowing down in the lift and speeding up in the sink. This soaring technique got its name from the vertical wavelike motion of the glider as it runs through cycles of lift and sink. Dolphin flight will only be possible over mountain ridges, cloud streets, or convergence zones at altitudes where the net upward vertical movement of the air exceeds your average sink rate. In light dolphin flight conditions you will need to slow to minimum sink speed to maximize your time in the lift and achieve the most altitude gain. Although your airspeed during dolphin flight may be slower than classic speed to fly theory, your average ground speed can be significantly higher because you are not pausing to circle in the lift. In booming conditions you may find you can run at a high speed without even bothering to slow down in the lift. Obviously, such dolphin flying is a magical occurrence and normally only possible in areas of abundant lift and during the strongest part of the soaring day. If you are lucky enough to enjoy dolphin flight in a paraglider then do not forget to keep a watchful eye out for signs of over development.

QUIZ:

To minimize altitude loss in sinking air you should

☐ increase
☐ decrease

your airspeed.

Ballast and Glider Sizing Effects

It used to be that paragliders were designed at a medium size and larger or smaller models were constructed by adding cells to, or removing them from, the center section of the glider. Thus, smaller gliders would have a lower aspect ratio and larger models

Flatland XC flying from Chelan Butte — Bo Criss photo

a higher aspect ratio than standard. Neglecting other effects, a higher aspect ratio glider will also have higher performance. Pilots realized they could get maximum performance by ballasting up and then flying a larger glider.

Nowadays, paragliders are laid out by computer and larger and smaller sizes are simply scaled up and down appropriately so the aspect ratio usually remains constant. Although the line lengths are also scaled, two relationships change slightly that can affect performance. First, since the pilot size remains constant (assuming the ballast is carried internally in the harness), the percentage of parasitic drag due to the pilot decreases with a larger glider. Secondly, although the total line length is greater on a larger glider, the ratio of total line length to wing area is less. Both of these factors, in theory, would indicate that a ballasted pilot on a larger wing will have better performance than flying unballasted on a smaller wing at an identical wing loading. This effect is likely minor enough that you should make your wing decision based more on handling and safety issues.

A glider's lift to drag ratio is unaffected by its weight but its flying speed, and hence, minimum sink rate are affected. The speeds increase by the square root of the ratio of the weight increase (i.e. if you double the weight then the stall, minimum sink, maximum L/D speeds, etc. will increase by a factor of 1.4). To put it more into perspective let's take the case of a 180 lb. pilot flying at a 225 lb. total weight on a glider that gets a minimum sink rate of 215 fpm at 18 mph and a maximum L/D of 8/1 at 23 mph. If he ballasts up with an extra 30 lbs. his sink rate will now be 228 fpm at 19 mph and his L/D will still be 8/1 but will occur at 24.5 mph. At first glance this may appear to be an insignificant speed increase for a 6% sink rate penalty but if you assume a six hour flight with only 1/3 of the time spent flying straight downwind the heavier glider will cover several extra miles, or more importantly, save ten to fifteen minutes.

Ballast can help your performance if the conditions are strong. You should fly with ballast that can be safely and easily dumped as the conditions weaken. Some pilots fly with sandbags although water is relatively heavy per unit of volume and has the extra benefit of being of potential use to you during and after the flight. The MSR Dromedary™ line of water bladders includes a large ten-liter version that can be fitted with a large diameter hose and shower valve enabling you to rapidly dump the over twenty pounds of fluid if needed.

Maximizing Your Distance

Flying the maximum possible distance on a given day is a one-on-one race against time. You need to start as early as you can sustain in the lift and strive to stay airborne until the last thermal of the day. It helps to set a realistic goal for the given conditions. Compute the trigger temperature not only for the start of the day but also for the end of the day and you will have an idea of the total available flight time. Now predict the prevailing winds for the estimated altitudes throughout the flight window. With an idea of the available time and winds, you should now plan the optimum route so as to take advantage of thermal sources and retrieval routes. By dividing your planned distance by the predicted time aloft, you will get the average ground speed required to make your goal.

One of the most difficult judgment decisions is to know when to transition from conventional speed-to-fly theory. In great conditions failure to transition to dolphin flight can cost you dozens of miles and in weak conditions failure to slow down and maximize your hunt time for the next thermal may cause an early landing. The pilot that depends only on his flight computer's speed-to-fly cueing typically makes consistent thirty mile flights while the pilot that knows how to interpret the current and forecasted conditions and applies speed-to-fly theory smartly is the pilot that makes impressive flights (and occasional short ones).

As the day wanes the thermals will start to lose strength, the heights reached will slowly decrease, and the time between successive thermals will increase. When this occurs you should try to bank as much altitude as possible in each thermal because it might be your last. A review of the altitude traces of numerous long distant flights reveals a common trait in that the last thermal of the flight is often one of the largest thermals of the flight – as if the earth gave out one last gasp of buoyant air. Once this happens it is likely time to go on final glide flying at the optimum speed.

Cross Country Adages

Here are a few tried and true XC adages as well as some lesser known recommendations.

1. Stay high. This is especially true when thermals are not strong or abundant (early or late in the day). When flying in a tailwind, staying high will usually maximize your ground speed due to the increase in the wind component and your true airspeed.

2. Do not leave lift early unless you are confident you will be able to find lift again when you need it. Many pilots have given up on weak lift at low altitude, only to find themselves on the ground wishing they had stayed with it. Be conservative early and late in the soaring day.

3. When high, fly the sky. When low fly the ground. If you are in the upper half of the height of the thermals then you should look skyward (and downwind) for signs of thermals (cumulus clouds or other soaring gliders). If you are in the lower half of the thermal band then look at the ground for probable thermal trigger spots.

4. Avoid wetlands. If you have no choice but to transit near large bodies of water, consider looking for potential trigger spots on the upwind side in humid areas and the downwind side in arid areas. (In arid areas the air flowing over the water will gain moisture and will have greater relative buoyancy when subsequently heated.)

9

5. Read the clouds. Building cumulus clouds have more defined edges and look like brains or cauliflowers. Dissipating cumulus clouds have more diffuse edges. Large decaying towering cumulus clouds can cause a "dead zone" shutting down thermals downwind for tens of miles.

6. Know when to leave the lift. If the thermals are good, plentiful, and predictable then leave the thermal when the climb rate decreases to less than the expected climb rate at the altitude of your next thermal encounter.

7. Do not outrun the lift. Many pilots have decked it by flying downwind past the end of a cloud street or convergence. Avoid areas devoid of clouds ("blue holes"). Be patient in convergence lift and run parallel to the front if possible.

8. Use microlift techniques to extend your flight. By following weak seams of lift at low altitude you may be able to stay airborne long enough to find another thermal or drift downwind to a better retrieval area.

Mark Stucky, Dean Stratton, and Bo Criss celebrate a successful retrieve with their chase driver, "Fast Eddie" Skow, after buddy flying for over one-hundred miles.

Top: XC flying requires careful weather observation. Half way through a 50 km flight, coauthor Mark Stucky uses speedbar to detour past an approaching gust front (note the dust cloud on the dry lakebed)

Bottom: Some clouds do have a silver lining. By having his chase driver position up ahead with a radio, he was able to ensure the conditions ahead were not deteriorating.

9

NOTES

_____

_____

_____

_____

_____

_____

_____

_____

_____

_____

_____

_____

_____

_____

_____

_____

Chapter Ten:
COMPETITION FLYING

PITTING YOUR WITS & SKILLS AGAINST OTHERS

A gaggle of paragliders jockey for position and altitude while awaiting the start window — Swing photo

Chapter 10 — COMPETITION FLYING

Pitting Your Wits and Skills Against Others

Flying in paragliding competitions can be a positive way to quickly advance your cross country skills and decision making processes. There are also some negative aspects of competition. Meet directors may feel pressured by sponsors, organizers, and some pilots to conduct tasks in potentially unsafe conditions. The additional pressure of competing also encourages some pilots to take risks they would never take in recreational flying. There can also be a pack mentality where the dangers may appear manageable simply because "everyone else seems to be doing it." Lastly, some competitors may resort to all kinds of antics to include unethical conduct and violation of FARs.

Just because you want to compete does not require that you purchase the latest and greatest DHV-3 Comp wing. There are numerous competitions that have separate classes for Serial-class gliders or recreational pilots.

Competition Formats
One-on-One

One-on-one competitions are occasionally seen at smaller competitions. The basic idea is to pit a pair of pilots against each other in a race along a closed course. Each pair must launch within a short window of time, the clock starting as soon as the window opens. To keep things interesting, the course includes a series of pylons with increasing difficulty. Each competitor must decide how many pylons they think they can make while still being able to reach the LZ. The winning pilot is the one that completes the entire course in the least amount of time or the most pylons. If both pilots round the same number of pylons then whoever does it the fastest is the winner.

Competitors await the opening of the launch window — Bo Criss photo

Total-Elapsed-Time (TET) Competitions

Most major competitions have evolved into some version of a TET format where the goal is to fly a predetermined course (it may be a direct route, dogleg, triangle, etc.) in the minimum amount of time. Some competitions may have a launch window that opens up for several hours and competitors may launch anytime. Pilots that fail to make goal are penalized. Pilots must decide what is the optimum time to head out on course, considering such factors as thermal strength and abundance, current and forecast winds, and chances of over development.

In recent years major competitions have begun using "start cylinders" with multiple start times (usually fifteen minute intervals). Pilots can choose to leave the cylinder and head out on course anytime, their elapsed time beginning from the most recent start time. If they choose to they may even return to the start cylinder to reset their start clock to the most recent start time.

Winning Strategies

Winning is a combination of flying (precision flying skills, canopy management, maximizing climb rate, adherence to best speed to fly), decision making (strategy, launch timing, route selection, thinking on the fly), risk management, and luck. A pilot who often takes big risks in competition is usually an inconsistent performer. The winner is often very good at managing the risks but is not the biggest risk taker. If you are losing, however, taking risk (soaring risks, not safety risks) may be the only possible "come from behind" strategy.

Scoring

To pick the best strategy you first need to be intimately familiar with the meet rules and scoring format. Examples of things you should know prior to the start include (but are not limited to):

- How are turn points verified (ground observers, photos, or GPS)?

- How are start and finish times measured and recorded?

- Are there any bonuses (e.g. early start time or spot landing)?

- What kinds of penalties are assessed for rules infractions or verification failures?

• What completion rate determines a valid task?

• How will those that fail to make the goal be scored?

An increasing number of major competitions are using automated scoring systems (such as GAP and OzGAP) that are very complex and sometimes give results that appear to be counter-intuitive. Knowledge of the scoring intricacies is important to maximize your performance.

One-on-One Strategy

If you are flying a glider with superior glide and speed performance then you can have the luxury of shadowing the other glider around the course. Try to get an altitude advantage and then maintain a "control position" by staying close behind. Ensure you stay close enough so that you can use your altitude and speed advantage to make a fast break for the last pylon and winning time.

If you are flying with a performance disadvantage then you must try to shake your opponent. If you are thermalling on a short course you may be able to make a run for the next pylon by using the element of surprise. Let him enjoy his altitude advantage but as you approach the altitude you think you can leave for the next pylon, start playing your turn rate so that you are following him. If that is not possible, then at least try to get opposite him in the thermal. Then make a break for the pylon as soon as he commits for another 360°. Some pilots will fail to recognize it until they have allowed a 10-15 second gap to occur. On a short course that could be enough of a head start to negate their performance advantage.

If you cannot pull off a fast break then another possibility (and one that requires luck and good fortune to be successful) would be to leave for the next pylon in conditions where your opponent thinks it is highly unlikely that either of you will be able to make it. In that situation it is prudent for him to let you go on your merry way while he hangs back for more altitude or better conditions. If you are completely outclassed then this may be your only option. You never know, you just might get lucky!

Conversely, if you are leading the competition (or day) then do not get so far ahead of your opponents that they realize they have absolutely no chance of winning without taking a big risk. They, too, just might get lucky.

TET Strategy

TET competitions encourage gaggle flying because of the synergistic effects. A gaggle can average a faster speed over the course because the multiple pilots tend to spot the best cores when in lift and possible escape routes when in sink. Unfortunately, the real race only begins once the gaggle reaches the point that one pilot thinks he can go on final glide to goal. Then the same small performance differences that were masked by the gaggle flying now become paramount once the sprint to the goal begins.

If the scoring system gives bonus points for an "early bird" start time then it may be tempting to get on course before the main gaggles but often these bonus points are more than offset by the loss of time inherent with trying to lead a race in weak conditions. If the conditions are strong and the soaring window is long then you should consider if you would benefit by leaving later and trying to make up time by using the gaggles as thermal markers.

Most TET formats use start cylinders. If you are going to commit to a start time then you should be close to the edge of the cylinder (in the direction of your first waypoint) as the start time approaches. A sloppy start can easily cost several minutes. If you have a bad start it may be beneficial to return to the start cylinder and pick up a later start window. You should also realize that you may choose to appear to have set out on course in an effort to get others to start racing. Once they pass you then you can sneak back to the start cylinder, get a later start time and try to chase down the gaggle.

Gaggle over launch at the annual Rat Race, Woodrat Mt. Oregon — Bo Criss photo

If you have a glider with excellent high speed capability then you may choose to stay with the lead gaggle until it is time to leave on final glide. If you have lesser speed capability then you have to leave first or try to get ahead of the gaggle.

Open Distance Strategy

Your strategy should be a race against time while making full use of the soarable window. This is no different than any time you are trying to maximize your XC distance. Refer to *Chapter Nine – Cross Country Flying* for optimal techniques.

Psyching Them Out

If you cannot win by skill and performance alone then you may want to try to achieve another type of advantage. Mental strength and clarity is important in all competitions and you can give yourself an advantage if you can cause your opponents to lose their focus. There are many ways to psych out opponents. If they are somehow convinced that you are invincible, they may feel compelled to take unnecessary risks to win. At the other extreme, if they decide you are inconsequential they may not worry about what you are doing until it is too late. There are all kinds of disinformation tactics. You might choose to purposefully leak a bogus strategy. If it's a weak day you may load up with an inordinate amount of ballast only to surreptitiously dump it when out of sight – the possibilities are endless.

If you are part of a team then there may be occasions where the team could benefit by using one member as a sacrificial lamb. If you have a teammate that is out of contention then perhaps he could sucker some opponents into following him early or taking a poor course line or encouraging the gaggle to stay in each thermal just a little too long…

Leaching

A leach is someone who never ventures out ahead or takes any risk, instead choosing to closely follow a contender. There is a fine line between gaggle flying and leaching off of others. It is OK to follow a mentor on a recreational cross country flight but most competitors have disdain for leaches.

NOTES

NOTES

_____

_____

_____

_____

_____

_____

_____

_____

_____

_____

_____

_____

_____

_____

_____

_____

_____

SAFETY & HOW TO PRACTICE IT

HOW TO SURVIVE A CAREER IN AVIATION

Light winds, a smooth grassy slope and a stable atmosphere are ingredients for a crystal-smooth relaxing flight. You can enjoy a career of injury-free flying if you arm yourself with the proper knowledge, skills, equipment, and judgement; and fly safe, proven sites in safe conditions.

Chapter 11
— SAFETY AND HOW TO PRACTICE IT

HOW TO SURVIVE A CAREER IN AVIATION

QUIZ:

Aviation is:

☐ A. Not inherently dangerous, but very unforgiving of incapacity or neglect

☐ B. Inherently dangerous and often forgiving of incapacity or neglect

☐ C. Inherently dangerous and forgiving of incapacity and neglect, but not often enough

---

The answer is (c). If you've been inside an aviation shop or office, you've probably seen a poster with answer (a) above. It's a favorite among pilots. It's a comforting sentiment, because it implies that what one does as a pilot is not really dangerous after all. It's one of those things that is so cleverly written and sounds so good that it ought to be true. But it isn't. Aviation is inherently dangerous; it's one of the most dangerous things you can do. It is sometimes forgiving; anyone who's been in aviation for very long can tell you endless stories of pilots who suffered spectacular crashes and walked away from them. (Indeed there is a whole genre of "there I was" stories that pilots entertain each other with when they're not flying.) But aviation does not forgive often enough, and it does not forgive with any sense of fairness. Pilots sometimes survive the grossest errors in judgment, while other times what seems like a simple mistake leads to a fatality.

You can survive a career in aviation. Furthermore what is required to survive is not any particular level of flying skill, or experience, or knowledge. Highly skilled, experienced and knowledgeable pilots kill themselves just about as often as pilots with less of all these attributes. Only three things are required to be a safe pilot; the desire to be a safe pilot, the understanding of where safety in aviation comes from, and the maturity and self discipline to act on your knowledge and desire.

It may be illuminating here to take a brief look at the history of hang gliding. In the early 1970's, hang gliding was a new sport, as paragliding is now. The statistical fatality rate was pretty high, and hang gliding acquired an image among the public as a "death sport." Then, over the years, the safety record improved. Today, hang gliding is statistically no more dangerous than any other "risk associated" sport, and by some measures is one of the safest forms of flying.

If you talk to professionals within the sport of hang gliding about the reasons for the improved level of safety, many will point first and foremost to the great improvement in equipment. Some mention will usually be made of better training methods. One of the most important factors is seldom mentioned.

The equipment argument is interesting to look at, though, especially in light of the current emergence of our new sport of paragliding. Early hang gliders, the argument goes, were very dangerous aircraft compared to today's vastly improved gliders. They featured low levels of static stability combined with highly flexible, billowy sails, unsupported by rigid ribs, which were prone to deflate spontaneously leading to large and rapid altitude losses, and sometimes crashes. Modern hang gliders are far more stable and far more rigid, and are not subject to deflation of the wing.

If this evolutionary change in equipment were really the primary factor responsible for the improvement in safety in hang gliding, those of us in paragliding ought to be seriously concerned. For how else are we to describe our present aircraft, but as being "highly flexible, unsupported by rigid ribs, and subject to spontaneous deflation leading to large and rapid altitude losses?" Is the safe practice of paragliding then impossible until paragliders evolve into modern high performance hang gliders?

If the "improved equipment was the cause of improved safety" argument was completely correct for hang gliding, we might properly be led to wonder whether paragliding was a viable sport for safety conscious pilots. But this common perspective on the equipment factor ignores some other factors, which are important and interesting to look at. Ironically, the changes to hang gliding equipment probably have been a major factor in making the sport safer, although not in the way many people think.

Hang gliders in 1975 were very simple, and the basic skills of hang gliding were very easy to learn, much like paragliding is today. The average hang glider pilot was in his early to mid 20's, was unmarried, and had about one year of flying experience, usually limited to hang gliders. He was probably self taught, or learned from a friend. His view of hang gliding was probably somewhat cavalier; many at that time preferred the term "Sky Surfing," as if hang gliding were not really an act of aviation but rather simply a three dimensional form of fun at the beach.

As the sport has evolved, the gliders have become higher performing, but also more complicated, more expensive, and a lot harder to learn to fly. Today the average hang glider pilot is in his mid to late 30's. He is married, probably with children. He has a substantial income (he needs it at today's hang glider prices). He has five to ten years of flying experience, including hundreds of hours, and his flying experience may even extend beyond hang gliders to sailplanes or airplanes. He probably learned to fly from a professional instructor in a fairly comprehensive training program, and he had to have a significant amount of personal dedication to stick with it through the learning process.

If you compare those two groups of pilots, it is obvious that the latter group could not help but be a statistically safer pilot population. The moral of the story is this: Pilot safety is a matter of individual pilot attitude. The nature of modern hang gliding and modern hang gliding equipment has changed to favor a population of pilots who are better trained, more mature, and take their flying more seriously. The specific type of attitude required for safe flying is one that a person tends to acquire with age and maturity.

To be a safe pilot, a pilot must be capable of the following:

- First, be able to recognize the limitations of his equipment, and of his personal skills and knowledge.

- Second, have the self-discipline to consistently operate within those limitations.

- Third, pay attention to the all of the little details of preflight procedures and equipment maintenance.

Safety will often be as simple an act as just deciding not to fly; because on that day, at that site, the conditions, or the site are just not comfortably enough within your abilities, or the capabilities of your equipment. Maybe it's a new site, and the launch is just a little too precipitous, and a little less forgiving than you feel comfortable with. Maybe you're unsure of the weather; the wind speed seems OK now, but it's marginally high and a little on the gusty side, and that cold front to the northwest on the weather map in the morning paper has you thinking that maybe conditions are going to build to an unsafe level after you're in the air.

Sometimes staying on the ground can be the hardest thing to do. As a beginning to intermediate level paraglider pilot, you know you should avoid flying in strong thermal conditions. Conditions which can cause a spontaneous major collapse of the canopy are extremely dangerous until you have completely mastered the techniques for controlling and reinflating your canopy during collapses. And when friends of yours with no more skill or experience than you have are out there gaining thousands of feet of altitude in middle-of-the-day-thermals, it may be hard for you to stay on the ground and wait for the smoother, and weaker lift at the end of the day. It will be especially hard, when you notice that they seem to be getting away with it and when you think about listening to their "there I was" stories that evening in the landing area. But if you really want to be a safe pilot, this is the kind of hard decision you have to be able to make. Look at it this way; during the next ten years you'll probably have at least ten thousand significant decisions to make as a pilot. (Do I fly today? Do I have enough room to turn back towards the hill in this thermal? In this one? Can I follow this thermal back and still have enough glide to get back over the ridge top and avoid the rotor?) If you make the go decision whenever you think you have a 90% chance of making it through all right, you won't make it 1000 times. If you raise your threshold to 99%, you still won't make it 100 times. If you raise it to 99.9%, you'll still be in serious trouble 10 different times. Your go / no go decision basis has to be a 100% certainty that you will make it. Nothing else is enough.

This is perhaps the most intractable problem in hang gliding and paragliding safety. The problem is that safety is virtually entirely determined by the quality of pilot decision making, and pilots get rewarded for bad decisions. Look at it this way. For every situation in which you find yourself, each option you can choose lies somewhere along a continuum of potential safety or danger. Good decisions are higher, bad ones are lower. Above some threshold level on that continuum, your success /survival rate is 100%.

However, at a point substantially below that threshold, it may still be 98%. As we explained above 98% is not good enough for long term safety. However, at 98%, the vast majority of your decisions will not result in a disaster and maybe not even any negative result at all. So what happens? You think you made a good decision. It had to be a good decision (the right decision), it worked out, didn't it? So when your decisions at the 98% quality point (which is already not good enough) get rewarded, you lower your threshold to 95%. These get rewarded also (nothing goes wrong) and so the threshold comes down further. Eventually, the laws of chance collide with your descending threshold, and you get caught. Maybe you're lucky and it's just an embarrassing accident that makes you look bad. Maybe you're not so lucky and you get seriously hurt, or even killed.

So how does one address this problem as a safety conscious pilot desiring to survive? What is required is that you be actively involved in critically analyzing your decisions both before and after the fact. You need to learn how to identify bad decisions that didn't result in bad results. Let's take a practical example. You're thermalling at your local site on a somewhat windy day, and you've climbed 1500' above launch and drifted almost a mile behind. You're trying to gauge how far over the back of the hill you can follow the thermal and still make it back. You've decided that for safety, you want to be able to glide back over the top with at least 800 feet to spare. You look at your glide slope and decide to head back out. You arrive 300 feet above the launch. It looks to everyone like you did fine, but in reality you made a bad judgment. You judged that you could get back with 700' of altitude loss and it took you 1200'. You have no way of knowing how much more it could have required; if it took 1200' it could have taken 1600' and you wouldn't have made it. You came out all right because your 800' goal was fairly conservative, but what you really wanted to achieve was to have that 800' as a minimum. You need to recognize the mistake you made and modify your decision making accordingly.

This doesn't mean that you will never try new things or never advance beyond where you are now. All pilots must "stretch the envelope" of their own skill and experience limitations in order to progress. But you can pick your spots; give yourself an especially large extra margin for error when you venture into unfamiliar territory, and evaluate the results of your decisions on a continuing basis.

Also, to be safe, a pilot has to take his flying and his safety seriously enough to pay attention to the more mundane aspects of safety, such as proper equipment maintenance, pre-flight checks, and so forth. If you can avoid stupid mistakes, and if you can consistently make the tough conservative decisions in your flying that keep you on the safe side of your limitations, you can have a safe aviation career.

And if you insist on a clever quotation about safety in aviation, try this one:

"Aviation has made the world a lot smaller, but it is still pretty hard to miss it if you fall."

Rules to Live By

There is a saying that good judgment comes from experience and experience comes from bad judgment. Unfortunately, there is a lot of truth to that statement and many pilots only get conservative after they have either seen or experienced a close call or accident first-hand. Taken to heart, the following recommendations can make you a safer pilot.

Leave Yourself An Out

As the saying goes, "don't put all your eggs in one basket." To help mitigate judgment errors, misreading of conditions, and random acts of nature; it is a good practice to always have a backup plan to leave yourself an "out." Here are some examples:

- Do not drift downwind of launch if there is any chance you will not be able to penetrate back to the front of the hill.

- Do not do a 360° turn near the hill in lift without having a way out if you encounter sink (either extra altitude or a clear vector to miss the terrain).

- Do not fly over neighborhoods or terrain that you could not safely land in if you had to.

- Do not fly in winds that require the use of the speed stirrup to penetrate forward.

- Do not do aerobatic maneuvers below an altitude that you could successfully deploy your reserve chute nor over terrain you would not be comfortable landing under your reserve in.

It Can Happen To You

It is likely that the majority of accidents happen to people that for some mistaken reason thought they were safe enough so as to avoid an accident. Think about it. Whether flying, driving, or crossing the street; if most people thought they would someday suffer a bad accident in any activity, then they would likely choose to no longer participate in it. But accidents do happen and the prudent individual anticipates them and formulates plans so as best to avoid or mitigate them. Even if you never plan on flying in turbulent conditions or pursuing acrobatics, you should still understand advanced canopy control maneuvers and recovery techniques. You can learn a great deal by visualizing emergencies and mentally reacting to them. Odds are you will never have a serious paragliding accident but you can better these odds if you realize that you just might.

Altitudes for Maneuver

Military fighter pilots live with rules of engagement (in peacetime they are now referred to as "Training Rules"). These rules set limits for how close aircraft can come to each other when mock dog fighting, which way to pass, minimum altitudes, weather and visibility limits, and so forth. They say these rules are "written in blood" because they are – likely each and every one of the rules was written as a result of death(s) by aviators who had not observed the limits. Even with these rules we still hear about the occasional crash but the overall accident rate has declined tremendously in recent years.

Other aspects of aviation can be made safer by adopting similar rules. Regardless of your aircraft, every pilot should have their own set of rules to live by. The USHPA has included a series of guidelines within their pilot rating scale regarding wind strength and how close one should fly to other gliders. These are a good starting point but a safe pilot needs to have rules that address all aspects of his flying.

Only recently (2002) are paraglider models being marketed specifically for aerobatic flight. Such flying can be extremely dangerous and is not recommended. No other style of flying has the potential for quickly turning what was originally a beautifully flying canopy into a free-falling tangled mess of fabric and lines. If you decide you must fly aerobatics then do not do so without proper instruction, with the proper equipment, at the appropriate site, and in the appropriate conditions.

Never fly in strong thermals, moderate turbulence, or perform aerobatics over any area or in conditions you would not be comfortable deploying your reserve parachute in (drifting downwind into a power line riddled neighborhood or a steep rocky face may be more death-defying than the original maneuver).

One of the most important aspects of setting rules to live by is to ensure these rules are rules you can live with. An overly conservative rule encourages breaking it and breaking safety rules should always raise a red flag in your mind. Continuing with the military fighter pilot example, historically one of the biggest causes of loss of life was a departure from controlled flight (i.e. stall and spin) with insufficient altitude for recovery. All too often the pilots would realize too late that they had insufficient altitude to recover and sometimes insufficient altitude to even eject.

The services set rules that they would not allow a dogfight to degenerate into slow speeds and high angles of attack below 10,000 feet AGL. They also decreed that if a pilot was not in control of his jet below this altitude that he must immediately eject. This was considered a good safe rule because all of the then-current fighter aircraft could recover from a departure in less than 10,000 ft.

The only problem was they continued to have loss of control accidents and pilots still were sometimes failing to eject in time (or at all). This would lead some people to think they should set the altitude limit even higher but eventually the military settled on lower limits.

One of the biggest problems with the original limits was the pilots knew they would likely be able to recover from all but the most severe departures in less than 10,000 ft. They also knew the ejection seat would provide a safe recovery from a significantly lower altitude. Since no pilot wants to lose a jet that they still might have a chance of recovering, they typically disregarded the rules and continued their efforts to recover the airplane at lower altitudes. The problem was they did not know just how low the actual limits were and were often unsuccessful at estimating them. The new rules allow dogfighting down to 5,000 ft as long as the pilots observe minimum speed and maximum angle of attack limits. The rules include an honest appraisal that some departures may take in excess of 6,000 ft to recover from and failure to eject by that altitude will likely be unsuccessful. The pilots now have rules they respect and the services are currently enjoying a safety record that is unequaled throughout aviation history.

Paragliding pilots need to follow specific guidelines with respect to minimum altitudes. You should set limits for yourself based on the site, the conditions, your glider, your skills and your style of flying. You should have a minimum altitude for which you practice advanced maneuvers, fly with speed bar, or consider taking a hand from a brake toggle (you may adjust these altitudes depending upon the site and conditions). Always have a minimum altitude at which you will immediately deploy your reserve parachute if you are not under full control of the canopy (see the Emergency Procedures section of *Chapter Seven*).

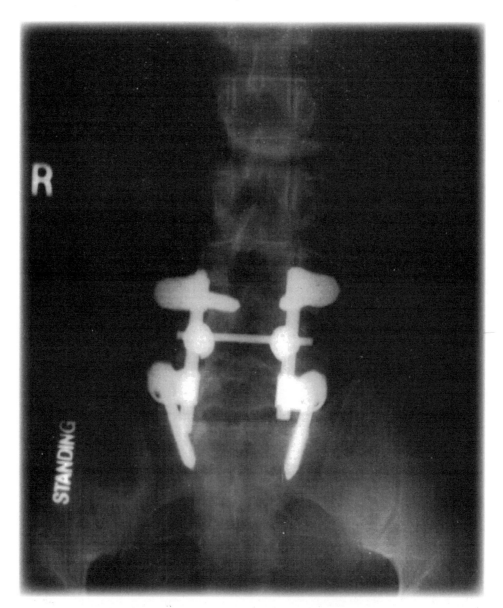

You can enjoy a career of injury-free flying if you arm yourself with the proper knowledge, skills, equipment, and judgement; and fly safe, proven sites in safe conditions.

Recommended minimum altitudes over normal terrain for proficient pilots exiting advanced maneuvers:

1,000 ft   Radical maneuvering to include aerobatics, full stalls and spins

500 ft   Extreme spirals, practice large asymmetric collapses

200 ft   Spirals, B-line stalls, practice small asymmetric collapses

100 ft   Lower limit for big ears (unless holding them in until the landing flare)

Recommended minimum altitudes for thermal flying:

500 ft   Strong or turbulent thermals or over terrain unsuitable for landing

200 ft   Smooth thermals over terrain in conditions that a safe landing or PLF could be accomplished

Recommended minimum altitude for deployment of reserve parachute:

500 ft   Initiate deployment if passing this altitude without signs of recovery after an extended loss of control (stall, spin, collapse, etc.)

400 ft   Failure to initiate deployment after a substantial collapse, stall, or spin below this altitude may result in ground impact prior to successful deployment

Recommended minimum altitude for use of the speed stirrup:

500 ft   In anything stronger than light turbulence

200 ft   In anything other than smooth air

WARNING

The decision to deploy a parachute must be based on altitude and not a visual interpretation of your altitude and rate of descent. Waiting to deploy until you sense the urgency of the situation (ground rush) is too late and will likely result in death or serious injury.

11

NOTES

NOTE:
The slower the aircraft's flying speed and the lighter the wing loading, the greater the amount of pilot prudence required with respect to flying conditions!

TOW LAUNCHING

LAUNCHING ALTERNATIVES FOR THE TOPOGRAPHICALLY CHALLENGED

Cheap Lift Ticket — Mark Stucky enjoys the view over Red Rock Canyon, California. This 33-mile flight began with a 600 ft. AGL tow

Chapter 12 — TOW LAUNCHING

LAUNCHING ALTERNATIVES FOR THE
TOPOGRAPHICALLY CHALLENGED

Let's face it, not all paraglider pilots have the luxury of living near mountain launch sites. Do not despair if you are topographically challenged, for towing can open up great flight possibilities for local and cross country soaring. Towing adds additional complexity to paragliding, which basically means there are more things that can go wrong. It can be done safely, however, if you have a basic understanding of tow theory, follow good established procedures, and have a knowledgeable pilot, safety observer, and tow operator.

Note – some paraglider models do not tow as well as others. Some require a special tow bridle that automatically reduces the angle of attack during tow. Consult your Owner's Manual, dealer, or manufacturer prior to attempting to tow your wing.

This chapter is intended to familiarize you with the theory, techniques, and procedures for safe towing. It is not intended as a substitute for professional instruction.

Safe towing requires adherence to the following guidelines:

1. The tow crew must be trained and knowledgeable on the proper tow procedures, signals and communications, and emergency procedures.

2. There must be a reliable means of communication.

3. Towline tension must be automatically regulated or monitored and manually regulated.

4. The tow force relationship to the center of gravity (CG) of the total system and the aerodynamic center (AC) is critical for ensuring controllability and stability. (It is common to read in hang gliding and paragliding literature that the tow force must act through the CG of the pilot but this is not true. In fact, if the CG and AC are excessively spaced then stability and control can be reduced. The practice of attaching the tow force to at or near the riser attachments puts the tow force close to the CG of the pilot and paraglider, which works well as long as the aerodynamic forces stay balanced.)

5. A proper weaklink must be used at the glider attachment so as to limit the possible load in the event of a failure to control towline tension.

6. The pilot must have a means to safely release the towline in all normal and emergency situations (to include a backup method).

7. The tow operator must have a means to rapidly release or cut the towline.

There are three generally accepted methods of towing a paraglider: using a vehicle-mounted payout winch, a stationary reel-in winch, or a simple length of towline behind a moving vehicle. Each method has its own advantages and disadvantages and the popularity of each tends to be based more on locality than overall superiority or safety. It is common to find fliers in one locale adamantly espousing the virtues of their tow method while those in other parts of the world may be just as vocal about the supposed superiority of their technique. The truth is, with the proper procedures and equipment any of these three methods can be used successfully.

Tow Forces and Changing Angles

12

At steep rope angles the tow tension is nearly vertical which loads the glider but provides little thrust. The lift vector is not tilted as far aft and the glider is more overhead the pilot.

Tow Theory

If you remember from the aerodynamics section of Chapter Four, a glider does not have thrust to counter its drag so it is continuously pulled downward and forward due to gravity. If you add sufficient thrust to the glider so that it becomes greater than the drag, then the lift vector will tilt upwards (and backwards) and you can now actually climb through the airmass. Towing works due to the longitudinal component of the tow force providing thrust to the aircraft in excess of the drag of the glider and towline. Note that when using a ground-based tow system, the longitudinal component of the tow force decreases during the later stages of towing when the angle of the towline becomes increasingly vertical.

The greater the forward tow force, the faster the climb rate. One of the greatest hazards of towing is overstressing the towed aircraft due to excessive tow force. The slower an aircraft flies and the smaller its speed range, the more

At low rope angles the horizontal tow tension provides maximum thrust to the paraglider. This angles the lift vector aft and the canopy reflects the loading by flying aft of the pilot.

critical variances in tow tension become. This principle is exacerbated by large changes in wind speed as a function of height (wind gradient).

Obviously, proper control of tow tension is of paramount importance when towing paragliders. Both payout and stationary winches are designed to regulate tension automatically but static line towing requires active speed control by the tow driver to control tension.

A tow to 2,000 feet AGL or higher is desirable in order to have a reasonable chance of finding a usable thermal. For a given glider and rope weight and diameter, the height that can be achieved on tow is dependent upon the length of the towline, the length of the tow road, and the wind velocity. As a rough rule-of-thumb, when limited by tow road length, the available height can be nearly doubled with a ten mph headwind. In most flat land locales, the minimum altitude for having a chance of finding a thermal from tow is 1,000 feet AGL.

The Dreaded Lockout

If the paraglider is allowed to get too far off-axis from the towline an unstable situation will result (similar to letting the canopy get too far off center while kiting). The towline tension, however, inhibits your ability to get back underneath the wing and properly control it. Without immediate action to recenter the canopy by the use of brakes the situation will rapidly develop to the point that brake control is insufficient to arrest the ever-increasing bank angle. At this point the glider is in a "lockout", the glider will continue its bank away from the towline and a high speed dive towards the ground will result.

There is a common misconception that a good winch with a proper weaklink will make it impossible to lockout. This is simply not true. Regulating the tow tension will help prevent sudden severe lockouts but it will not prevent a lockout due to poor piloting.

The procedures for dealing with a lockout are contained in the Tow Emergencies section at the end of this chapter.

Payout Winch Towing

The payout winch is technically a misnomer in that it does not winch the line in during tow, instead it operates as a reel and the towline pays out, increasing in length throughout the tow. A typical payout winch consists of a spool of line controlled by an automotive hydraulic disk brake. The hydraulic pressure is set to a specific value so the brake controls the line tension. The drum may contain up to several thousand feet of towline although only a relatively short length of line is initially used for launching. The winch is mounted on a vehicle and towed at a speed that causes tension greater than the threshold set for the disc brake. The towline unwinds from the drum and the glider climbs out with nearly constant tension. As a rule of thumb in no-wind conditions, if you are not limited in the length of your towline then you should be able to reach a height equal to approximately 20% of the length of the tow road.

Advantages of using a payout winch are they are relatively affordable (inexpensive to make if you are good at scrounging parts or have access to a machine shop), have a proven track record, and are portable. The primary disadvantage is it requires a smooth tow road at least one mile in length and clear of nearby obstructions.

There are many variations in payout winches, the most notable being the size and style of the drum. The original winches were quite large since they had to hold several thousand feet of the 3/8" diameter polypropylene towrope. Nowadays suitable strength and durability can be achieved from 1/8" diameter spectra so the winch size can be reduced dramatically. The major variance is whether the winch is wide with a relatively thin layer of line, or narrow with a thicker layer of line. The wider winches are costlier because they must contain a level-wind mechanism for ensuring the towline is rewound symmetrically along the spool.

Thin winches can be made much less expensive because they do not require the added complexity of a level-wind. The disadvantage, however, is the relative thickness of the towline axle changes greatly throughout the tow so that for a given brake setting, the line tension increases as the line pays out and the hub thickness decreases. Additionally the weight distribution and therefor the rotational inertia will also change more during the tow (although with proper procedures this effect can be minimized).

12

12

The Stationary Reel-in Winch

A stationary winch uses an engine to reel in an initially long length of towline. Top-end systems use automotive engines powering hydraulic motors for very smooth and precise control. Some innovative designers have constructed winches powered by a car's drive wheel (similar to a dynamometer). Simple stationary winches have been made using motorcycle scooters. The scooter's centrifugal clutch regulates the tow tension within suitable limits and the hand disk brake can regulate the reel-in at the end of the tow.

The tow area needs to be clear of obstructions and is normally a large field. The winch is setup at the upwind edge of the tow field and the line stretched to the limit of either the field or towline length. Radio communication is highly recommended because of the large separation between the paraglider and tow operator.

After release the line is rewound on the drum. A scooter or ATV is commonly used for stretching the line back to the starting point for subsequent tows.

Static Line Towing

Towing a glider behind a vehicle with a fixed length of towline requires the use of a gauge that measures the tow tension and displays it to the tow driver. An inline hydraulic cylinder that has been calibrated to read tension instead of pressure is typically used although modern light weight electronic tension gauges are now commercially available.

A towline length of 40% of the available tow run is a good start for no-wind conditions. (If there is wind then you can use a longer towline.) If there is more than a few mph of wind then the tow driver must be especially observant for wind gradient effects and be ready to slow down and possibly even back up to maintain tension limits.

Mark Stucky performs a no-wind tow launch as part of a NASA research flight at Edwards AFB in 1998. Photo series courtesy of NASA.

Precise regulation of towline tension is more difficult because of delays due to driver reaction time as well as due to the inertia of the tow vehicle. Some means of damping these tension spikes is advisable, especially in thermic conditions. Adding a couple of hundred feet of 3/8" polypropylene water ski rope at the paraglider end is a simple way to add shock absorption to the tow system. Having too much shock absorption can also cause problems by inducing excessive delays between tension changes at the ends of the towline. This is usually not a problem but can occur with long lengths of nylon or very long lengths of polypropylene. This can cause the driver to make corrections that are too late or even out of phase with the glider, leading to increasingly severe tension oscillations.

In the situation where there is extra towline available (the tow run is limited by road length), then additional height can be gained by running the towline through a pulley that is anchored at the upwind end of the road. The car now drives toward the launching paraglider and a greater height is achieved for a given amount of driving. There is also the added benefit that the driver has a much better view of the launching paraglider. Take care to use a pulley that has the proper bearings to handle the load and that the towline cannot jam between the pulley and housing. Having an observer located with a hook knife located next to the pulley is always a good idea. Radio communication is highly encouraged.

The Tow Train

The tow train consists of the towline and all hardware to include any drogue chute, leader, weaklink, release, tow bridle and any attachment hardware.

The Towline

A good towline should have high strength, low stretch, and good resistance to UV rays and road rash. Most tow operators use modern high-performance small-diameter synthetic ropes to minimize rope drag and winch size. Spectra™ (1/8-3/16" diameter) is preferred due to its high strength to weight ratio and low stretch. Others choose Ultraline™ because it is only slightly larger (3/16-1/4" diameter) and significantly cheaper. The use of thin steel cable is popular on stationary winches in Europe but less common in the U.S. Inexpensive nylon and polypropylene ropes have fallen from favor because of their large diameter and excessive stretch. Some shock absorption is desirable so a length of high stretch rope may be added at the glider end for added damping, particularly with static line tows.

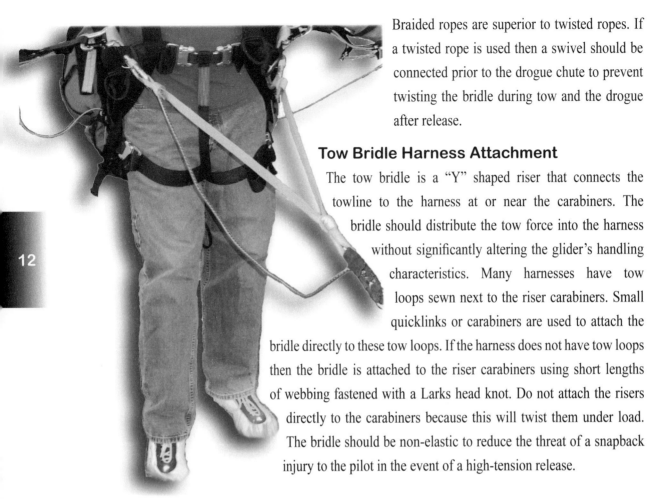

Braided ropes are superior to twisted ropes. If a twisted rope is used then a swivel should be connected prior to the drogue chute to prevent twisting the bridle during tow and the drogue after release.

Tow Bridle Harness Attachment

The tow bridle is a "Y" shaped riser that connects the towline to the harness at or near the carabiners. The bridle should distribute the tow force into the harness without significantly altering the glider's handling characteristics. Many harnesses have tow loops sewn next to the riser carabiners. Small quicklinks or carabiners are used to attach the bridle directly to these tow loops. If the harness does not have tow loops then the bridle is attached to the riser carabiners using short lengths of webbing fastened with a Larks head knot. Do not attach the risers directly to the carabiners because this will twist them under load. The bridle should be non-elastic to reduce the threat of a snapback injury to the pilot in the event of a high-tension release.

Tow bridle attachment

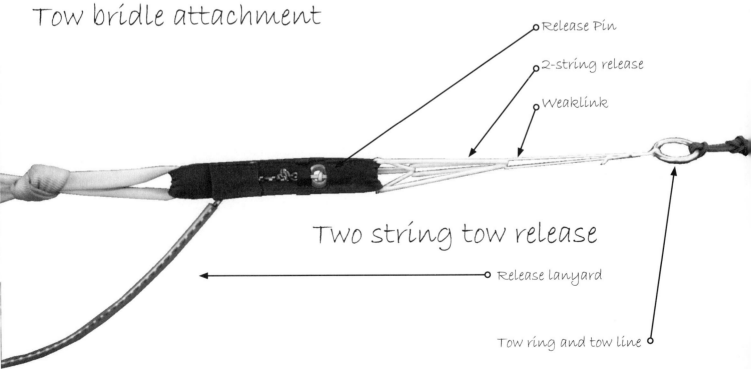

Release Pin

2-string release

Weaklink

Two string tow release

Release lanyard

Tow ring and tow line

The tow release mounts at the single leg of the Y and connects to the towline weaklink. The release must operate regardless of the angle of the towline and the tension level. Simple two or three-string looped releases are common and they are inexpensive, reliable, and help mitigate snapback dangers. Releases are normally actuated by hand and the ability to release using either hand (or even a kick of the foot) is desirable.

The weaklink functions similar to a fuse, preventing tow loads from exceeding acceptable values. A proper weaklink can reduce the chances of overstress due to excessive tow speeds, tension, or extreme lockouts. A weaklink is always required – regardless of the tow method – because machinery can malfunction, lines can jam, and people can make mistakes. Weaklinks should be set to break at between 70% and 80% of the full load of the pilot, glider, and all equipment. Popular weaklinks are constructed from #205 leech line using double grapevine knots to secure. The breaking strength of a corded weaklink is highly dependent upon the configuration, locations of knots, and radius of attachment points. You should test your weaklink under loading conditions identical to what you will experience in flight. A test rig can be fashioned by hanging your harness (with bridle, release, and weaklink) by a short length of towline and slowly adding weight until the link fails. You can reduce the strength of the weaklink by 30% by tying a simple overhand knot in the tension-bearing portion of the link

For static line towing a second weaklink that is fifty percent stronger than the pilot's weaklink should be mounted at the vehicle to protect from towline damage due to snags.

Towline Drogue Chutes

Small parachutes near the glider end of the towline are recommended for use with any type of motorized rewind system. The drogue chute slows the fall of the line after it is released, allowing for the tow operator to rewind the entire line length without it ever touching the ground. In the event of a sudden release, the drogue helps prevent the towline from snapping back and fouling the winch. There are several different designs for drogues, including parafoil and conventional round chutes. Parafoils provide more lift and hence can be smaller but they are more susceptible to problems such as uncommanded turns and failures to inflate.

The drogue must remain in a low drag position until automatic deployment when the towline releases. The simplest setup uses a robust drogue that is a tension bearing member of the towline. The tow tension keeps the chute deflated until release. More complicated arrangements use in-line deployment bags that house the drogue and spring open once tension is released. This method requires a means to keep the deployment bag closed during preflight ground operations. The tow should be immediately terminated if the drogue deploys at low altitude (less than 200 ft). Above that altitude the tow team may consider continuing the tow and accepting the lower final altitude due to the increased drag.

The drogue should be near the end of the towline but not so close that it could envelope the pilot or interfere with his visibility in the case of a premature opening or towline break. Normally a short leader of line is attached to the apex of the chute and runs to the pilot's release.

If you tow over extensive vegetation then you may it near impossible to keep a drogue from getting entangled with the foliage. This is problematic and usually requires repeated untangling by hand. You will likely find it easier to use a more robust tow line without a drogue. The line will lie over the foliage but will normally rewind without becoming ensnared.

Miscellaneous Equipment

The pilot and winch operator should wear protective eye wear to prevent injury due to a sudden snapback of a broken or suddenly released towline. The tow pilot must have a hook knife that is easily accessible for rapidly cutting the towline in the event of a release failure. The winch operator must also have a hook knife or some type of guillotine setup for rapidly cutting the towline at the winch.

The Tow Crew

In a perfect world all tows would be conducted with a trained and knowledgeable team with separate roles and responsibilities.

The safety observer also functions as a launch director and is located near the launching glider. His mission is to help facilitate the safety of the operation by ensuring the proper checklists and procedures are being followed, monitoring the launch and tow, and providing direction to the pilot or tow operator as appropriate.

A safety observer is of greatest value when the tow operator is located a long distance away from the glider such as during stationary reel-in and static line tows. In the absence of radio communications, the safety observer will relay the appropriate visual signals to the tow operator.

In some situations towing is done without a dedicated safety observer. This is only acceptable if both the tow operator and pilot are competent in the tow operation and the tow operator can observe the glider throughout the tow (either directly or through a suitable mirror).

Tow Signals

Radios are invaluable for towing operations and mandatory for tow training. Although experienced pilots might not feel there is a requirement to use radios, their use can help maximize tow altitude by fine tuning the tow pressures and reducing reaction times during step towing. The pilot should have a convenient push-to-talk switch that does not require removing hands from the brakes. At locations with multiple pilots, each tow operation should have its own dedicated frequency to avoid confusion. Some operations have had success with using cellular telephones with hands-free headsets for tow communication. Legally, the FCC restricts cellular telephones to ground usage but their use during tow operations is unlikely to cause any problems to the cellular system.

Safe towing requires the use of clear and concise aural and/or visual signals. Voice call outs will either be directive or descriptive in nature while visual signals are normally reserved for directive commands. There are many lessons that have been learned over the years in aviation and other disciplines that have application for us. Specifically, terminology should be selected to minimize the chance of a directive command being confused with a question.

Let's use an example of bad communication. In this scenario, the tow driver is impatiently waiting for the signal to start the tow and finally asks, "ready to tow?" Our intrepid paraglider pilot is still busy getting his brakes and PTT in the proper hands and radios back, "not ready". Unfortunately, he did not push the PTT early enough and all the driver hears is "...ready." The driver starts speeding away and

the surprised pilot who still doesn't have the PTT velcroed to his finger decides to go ahead and pull up the glider.

Our impatient tow driver now sees what looks like a good inflation and is irritated when he doesn't get the command to increase the tow pressure. He chalks this one up to pilot inexperience and sets the tow pressure anyway (besides, if the pilot had a problem he would speak up wouldn't he?). The pilot meanwhile is climbing out smoothly but decides it would be best not to worry about the PTT and lets it dangle from his sleeve. The tow progresses with each person thinking the other is an idiot. There are many different possible endings due to poor communication procedures and most of them have potentially disastrous results.

Voice Communication Rules

To promote good communications we recommend the following rules:

1. The driver and pilot must acknowledge all directive and preparatory communications.

2. Flight critical commands should only be used as a command, never as a question or description. Examples of flight critical commands include "abort" (stop the tow), "release" (pilot should release), and "cut" (towline released immediately at the tow end using the most expeditious manner).

3. Flight critical commands should consist of single words and should be repeated three times to ensure reception. Examples include, "release, release, release" and "abort, abort, abort".

4. The word order of non-critical directive commands used by the pilot and tow operator should be different so as to reflect compliance with the command. Example: pilot commands "increase pressure", operator increases the pressure (assuming it was not at the upper limit) and responds "pressure increased".

5. If either the pilot or tow operator is waiting for a response he should make the situation known by commanding "Pilot (or tow operator) waiting." The other person should then respond as appropriate or, if he missed the original request, transmit "say again?"

Visual Signals

Visual signals are normally used as backups to directive communication. These signals should be easy to recognize at great distances and, in the case of pilot signals, should be easy to accomplish while maintaining control of the glider. Visual signals by the launch observer should be augmented with the use of a brightly colored flag (such as a glider bag).

Standardized Signals

Although some tow operators may use different signals and commands, the following standardized directive communications and visual signals are recommended and given in the normal order they would occur. These commands were developed using the previously mentioned guidelines. Because paraglider towing is relatively new in the United States, effort was made to devise signals and commands that were also compatible with hang glider and sailplane towing.

Proper communication through clear and concise signals is of paramount importance for safe towing.

— *Official NASA photo*

The thrust force of a tow tilts the lift vector (and canopy) backwards

DIRECTIVE COMMUNICATIONS AND VISUAL SIGNALS

TAKE UP SLACK

Pilot	Observer	Driver/Operator
Lifts and lowers one leg repeatedly to the side.	Waves flag back and forth below the waist	For forward inflations, removes slack with 20 lb. of tension. Tension may be increased to 50 lb. to account for line drag with static line and stationary winches. Note—for reverse inflations there should be enough slack near the pilot to allow for movement toward the canopy during the inflation

Leans back to brace himself for up to 20 lb. of tension.

HOLD POSITION — Winch/Tow-Driver STOPS.

Pilot	Observer	Driver/Operator
Single arm held stationary overhead	Single arm or flag held stationary overhead	Stops taking up slack and holds position

GO TO CRUISE		Canopy inflation...
Pilot	Observer	Driver/Operator
Slow bow at the waist (3 times)	*Waves flag in a vertical half-circle from straight up to straight down*	*Accelerates to 15-20 mph airspeed*

ABORT! ABORT! ABORT!		Emergency stop...
Pilot	Observer	Driver/Operator
Pilot dumps canopy	*Waves flag back and forth overhead*	*Dumps tow pressure and stops vehicle immediately*

ACCELERATE

Pilot	Observer	Driver/Operator
Flaps elbows	*Waves flag in a continuous vertical circle*	*Sets tow tension and accelerates to 25-30 mph airspeed*

INCREASE TENSION

Pilot	Observer	Driver/Operator
Moves legs in a running motion		*Ensures proper tension and speed was set and increases if safe to do so*

DECREASE TENSION

Pilot	Observer	Driver/Operator
Moves legs in a "jumping jack" motion		*Decreases tension and/or speed as appropriate*

Tow Phases

The best tow procedures break the tow into five distinct phases:

1. Preflight operations

2. Paraglider inflation

3. Launching and initial climbout

4. Climbout

5. Release

All equipment should be properly preflighted, the towline laid out, properly attached, and prelaunch checklists completed prior to inflating the canopy. It is good procedure to ensure a careful preflight of the canopy, risers, lines, and harness attachments is completed prior to hooking the towline to the bridle.

Removing Towline Slack

The exact procedure for removing the slack and setting the initial tow tension is dependent upon whether a forward or reverse inflation is planned. The slack should be completely removed prior to a forward inflation. In high winds a small amount of slack near the pilot is beneficial during a reverse inflation so the pilot is free to quickly step towards the canopy during the pull up. Failure to do so during the inflation will likely result in the towline tension pulling your feet out from underneath you as it spins you around and drops you on your butt. The tow observer should help hold the slack towline clear of the pilot's feet during reverse inflations.

The initial tension during slack removal and inflation should be set to a low enough value so there is no possibility of pulling the pilot before he is ready or dragging him in the event of a botched inflation or fall during the launch sequence.

At the command to remove the slack, the tow operator should add a small amount of tension and slowly drive forward. For payout winches a value of approximately 20 lb. is good. If using a stationary winch or static line then the tension should be increased to 50-60 lb. to counter the effect of rope drag. When using a payout winch the proper tension is verified by leaning backward against the tow pressure. The winch should start to release line when the pilot is reclined approximately twenty degrees.

The Towed Forward Inflation

After the slack is removed the traffic pattern must be verified to be clear of all ground and airborne traffic (usually the observer and pilot exchange "thumbs up"). The pilot will issue the "go to cruise" command. The tow driver will quickly accelerate to 15-20 mph airspeed and expect the pilot to pull up the glider in short order. With stationary or static towing the pilot should resist the tow force initially, starting the inflation as it gets difficult to hold position. If using a payout winch the pilot can maintain his backwards lean as the line spins off the drum and inflate at his leisure. The tow force aids the inflation and you will find even calm wind forward inflations relatively easy to perform.

After the canopy is up overhead the tow tension will be enough to cause you to be light on your feet. Verify the glider is ready for flight, maintain your forward lean and run, and give the launch command "accelerate".

The Towed Reverse Inflation

After the pull up you should spin around (in the direction of the bridle!) to face forward. Lean forward and kite the glider as you step backwards to remove the slack from the line. Do not give the "accelerate" (launch) command until the towline is tight.

The Towed Launch and Climbout

The command "accelerate" should be given after verifying a good inflation and tight towline. The tow driver should respond "accelerating" and as quickly as possible set the initial climbout tension and accelerate to greater than 25 mph airspeed. For static line or stationary winch towing the initial climb tension should be set. Keep your feet underneath you for several seconds until you verify you are safely climbing away.

Once airborne you should be able to climb with minimal to no brake application. If you feel the need to hold brakes toward the minimum sink position then you should call for increased tow tension. Proper tow tension is set when you are climbing with the brakes at the best L/D brake position (normal trim condition with brakes off). Make turn corrections, by using weight shift as much as possible and minimal brakes if required. In a crosswind you should allow yourself to drift downwind. In all conditions you maximize your climb by keeping the towline square to your harness. You may need to crab during the initial tow if there are obstructions (such as trees or power lines) on the downwind side of the tow lane. In that case the towline will not be perpendicular to your harness. A proper crab is done with the wings level, not banked away from the tow.

After the canopy is inflated the proper tow tension should be based on achieving a suitable rate of climb with proper controllability and safety. During towed flight the canopy will be aft of the overhead position mainly due to the backwards tilting of the lift vector and additionally due to the vertical offset between the tow force and the canopy drag. If the tow force suddenly stops (due to weaklink break, release under tension, tow engine failure, etc.) then the canopy will need to surge forward to regain proper orientation. Because of the dangers of a low altitude surge and pendulum, the initial launch tension should be set so that the canopy is not more than twenty degrees aft of vertical. The tow pressure can be increased above two hundred feet AGL if the pilot is experienced with proper surge control and is comfortable with the increase. At no time should the canopy be inclined greater than thirty degrees aft of vertical.

Tow theory shows us that maximum thrust is achieved when the tow force is aligned with the longitudinal axis of the glider, thus the maximum rate of climb will be achieved when the towline is close to horizontal. This is obviously only possible with an infinitely long towline or with an aerotow. A common technique for maximizing tow height is to increase the tow tension during the latter stages of the tow as the rope angle gets progressively steeper. This may buy a bit more altitude but it is a case of diminishing returns because past a certain point, increasing altitude requires exponentially increasing tow tension. Even ignoring the drag and weight of the towline, at a rope angle of sixty degrees only half of the tow tension is thrust, while 87% loads the glider vertically (increasing the induced drag). In fact, including the drag and weight of the towline, the glider is likely supporting a 2-g loading at rope angles greater than 60°. It may be prudent to avoid unnecessary wear and tear on your equipment by resisting the urge to crank up the tension for an extra few feet of altitude.

If you are using a payout winch then the limiting factor is normally either the available length of tow road or the available length of the towline. In these two cases you can maximize your tow altitude by initially driving at an excess speed so the rope angle stays low for the majority of the horizontal tow distance. As either of the limiting factors (available rope and/or road length) approaches, the vehicle should be slowed down to a speed so that the towline is only slowly unwinding. For a given length of road, the maximum height will occur when the total length of line is extended and the glider has reached the maximum vertical angle. The exact point that the driver should slow down depends on the winds. He should slow down earlier in calm conditions and later if it is breezy. In fact, if it is breezy, the driver may stop moving all together and with some designs even back up if the towline end is approaching and the rope angle is still low.

Releasing From Tow

Releasing under high tension should be avoided so the pilot does not have to deal with a strong wing surge. If possible you should always give a preparatory "drop pressure" command so the tow operator can reduce tension prior to releasing. The operator should respond with a "pressure dropped" call although you will likely be able to feel the reduction. Actuate the release and immediately turn away to clear the towline and make it obvious a release has occurred.

Circuit Towing

Circuit towing involves towing in a circular or box pattern which is possible if the winds are light and you have a suitable tow field or series of compatible roads. Payout winches work best for circuit towing although a static towline can be used in very light winds. The glider should follow the tow vehicle, avoiding slack in the towline during turns by staying slightly to the outside. During turns the towline will lag the tow vehicle with a horizontal bow that is similar to the vertical bow during a straight tow. The pilot should ensure the towline remains square to the bridle and canopy while he lags the tow path. If an excessive bend occurs you should anticipate when it will start to pull straight and be in position to be square to the line. The tow operator can help remove line slack by momentary actuations of the rewind motor (doing so would first require dumping the brake pressure and then resetting it after the slack was removed).

Step Towing

Step towing is a technique possible with stationary winches in which maximum height is achieved by performing multiple tow runs. Instead of releasing when nearing the top of the tow, the pilot calls for a release in pressure and then turns downwind. The tow operator sets a low pressure to avoid getting slack in the line and the line pays out as the pilot flies downwind. In many situations the pilot is able to extend downwind past the starting point as long as he can ensure the rope will stay clear of any obstacles. In any case at no lower than 300 feet AGL he reverses his turn to face back into the wind. The tow operator then resets the tow pressure and resumes the tow. In light winds step towing can reach an altitude equal to the length of the tow field after three upwind segments.

Step towing is an advanced maneuver for both the pilot and tow operator. Proper communication is required for safe and proper step tows.

The Future Is Aerotow

Done properly, the concept of towing behind an aircraft offers many exciting possibilities. Instead of a long road that faces the prevailing wind and is free of obstacles and traffic, aerotowing requires only a suitably large field. In fact, the sport of hang gliding has seen the development of several commercial aerotow flight parks. Aerotow operations can normally better handle changes in wind direction, can tow to a higher altitudes, and – best of all – can tow you directly to a thermal! In recent years aerotowing has been used for major competitions as well as to set numerous world records.

There has been some experimentation with aerotowing of paragliders but the concept will not enjoy real success until a suitable tow aircraft is developed than can tow at the speeds appropriate for a paraglider with procedures that are safe and easy to use.

12

Tow Emergencies

Blown Launch

A botched inflation or trip during the launch run is of little consequence if the proper "go to cruise" (low tension and airspeed) procedure is used. With a winch the pilot should be able to simply sit down without fear of being dragged. During static line tows the driver must devote almost full attention to maintaining proper tension during the inflation and launch and must be prepared to stop or even back up if required.

Low Altitude Loss of Tension

This could be caused by a weaklink or line break, inadvertent release, or tow failure. You should always anticipate a sudden release, especially at low altitude. Keep your feet under you until you are safely climbing away and have sufficient time to get them back underneath you if required. If a sudden loss of tension occurs, brake aggressively to keep the canopy from surging significantly forward of vertical. Be ready to then reduce the brakes to transition to gliding flight.

Lockout

You can proactively avoid lockouts by proper control of tow tension and maintaining the towline square to the canopy. Failure to do so can cause a lockout and normal control can only be regained by an immediate reduction or release of tow force. Failure to recognize a low altitude lockout until after it has occurred can place the pilot in an extremely dangerous position from which recovery may not be possible. A competent tow operator can help remedy an incipient lockout with a timely dump in tow pressure, only increasing the pressure once the glider has regained proper orientation to the towline. Inexperienced tow pilots may fail to react in time or just plain freeze up, making a radio-equipped launch observer especially valuable.

Note: The use of checklists is required for towing due to the added complexity and reliance on others.

TOW DRIVER/OPERATOR PARAGLIDER LAUNCH CHECKLIST

1. Winch preflighted?

2. Are roles and responsibilities defined (driver, winch operator, observer)?

3. Hook knife for operator?

4. Communication checked and visual signals reviewed?

5. At "TAKE UP SLACK" command (pendulum swinging of flag below the waist), verify pressure is set for 20 lb. of tension. Drive forward until the rope is tight.

6. Traffic clear (road, spectators, sky)?

7. At "GO TO CRUISE" signal (waving of flag in a vertical half-circle) accelerate to 15-20 mph airspeed.

8. At "ACCELERATE" signal (swinging of flag in a vertical circle facing driver) accelerate to >25 mph airspeed and set tow pressure.

9. After a clean launch and with proper canopy position, accelerate to maximize the amount of line pay out during the first 2/3 of the tow run.

PARAGLIDER TOW LAUNCH CHECKLIST

1. HARNESS – leg, chest, cross-straps, speed stirrup, buckles, and reserve chute properly routed and secured?

2. RISERS – correctly attached to harness and without twists?

3. TOW BRIDLE – attached to harness correctly and symmetrically?

4. RELEASE MECHANISM – set correctly?

5. RELEASE LINE – properly routed and accessible?

6. RETRIEVAL CHUTE – stowed and connections correct?

7. SAFETY LINK – properly sized, routed, and in good condition?

8. HOOK KNIVES – available for both pilot and winch operator?

9. RISER AND TOGGLES – in pilot's hands without tangles?

10. PILOT CENTERED – in canopy?

11. LINES CLEAR – of harness, reserve chute, instruments, and feet?

12. TOWLINE LEADER – length correct for conditions?

13. TOWLINE ROUTED & PRE-TENSIONED correctly?

14. RADIOS checked?

15. COMMAND "TAKE UP SLACK" – Driver creeps forward to tension the line.

16. TRAFFIC clear – road, people, and sky?

17. WIND speed and direction acceptable?

18. COMMAND "GO TO CRUISE" & INFLATE THE CANOPY – driver sets 15-20 mph airspeed

19. COMMAND "ACCELERATE" – driver sets tow pressure & accelerates to > 25 mph airspeed

NOTES

12

QUIZ:

Label each of the tow signals below

NOTES

12

Chapter Thirteen:
MOTORIZED PARAGLIDING

AN INTRODUCTION TO THE LIGHTEST MANNED AIRCRAFT

— Jeff Goin, USPPA

Chapter 13 – MOTORIZED PARAGLIDING
AN INTRODUCTION TO THE LIGHTEST MANNED AIRCRAFT

With the addition of a motor and propeller you can turn a paraglider into a paramotor, a simple airplane with the capability to takeoff from level ground, climb thousands of feet and fly for miles on a small tank of gas. Do not be confused, however, by some high-end sports catalogues that tout motorized units to the general public as incredibly safe and easy to fly. In the right conditions, paramotoring can be a safe and enjoyable activity. It is, however, more complicated than simply adding a motor to your back. The weight, bulk, and torque effects of the paramotor change the way the glider launches, handles, and lands; it is not something to teach yourself. The exaggerated forward lean that is so important when launching a free flight paraglider changes with the addition of a motor since an upright upper body is required for proper thrust orientation (failure to remain upright when adding power will usually result in an immediate face plant). A novice paraglider pilot should be able to learn to fly a paramotor after only several hours of professional instruction.

Paramotors range in weight from under fifty pounds to nearly one hundred pounds. The larger models require unique harnesses to distribute the weight and thrust forces of the engine. The higher weight of the motor normally dictates a larger canopy than you would use for unpowered flight. In fact, there are paraglider canopies that have been designed specifically for paramotoring. Other common features of paramotor canopies is the addition of trimmers to the rear risers so that the torque of the propeller can be trimmed out.

Soaring flight is possible with the engine off or idling but it is unrealistic to expect the same level of soaring performance possible without the extra weight and drag. On good soaring days, however, the paramotor may be just the ticket to get you up to where you want to go.

Paramotoring Safety

A review of accidents and incidents in paramotoring reveal some common threads.

• Flat hatting accidents. Just like other forms of powered flight, too many accidents occur due to flying too low or doing aggressive maneuvering too close to the ground or water. Never fly at an altitude that you cannot glide to a safe landing in the event of a sudden loss of power. Never fly over water without proper flotation equipment (sufficient to maintain your head above the water without effort). Those with experience in single engine two-stroke aircraft know it is not a matter of if they will have a power failure, it is a matter of when so always leave yourself in a position to handle it. If you must fly low then remember that by flying into the wind you will slow your groundspeed, giving yourself more time to see hazards and making an immediate landing much less hazardous than if you were flying downwind. Remember, impact energy goes up with the square of your inertial velocity. If you are flying in only a ten mph wind and hit the ground flying downwind then you will impact with a minimum of four times the energy than if you were flying upwind. Low altitude downwind flight also increases your chances of trying to turn too hard to get back into the wind and losing climb performance due to the steep bank. The highest single risk for a fatal accident while paramotoring comes with extreme maneuvering close to the ground. The urge to showboat often goes hand in hand with the urge for low altitude flight. Many accidents have occurred due to pilots maneuvering hard in front of friends and family. Flying for a camera increases risk and the biggest red flag of all should be raised if you ever hear the infamous words "watch this!"

- Launch accidents. Numerous accidents have occurred due to pilots not having adequate clearance from upwind or nearby obstructions. The launch area should be smooth and offer good footing. A furrowed field may be perfectly suitable for tow launching but be too difficult to negotiate with eighty pounds on your back and 100 pounds of thrust. A simple misstep while launching a paramotor often ends with some degree of damage to the pilot or equipment.

—Jeff Goin, USPPA

- Landing accidents. A mistimed flare is usually not too big of a deal in paragliding but can easily lead to leg and back injuries due to the added weight of a paramotor. A paramotor pilot must also ensure he lands upright with the motor over his feet or else he will likely fall backwards and risk damaging the cage structure and propeller.

- Stalls. Trying to maximize climb performance means flying close to a stall. A sudden tailwind gust or even loss of headwind can be enough to cause a stall. Because the thrust line is so far below the canopy, adding or maintaining high thrust can aggravate the stall. Remember, if the wing is going back then your hands should go up and your power back. Add power judiciously once the wing is back overhead.

- Turbulence. Be especially cautious if your launch area is ringed with large trees or buildings that may block the surface wind but generate bad mechanical turbulence shortly after launch. Remember, flying low exposes you to low altitude turbulence such as wind shears and rotors as well as reduces your time available to deal with a problem. A simple rule-of-thumb is the slower your flying speed then the greater the amount of pilot judgment required to avoid hazardous weather. Avoid strong winds and turbulence by avoiding the heat of the day.

- Misjudging the climb gradient. Do not launch from a spot that you cannot safely do a rectangular pattern in while still maintaining a positive climb gradient. The difference between upwind and downwind climb gradients is dramatic on a paramotor. In a ten mph headwind, a paramotor that has a climb rate of only 300 fpm at 20 mph of airspeed will climb at an impressive 20° angle. If the same paramotor turns downwind the climb angle drops to less than 7°.

- Flying low also exposes you to the invisible but deadly hazard of power lines. If you maintain greater than 200 ft above the highest terrain then you will greatly reduce your chances of encountering an unseen wire. If you must cross power lines then fly directly over the towers (to ensure you don't encounter an unseen wire). If possible, plan to cross at a minimum of twice the height of the tower, perpendicular to the wires so as to minimize your exposure time.

- Serious cuts and partial finger amputations. A number of pilots have learned firsthand the hazard of a moment's inattention when reaching back to grab a brake handle or line that is in close proximity to a high-speed propeller. The cages surrounding the propeller are wrapped in netting that is designed to keep lines out of the prop. If you thrust your hand hard enough you can reach the spinning prop.

For additional information on paramotoring check out the United States Powered Paragliding Association at: http://www.usppa.org

— Jeff Goin, USPPA

NOTES

13

Chapter Fourteen:

STAYING LEGAL

PARAGLIDING & THE FAA; PILOT RATINGS & THE USHPA

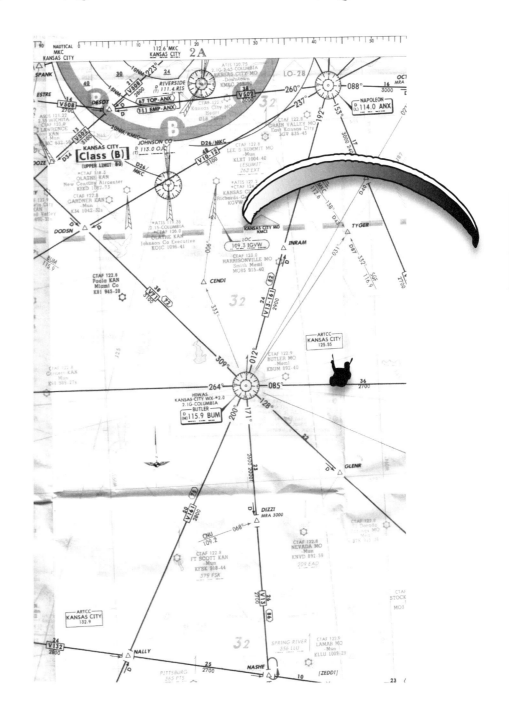

Chapter 14 — STAYING LEGAL

PARAGLIDING & THE FAA; PILOT RATINGS & THE USHPA

Paragliders, like hang gliders fit within the definition of an "ultralight vehicle" as contained in Federal Aviation Regulation (FAR) Part 103. Flight by ultralight vehicles in the United States is governed by FAR Part 103. Compared to the regulations governing other forms of aviation, Part 103 is brief and simple. Its essential effect is to leave ultralight flying largely self regulated. We are not required to have a pilot's license or medical certificate, and our aircraft don't need registrations or airworthiness certificates. FAR Part 103 does, however, prescribe certain restrictions by which we as ultralight pilots must abide. It is the responsibility of every paraglider, hang glider and powered ultralight pilot to familiarize himself with those regulations and fly in accordance with them in such a way as to protect our unique and privileged self regulated status.

The complete FAR Part 103 is contained in Appendix Two. A more simple paraphrased version follows:

1. Ultralights are not required to have and do not have any U.S. or foreign airworthiness certificate; and

    A. if unpowered, weigh less than 155 pounds; or

    B. if powered:

    1. weigh less than 254 pounds empty weight, excluding floats and safety devices which are intended for deployment in a potentially catastrophic situation (reserve parachutes);

    2. has a fuel capacity not exceeding 5 U.S. gallons;

    3. is not capable of more than 55 knots calibrated airspeed at full power in level flight;

    4. and has a power-off stall speed which does not exceed 24 knots calibrated airspeed.

2. They are to be flown single place. A USHPA exemption allows for USHPA Tandem Rated hang glider and paraglider pilots to operate hang gliders and paragliders tandem for instructional and recreational purposes. Without a

specific authorization to fly tandem from a recognized exemption holder, it is a violation of Federal Aviation Regulations to fly tandem.

3. They are to be used for recreation or sport purposes only. (No commercial operations, although instruction is not considered a commercial operation.)

4. No operation is permitted which creates a hazard to other persons or property (e.g. you cannot buzz bystanders or drop bricks on that annoying landowner's house).

5. They are restricted to daylight operation between the hours of sunrise and sunset except as follows:

A. They may be operated during the twilight periods 30 minutes before official sunrise and 30 minutes after official sunset or, in Alaska, during the period of civil twilight as defined in the Air Almanac, if:

1. the vehicle is equipped with an operating anti-collision light visible for at least 3 statute miles; and

2. all operations are conducted in uncontrolled airspace.

6. No operation is permitted over any congested area of a city, town, or settlement, or over any open air assembly of persons.

7. Each person operating an ultralight vehicle shall maintain vigilance so as to see and avoid aircraft and shall yield the right-of-way to all aircraft. No person may operate an ultralight vehicle in a manner that creates a collision hazard with respect to any aircraft. Powered ultralights shall yield the right-of-way to unpowered ultralights.

8. Operations are restricted in certain airspace, as specified below. In order to know where these airspace areas exist, you will need to refer to a Sectional Aeronautical Chart. Sectionals are published by the FAA, and show the locations of airports, air traffic routes, navigational aids, designated airspace areas and other information required by pilots for navigation and compliance with FAA regulations. They can be purchased from any pilot supply shop (usually located at or near airports that offer flight instruction). You can also find FAA aeronautical charts from several online sources. Some allow you to use small portions of the charts at no charge (e.g. SkyVector.com).

14

The national airspace system is broken into "classes" of airspace according to the types of operations expected to be conducted therein. The majority of airspace is "controlled airspace" meaning air traffic control services are available. In addition to a radio, an air traffic controller requires either a radar or a visual on the aircraft that he's controlling. Therefor uncontrolled airspace is limited to low altitude rural areas or desolate mountainous regions in the western U.S. Controlled airspace is broken into classes from "A" to "E". Uncontrolled airspace is called Class G airspace. (There is no Class F airspace in the U.S.)

a. Class A airspace is all airspace over the continental U.S. and Alaska from 18,000 feet above sea level on up (to 60,000 feet). Since Class A airspace is normally well above the altitudes of a typical paraglider flight, an easy way to remember it is to think of "A for above." This area is restricted to air traffic flying under instrument flight rules. Think of it as the high altitude sanctuary where only airliners tread. A paraglider may not enter Class A airspace without prior permission from the controlling agency. On occasion, major competitions located in mountainous areas known for "big air" secure permission to use a small box of Class A airspace overlying the competition area. Do not forget your oxygen!

b. Class B airspace is the big daddy of low altitude controlled airspace; it surrounds the nation's busiest airports like Los Angeles International (KLAX), and is indicated on a sectional by a circular series of solid blue lines. Think "B for big city airports." Class B airspace is shaped something like an inverted wedding cake (though the areas are not necessarily regular cylinders); the central core extends all the way from the top to the surface, but the outer areas only include the higher altitudes. Each Class B is tailored for the specific airport but a typical Class B ceiling is 10,000 ft MSL and the radius of the outer ring around 20 miles. The floor and ceiling altitudes (in hundreds of feet) are indicated as fractions in blue numbers for each sector. For example, 100/70 means that section of airspace has a ceiling of 10,000 ft MSL and a floor of 7,000 ft MSL. A paraglider may not enter Class B Airspace without prior permission from the controlling agency. A paraglider may, however, legally fly underneath an outer ring of a Class B airspace. (It might not be the wisest thing to do but it is legal.) Class B airports have a continuous stream of major airliners entering and leaving. Unauthorized entry into Class B airspace is dangerous and will subject the violator to severe penalties and jeopardize nearby flying sites. In some situations a paraglider may even be able to climb over the top of a corner of Class B airspace. This should only be done with extreme caution and exact knowledge (aviation GPS recommended) of the airspace. Do not forget paragliders are not allowed to operate over congested areas. Urban areas are depicted as bright yellow areas on sectionals – probably a good rule-of-thumb for a congested area.

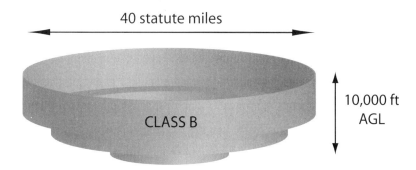

c. Class C airspace surrounds airports that service medium-sized cities such as Santa Barbara, CA (KSBA). Think of it as a scaled down Class B. The airspace is designated by concentric magenta lines, usually basically circular with some alterations. The airspace extends down to the surface in the central core, but only down to some specific altitude in the outer ring. The top of Class C airspace is normally 4000 feet above the ground and the floor of the outer ring is normally 1200 ft AGL. These altitudes are depicted in MSL as magenta fractions on the sectional. A paraglider may not enter Class C Airspace without prior permission from the controlling agency.

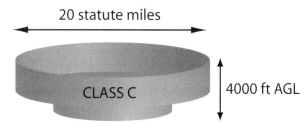

d. Class D airspace is a volume of airspace around smaller airports (but large enough to warrant control towers). An example is Bakersfield, CA (KBFL). The airspace extends from the surface to [normally] 2,500 feet above the ground. The ceiling, in hundreds of feet, is indicated by a number within a dashed box. Class D airspace is depicted on a sectional by a dashed blue circle with a 5 mile radius. There is sometimes an extension on one side (to serve as a corridor for arriving aircraft), so the shape looks somewhat like a keyhole. A paraglider may not enter Class D Airspace without prior permission from the controlling agency. Think "D for dinky" towns.

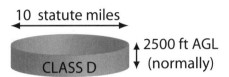

e. Class E airspace is controlled airspace that falls outside of all the other types of controlled airspace. In layman's terms it is the majority of our airspace below 18,000 ft. Think of "E for everywhere else." Class E airspace normally extends upwards from low altitude until it hits a more stringent class of airspace. The normal floor is 1,200 ft AGL and it is not depicted on sectionals unless it abuts uncontrolled airspace. Near small airports (without control towers) the floor may be 700 ft or even extend to the surface. In some mountainous regions the floor may be referenced to MSL altitudes and might be as high as 14,500 ft. The depiction of Class E airspace boundaries is one of the most confusing aspects of reading a sectional chart. (Thankfully, it's also about the least important part of reading a sectional!) Changes in the floor boundaries are normally shown with broad lines, magenta for 700 ft AGL and blue for 1,200 ft AGL (the lower floor is the fuzzy side of the line). Floors that reference MSL are depicted by a staggered blue line. For an example look just north of Chico, CA (KCIC). With one exception, there is no prohibition against our operating in Class E airspace. The exception is FAR 103.17 which prohibits operating within the "lateral boundaries of the surface area of Class E airspace designated for an airport unless that person has prior authorization..." Airports that only have Class E surface areas depict that area similar to Class D airspace (except it is a dashed magenta line, not blue).

f. A Prohibited or a Restricted Area. Prohibited areas and restricted areas are shown on the sectional as generally rectangular areas bordered by a solid thin blue line, the inside of which is bordered by short diagonal blue hash marks, and are labeled as "Restricted" or "Prohibited." Restricted areas are generally connected with hazardous military operations. A paraglider may not enter a prohibited or restricted area without prior permission from the controlling agency. Many restricted airspaces are not continuously active. If the airspace is "cold" then ultralights may be able to transit the airspace. Contact the nearest FSS for the status of such areas.

g. Wildlife and recreational areas are depicted by blue lines with an inner dotted boundary. All aircraft are requested to remain outside of 2,000 ft AGL or 2,000 ft laterally from terrain. Such areas can range from National Parks where launching or landing is expressly forbidden without permission to less known areas where the rangers may help you launch!

h. National Security Areas are small areas depicted by a dashed magenta line and are usually located around nuclear or weapons storage facilities. Sectionals depict the airspace with a note requesting aircraft avoid overflying below a specified altitude.

i. Ultralight aircraft cannot operate in certain areas designated by NOTAMs, or Notices to Airmen, which designate a temporary flight restriction (TFR) in an area where special operations are occurring. Examples include space flight operations, where the U.S. president is traveling, fire fighting operations, and even sporting events. You can find out about such NOTAMS in your flying area by contacting an FAA Flight Service Station by telephone. You should specifically ask for NOTAMs and TFRs that affect part 103 operations. A paraglider may not operate in such airspace without a specific waiver or prior permission from the approving agency.

j. Military Operating Areas (MOA) and Alert areas are volumes of airspace that the military uses for high intensity flight operations. Unlike Restricted and Prohibited areas, civilian aircraft, including ultralights can legally fly in a MOA or Alert area. A MOA is depicted on a sectional by a magenta line ringed internally with hashed lines. Much of California's famous Owens Valley XC route lies within MOA airspace (which is also Restricted airspace above 18,000 ft MSL). Like Restricted and Prohibited airspace, an alert area is depicted in blue but with the letter "A". You can check the status of these areas by calling a FSS.

9. You must operate only with visual reference to the surface; i.e. you must be able to see the ground.

10. You must maintain the standard Visual Flight Rules visibilities and clearances from clouds, as given below:

AIRSPACE	FLIGHT VISIBILITY	DISTANCE FROM CLOUDS
CLASS A	NOT APPLICABLE	NOT APPLICABLE
CLASS B	3 STATUTE MILES	CLEAR OF CLOUDS
CLASS C	3 STATUTE MILES	500 FT BELOW, 1000 FT ABOVE, 2000 FT HORIZONTAL
CLASS D	3 STATUTE MILES	500 FT BELOW, 1000 FT ABOVE, 2000 FT HORIZONTAL
CLASS E BELOW 10,000 FT MSL	3 STATUTE MILES	1000 FT BELOW, 1000 FT ABOVE, 2000 FT HORIZONTAL
CLASS E ABOVE 10,000 FT MSL	5 STATUTE MILES	1000 FT BELOW, 1000 FT ABOVE, 1 STATUTE MILE HORIZONTAL
CLASS G 1200 FT OR LESS AGL	1 STATUTE MILE	CLEAR OF CLOUDS
CLASS G MORE THAN 1200 FT AGL AND LESS THAN 10,000 FT MSL	1 STATUTE MILE	500 FT BELOW, 1000 FT ABOVE, 2000 FT HORIZONTAL
CLASS G MORE THAN 1200 FT AGL AND MORE THAN 10,000 FT MSL	5 STATUTE MILES	1000 FT BELOW, 1000 FT ABOVE, 1 STATUTE MILE HORIZONTAL

As we have said, paragliders are in no way prohibited from operating in controlled airspace but flying in controlled airspace that is not Class E airspace requires permission from the controlling agency. The only practical affect of flying in controlled airspace is that the visibility and cloud clearance requirements, as stated above, become more restrictive. The prohibitions for certain specific airspace areas above have nothing to do with the concept of "controlled airspace." It is possible to use a sectional to determine what airspace regions are controlled and which are uncontrolled, although it is not readily apparent on the sectional. For more information on controlled airspace and FAA regulations in general, we recommend that you obtain a copy of the current FAR's and the Airman's Information Manual (both come in one book) at a pilot's supply shop. You can also see the current part 103 regulations online at either the FAA or USHPA websites.

Pilot Ratings and Legal Regulation of Flying Sites

While paraglider and hang glider pilots are not required to have FAA issued pilot licenses, there are pilot skill rating programs administered hang glider pilots and paraglider pilots by the United States Hang gliding and Paragliding Association. In many areas, the use of flying sites is under arrangement with a local, state, or federal governmental agency. In such a case the local hang gliding or paragliding club which administers the site will have a requirement that the pilot possess a specific rating in order to fly the site, and such a requirement will carry the force of law.

Pilots are encouraged to join the USHPA and obtain pilot ratings as they progress through the sport. The USHPA Paraglider Pilot Rating System is included as an appendix in the rear of this manual.

Torrey Pines Gliderport is a regulated site. Paraglider pilots must be a current USHPA member with an intermediate rating. The launch site (delineated on the sectional by a glider symbol with an "H") lies within the lateral boundaries of the San Diego Class B airspace. How high can the paragliders legally fly over launch?

Answer: The Class B airspace overlying the launch site is the long, diamond shaped area defined by the broad, dark gray line (blue on an actual sectional chart). As per the boxed fractional numbers above the area, which are associated with the dotted line ending in an arrowhead, this space has a floor of 1800 ft MSL - which means about 1400 feet above the cliff top. It is unique in that there is a corridor between 3,200 ft MSL and 6,800 ft MSL where it would also be legal to fly to a paraglider (assuming you had a way to get into that space without passing through the space below it, and that you had a way to maintain that altitude).

NOTES

14

USHPA PROFICIENCY RATING SYSTEM

PARAGLIDER PILOT RATING STANDARDS

UNITED STATES HANG GLIDING ASSOCIATION, INC.

This Certifies that LAURENCE D ARVADA
9723 W 83RD AVE
ARVADA CO 80005

is a full member and is rated as a _Advanced PG_ pilot

By: W LAURENCE Date: 08/08/65 USHGA# 58959

Special Skills:

Ratings: FL TOW TANDEM 1-FL

Appointments:

REG-04

01/31/10

Expiration Date

Rating System - Pilot Proficiency System - SOP 12-2   Revised 06/06

United States Hang Gliding and Paragliding Association, Inc.
Standard Operating Procedures - 12-2

PART 104 - PILOT PROFICIENCY SYSTEM

INTRODUCTION

USHGA pilot ratings are issued to reflect completion of WITNESSED tasks. Some tasks may seem to require excessive precision or attention to detail, but the practice preparing for them will prove beneficial. A rating gives a pilot an introduction to local people at a different site. Flying sites are labeled according to the approximate skill level required to fly there safely. A pilot may fly the hill only if the local people feel he is capable of doing so. *It is recommended that all pilots maintain a flight log.*

104.01 - ADMINISTRATION

A. Administration Procedures

1) Flights offered in evidence of a skill must have been made in accordance with regulations and requirements of the USHGA in effect at the time of the flight.

2) Ratings shall be obtained in order, starting with the Beginner Rating, and each assumes the applicant has the ability to perform the tasks required by all lower ratings. Beginner and Novice ratings may be issued simultaneously.

3) Ratings Beginner and Novice may be issued by the USHGA upon recommendation of USHGA Basic or Advanced Instructors. The Instructor shall provide the applicant with a rating application, a standard USHGA rating application waiver, and a 30-day temporary rating from the application. The applicant shall send the signed application, the required application fee, and the completed waiver to USHGA Headquarters and provided that all the requirements are met, the USHGA shall issue a permanent rating.

4) Ratings Intermediate and Advanced may be issued by the USHGA upon recommendation of USHGA Observers and Advanced Instructors. The Observer or Instructor shall provide the applicant with a rating application, a standard USHGA rating application waiver, and a 30-day temporary rating from the application. The applicant shall send the signed application, the required application fee, and the completed waiver to USHGA Headquarters and provided that all the requirements are met, the USHGA shall issue a permanent rating.

5) Master ratings may be issued by the USHGA upon recommendation of USHGA Regional Directors. The applicant shall send the signed application form, the required application fee, and the completed waiver to USHGA Headquarters and provided that all the requirements are met, the USHGA shall issue a permanent rating.

6) Examiners may recommend applicants for the Instructor Certification Program, may appoint Observers and may recommend Advanced Pilots for the Master Rating. All recommendations are submitted to the USHGA office.

7) All pilots applying for ratings MUST be current Full Members of USHGA.

8) Before the USHGA issues any rating, and as a condition precedent to the issuance of any rating, the applicant must agree to all the provisions of the USHGA standard waiver and assumption of risk agreement and deliver an original signed copy to the USHGA office.

104.02 RATING FILING FEES: *Effective June 1, 2004*

A. Rating Fees

Fees are collected for each level of rating, to cover administrative costs.

1. Beginner (H-1, P-1)	-- $ 15.00, payable to USHGA
2. Novice (H-2, P-2)	-- $ 15.00, payable to USHGA
3. Intermediate (H-3, P-3)	-- $ 15.00, payable to USHGA
4. Advanced (H-4, P-4)	-- $ 15.00, payable to USHGA
5. Master (H-5, P-5)	-- $ 15.00, payable to USHGA
6. Tandem I	-- $ 15.00, payable to USHGA
7. Tandem II	-- $ 15.00, payable to USHGA
8. Basic Instructor	-- $ 15.00, payable to USHGA
9. Advanced Instructor	-- $ 15.00, payable to USHGA
10. Tandem Instructor	-- $ 15.00, payable to USHGA
11. Instructor Re-certification	-- $ 15.00, payable to USHGA
12. Portable Radio Authorization (PA)	-- $ 15.00, payable to USHGA
13. Vehicular Radio Authorization (VA)	-- $ 15.00, payable to USHGA
14. Aero Tow Tug Pilot (ATP)	-- $ 15.00, payable to USHGA

104.03 - RATING REQUIREMENTS

General Information - Launch Skill Requirement - Foot Launch and/or Tow Launch

A USHGA rated pilot must be rated for **at least one Launch Skill**, either Foot Launch (FL) or one of the tow launch methods, and may be rated for both. The holding of a tow launch method does not give the skills necessary to operate a tow system. The operation of a tow system is a difficult and demanding task requiring special training. A pilot is not rated for aero towing behind a flying tow vehicle without an *AEROTOW Special Skill signoff.*

Code	Name	Rating Class	Rating or Skill
AWCL	Assisted Windy Cliff	Solo	Special Skill
CL	Cliff Launch	Solo	Special Skill
FL	Foot Launch	Solo	Special Skill
FSL	Flat Slope Launch	Solo	Special Skill
HA	High Altitude Launch	Solo	Special Skill
P-1	Beginner	Solo	Rating
P-2	Novice	Solo	Rating
P-3	Intermediate	Solo	Rating
P-4	Advanced	Solo	Rating
P-5	Master	Solo	Rating
PS	Para-Ski	Solo	Special Skill
RLF	Restricted Landing Field	Solo	Special Skill
RS	Ridge Soaring	Solo	Special Skill
ST	Surface Tow	Solo	Special Skill
T-1	Tandem 1	Tandem	Rating
T-2	Tandem 2	Tandem	Rating
TFL	Tandem Foot Launch	Tandem	Special Skill
TST	Tandem Surface Tow	Tandem	Special Skill
TUR	Turbulence	Solo	Special Skill
X-C	Cross Country	Solo	Special Skill

A1

Appendix 1: USHPA PARAGLIDER PILOT RATING SYSTEM

104.13 BEGINNER PARAGLIDING RATINGS

General Description

A Beginner pilot has the knowledge and basic skills necessary to fly and practice under direct instructor supervision and within significant operating limitations. The pilot understands the USHGA paragliding rating systems and recommended operating limitations.

13.01 Beginner Rating - Required Witnessed Tasks

A. Attends and completes a basic ground school.
B. Layout and preflight of canopy and harness.
C. Demonstrates canopy handling skills sufficient to launch - under control.
D. With each flight, demonstrate method(s) of establishing that pilot is properly connected to the canopy, with cleared lines and risers, just prior to inflation.
E. Launch unassisted showing:

   1. Aggressive inflation and run.
   2. Pendulum control during launch.
   3. Directional control.
   4. Smooth transition from running to flying, during launch.

F. Airspeed recognition and control,

   1. Two flights, predetermined to show:
      a. Constant airspeed.
      b. Smooth straight flight.
      c. Safe, smooth landing, on feet, into wind.

   2. Two flights, predetermined to show:
      a. Confident, slight variation in airspeed showing awareness of control inputs and pendulum control.
      b. Smoothly increasing airspeed, and smoothly slowing airspeed showing good control.
      c. Safe, smooth landing, on feet, into wind.

G. Shows the ability to recognize and understand how different wind conditions at this site will affect their flights.

   1. Wind direction.
   2. Wind velocity.
   3. Terrain shape.
   4. Obstructions.

H. On each flight, demonstrates proper post-landing procedure, to include, but not limited to:

   1. Canopy deflation.
   2. Canopy immobilization.
   3. Checking traffic.
   4. Removal of canopy from landing area.
   5. Disconnection from the canopy.

Reprinted with permission of the United States Hang Gliding and Paragliding Association

I. Demonstration of understanding of the importance of proper packing, storage, and care of the canopy.
J. Has read and understands USHGA statements regarding good judgment and maturity.
K. Must pass the USHGA Beginner Paragliding written exam.
L. Must agree to all the provisions of the USHGA standard waiver and assumption of risk agreement for the Beginner rating and deliver an original signed copy to the USHGA office.

13.03 Recommended Operating Limitations for Beginner Pilots:

A. Should exceed these limitations only after demonstrating complete mastery of the required Beginner paragliding tasks (above), and only after acquiring a full understanding of the potential problems and dangerous situations which may arise from exceeding these limitations.
B. All flights be made under the direct supervision of a USHGA Certified Basic or Advanced Paragliding Instructor.
C. Should fly only in steady winds of 12 m.p.h. or less.
D. If foot launching, should only foot launch only on slopes of 3:1 - 4:1, where wind is within 15° of being straight up the slope.
E. Should launch only when there are no obstructions within 60° to either side of the intended flight path.
F. Should fly appropriate sites for this skill level.
G. Should fly a canopy recommended by the manufacturer as suitable for Beginner or Novice pilots.

104.14 - NOVICE PARAGLIDING RATING

General Description

A Novice paraglider pilot has the knowledge and basic skills necessary to fly and practice without direct instructor supervision but within significant operating limitations. The pilot understands the USHGA paragliding rating systems and recommended operating limitations.

The pilot shall use good judgment and have a level of maturity commensurate with the rating. Pilots must demonstrate Beginner level skills and knowledge before obtaining the Novice rating. All witnessed flights must be pre-planned by the pilot and discussed with the Instructor or specially qualified Observer.

14.01 Novice Rating - Required Witnessed Tasks

A. Logged Requirements

1. Attends a minimum of 8 hours of ground school.
2. 25 flights. At the discretion of any paragliding instructor or special observer, powered paragliding flights can be used to fulfill this requirement. Use of a powered paraglider to demonstrate the required witnessed tasks is allowed, as long as the engine is stopped at no lower than 200 feet AGL and remains off.
3. 5 flying days.

B. Demonstrated Skills and Knowledge

Reprinted with permission of the United States Hang Gliding and Paragliding Association

1. Demonstrates layout and preflight of the canopy, harness, and backup reserve parachute.
2. Gives a reliable analysis of general conditions of the site and self, and a flight plan including flight path, areas to avoid in relation to the wind flow, and obstacles to stay clear of.
3. Demonstrates 5 consecutive forward inflations with a visual check of the canopy each time.
4. Demonstrates 5 consecutive controlled reverse inflations with proper surge dampening.
5. Demonstrates controlled kiting of a glider overhead for 2 minutes in a steady wind.
6. Demonstrates 2 clean, smooth reverse inflations/reversals prior to launch.
7. With each flight, demonstrates a method of establishing that the pilot is properly connected to the glider, with cleared lines and risers just prior to inflation.
8. Demonstrates 2 successful, aggressive, confident inflations/launches, where the wind is at least 15° cross to straight up the hill in wind not exceeding 5 m.p.h.
9. Demonstrates 2 no-wind (0-5 m.p.h.) inflations/launches.
10. Demonstrate how to brief and instruct a ground crew and explain when an assisted launch is necessary.
11. Demonstrates 2 high-wind (10-15 m.p.h.) inflations/launches.
12. Demonstrates flight with smooth variation in airspeed, from above minimum sink to fast flight, while maintaining a heading.
13. Demonstrates flight showing the ability to comfortably and precisely slow the glider to minimum sink and smoothly increase to normal airspeed while maintaining a heading. The pilot should not slow the glider to near the stall speed.
14. Demonstrates flight(s) along a planned path alternating 'S' turns of at least 90° change in heading. Flight heading need not exceed 45° from straight into the wind. Turns must be smooth with controlled airspeed, ending in safe, stand up landings on a heading.
15. Demonstrates 360-degree turns in both directions, and at various speeds and bank angles.
16. Demonstrates hands-off flying, one handed flying skills, weight-shift turns, and rear-riser turns.
17. Demonstrates symmetric and asymmetric tip folds for increased descent rate.
18. Demonstrates the ability to judge and allow for proper clearance from a ridge and other aircraft.
19. Demonstrates 5 landings within 25' of a target, safe, smooth, on the feet and into the wind. The target must be sufficiently close to launch such that turns are required to set up an approach and avoid over-flying the target. The target should be at least 100' below the launch point.
20. Explains proper strong wind landing procedures and how to keep from being dragged back.
21. Explains correct canopy maintenance.
22. Explains how to lengthen and shorten the flight path.
23. Explains the right of way traffic rules.
24. Explains the use of a speedbar/accelerating system.
25. Demonstrates reserve deployment while hanging in a harness in simulated turbulence or malfunction conditions.
26. Gives a thorough verbal demonstration of knowledge of how to:

    a. Maintain directional control during and correct for an asymmetric wing fold of 25% of the wing span.
    d. Fly at minimum sink while precluding any chance of inadvertent stall or spin.
    e. Increase descent rate and/or forward speed.

27. Demonstrates proper and effective PLF technique.
28. Must pass the USHGA Novice Paragliding written exam.
29. Must agree to all the provisions of the USHGA standard waiver and assumption of risk agreement for the Novice rating and deliver an original signed copy to the USHGA office.

30. Acknowledges and understands the need to become familiar with site-specific restrictions and launch or landing access limits, consistent with preservation of flying privileges at a site.

14.03 Recommended Operating Limitations for Novice Paragliding Pilots

A. Should exceed these limitations only after thoroughly mastering all required tasks, and after acquiring a full understanding of the potential problems and dangers involved in exceeding these limitations.
B. Maximum base wind of 12 m.p.h.
C. Maximum peak gusts to 15 m.p.h.
D. Maximum gust rate of 5 m.p.h. in 5 seconds.
E. Should not fly in thermal lift where peak climb rates exceed 200 fpm.
F. If foot launching, should launch only on slopes steeper than 4:1, where the wind is within 25° of being straight up the slope.
G. Visual contact with the landing zone.
H. Avoid application of either brake beyond 2/3 of the way from slack to stall position.
I. Limit turns to 30° of bank, limit speed in turns to 1.5 times the straight line, brakes off, cruise speed, and smoothly exit any spiral turn which shows a tendency to steepen or accelerate.
J. Should fly a canopy recommended by the manufacturer as suitable for Beginner to Intermediate pilots.

104.15 - INTERMEDIATE PARAGLIDING RATING

General Description

The pilot has the knowledge and skills to fly most sites in mild to moderate soaring conditions, and to judge when the site and conditions are within the pilot's skill, knowledge, and experience level. The pilot understands the USHGA paragliding rating system as recommended operating limitations, and the FARs and other flying rules applicable to his/her flying (ridge rules, thermal right of way, FAR 103, aircraft sectional use and regulated airspace avoidance, etc.).

The pilot shall use good judgment and have a level of maturity commensurate with the rating.

15.01 Intermediate Rating - Required Witnessed Tasks

A. Logged Requirements

1. Must have logged a minimum of 30 flying days.
2. Must have logged a total of at least 90 flights.
3. Must have logged a minimum of 20 hours of solo airtime.

B. Demonstrated Skills and Knowledge

1. Has received training in and/or understands the importance and significance of:

a. Right of way rules.
b. FAA Regulations and aircraft sectional charts
c. Airspeed control, stalls, spins, and turbulence-induced collapses and recoveries.
d. Canopy owner's manual.

Reprinted with permission of the United States Hang Gliding and Paragliding Association

A1

Appendix 1: USHPA PARAGLIDER PILOT RATING SYSTEM

  e. USHGA Accident Report results currently in print.

2. Can give verbal analysis of conditions on the hill, demonstrating knowledge of wind shadows, gradients, lift, sink, laminar air, turbulence and rotors, and the effect these items have on an intended flight path and turns.

3. Must give a verbal flight plan for each observed flight.

4. Must show thorough preflight of the harness, canopy, and backup reserve parachute.

5. With each flight, demonstrates a method of establishing that the pilot is properly connected to the glider, with cleared lines and risers just prior to launch.

6. All inflations/launches should be aggressive, confident, and with a smooth transition from running to flying. Flights with slow, unstable inflations/launches will not be considered adequate for witnessed tasks.

7. For witnessed tasks, all landings must be safe, smooth, on the feet, and in control.

8. Demonstrates the ability to differentiate airspeed from ground speed.

9. Demonstrates linked 180° turns along a predetermined ground track showing smooth controlled reversals and proper coordination at various speeds and bank angles.

10. Demonstrates 360° turns in both directions, and at various speeds and bank angles.

11. Demonstrates symmetric and asymmetric tip folds (25% per side, 50% total) or some other method of canopy reduction for increased descent rate.

12. Demonstrates one method to increase forward speed.

13. Demonstrates proper surge control of canopy using properly timed brake application.

14. Gives a thorough verbal description of how to maintain directional control during and correct for an 50% asymmetric wing collapse.

15. Explains characteristics of impending stall and impending spin.

16. In 8 to 15 m.p.h. winds, demonstrates the ability to maintain airspeed at or near minimum sink during crosswind and upwind legs, without any evidence of stalls.

17. Demonstrates 5 landings within 10' of a spot after flights requiring turns on approach.

18. Demonstrates proper airspeed control on landing approach when descending through a gradient.

19. Demonstrates proper airspeed for maximum distance flown into a significant headwind.

20. Demonstrates complete understanding of all Paragliding Tow Discussion Topics (for tow rated pilots only).

21. Must pass the USHGA Intermediate Paragliding written exam.

22. Must agree to all the provisions of the USHGA standard waiver and assumption of risk agreement for the Intermediate rating and deliver an original signed copy to the USHGA office.

23. Acknowledges and understands the need to become familiar with site-specific restrictions and launch or landing access limits, consistent with preservation of flying privileges at a site.

15.02 Recommended Operating Limitations for Intermediate Paraglider Pilots

A. Maximum base wind of 15 m.p.h.

B. Maximum peak gusts to 18 m.p.h.

C. Maximum gust rate of 5 m.p.h. in 5 seconds.

D. Avoid steep turns close to the ground.

E. Avoid application of either brake beyond 3/4 of the way from full off to stall position.

F. Limit turns to bank angles recommended by the manufacturer, limit speed in turns to 2 times the straight line, brakes off, cruise speed, and smoothly exit any spiral turn that shows a tendency to steepen or accelerate.

G. Should initiate downwind turns only with 300' of clearance outward from the hill or ridge in winds above 15 m.p.h., and 200' of clearance in winds above 10 m.p.h.

Reprinted with permission of the United States Hang Gliding and Paragliding Association

H. Should not fly in thermals where peak climb rates exceed 500 fpm or where significant vertical cloud development exists.

I. Upon mastering the above skills, an Intermediate Paragliding Pilot should pursue new maneuvers, sites, and conditions with the guidance of a USHGA Certified Advanced Paragliding Instructor or Observer.

104.16 - ADVANCED PARAGLIDING RATING

General Description

The pilot has the knowledge and skills to fly technically demanding sites in strong soaring conditions, and to judge when the site and conditions are within the pilot's skill, knowledge, and experience level. The pilot understands the USHGA paragliding rating system and recommended operating limitations, and the FARs and other flying rules applicable to his/her flying.

The pilot will fly using good judgment and have a level of maturity commensurate with the rating.

16.01 Advanced Rating - Required Witnessed Tasks

A. Logged Requirements

1. 250 flights.
2. Must have made 5 flights at each of 5 different sites in Intermediate level conditions, of which 3 were inland.
3. Must have logged a minimum of 80 flying days.
4. Must have at least three, 1-hour flights in thermal lift without sustaining ridge lift. Flights must originate from at least two different sites in Intermediate level conditions.
5. Must have at least one, 1-hour flight in ridge lift without sustaining thermal lift.
6. Must have logged a minimum of 75 hours total airtime, with no more than 25 of these hours to be tandem. Of these 75 hours, 25 must be in thermal lift, with no more than 10 of these 25 hours to be tandem flights.
7. Must have flown a minimum of 5 different canopies.

B. Demonstrated Skills and Knowledge

1. Preflight of the harness, canopy, and backup reserve parachute.
2. Verbal analysis of conditions.
3. Flight plan.
4. With each flight, demonstrates a method of establishing that the pilot is properly connected to the glider, with cleared lines and risers just prior to launch.
5. All inflations/launches should be aggressive, confident, and with a smooth transition from running to flying. Flights with slow, unstable inflations/launches will not be considered adequate as witnessed tasks.
6. All landings must be safe, smooth, on the feet and in control.
7. Demonstrate ability to allow clearance when doing 360 degree turns by demonstrating figure eights:

a. In a wind sufficient to cause drift, two points will be selected on a line perpendicular to the wind.
b. The pilot will fly along a line parallel to that joining the pylons, slightly downwind of the

Reprinted with permission of the United States Hang Gliding and Paragliding Association

PARAGLIDING: A Pilot's Training Manual   **287**

pylons, toward a point midway between them. During the crosswind leg, the pilot will establish the degree of wind drift. At the midpoint between the pylons, the pilot will make a smooth, deliberate upwind turn and enter a figure eight course consisting of smooth turns of constant ground track radius around the pylons (centered on the pylons) with straight segments at the midpoint between the pylons.

   c. The pilot must complete two consecutive figure eights in which the airspeed, bank angle, and turn rate are altered smoothly around the course such that the proper ground track is held and the drift is compensated for, without overcompensation or hesitation.

8. Demonstrate three consecutive spot landings within 10' of a target after a flight which requires turns on approach. In smooth conditions, the spot location should be changed by the Observer, for each of the three flights. Flights should be a minimum of one minute and 200' AGL.

9. Demonstrate smooth coordinated 360 degree turns in both directions, with reversal at various speeds and bank angles appropriate to the rating level.

10. Demonstrates significant asymmetric wing collapses (50% of the wing span) with directional control.

11. Demonstrates complete understanding of all Paragliding Tow Discussion Topics (for tow rated pilots only).

12. Must pass the USHGA Advanced Paragliding written exam.

13. Must convince the Instructor or Observer that he can check in and fly Advanced rated sites without endangering spectators, other pilots, or jeopardizing the site.

14. Must agree to all the provisions of the USHGA standard waiver and assumption of risk agreement for the Advanced rating and deliver an original signed copy to the USHGA office.

16.02 Recommended Operating Limitations for Advanced Paraglider Pilots

   A. Should not fly within 30' of another glider in smooth air, or within 100' of another glider in moderately turbulent air.

104.17 - MASTER PARAGLIDING RATING

General Description

For pilots who wish to further diversify their skills in the sport of paragliding, and to recognize the achievement of the expert skilled pilot who has experience beyond the Advanced level, there is a designation of Master Pilot. No site will be designated as requiring Master skills. The pilot will fly using good judgment and have a level of maturity commensurate with the rating.

17.01 Master Rating - Required Witnessed Tasks

   A. Logged Requirements
      1. Must be a current USHGA Full Member.
      2. Must have all Special Skills witnessed except Para Ski (PS).
      3. Must have a minimum of 1,450 points in at least 6 categories (see chart below). Must have a minimum of 400 hours airtime with at least 200 hours in thermals, and at least 500 logged flights.
      4. Must obtain at least 3 letters of recommendation from USHGA Paragliding Observers, Examiners, or Advance Instructors, who will attest to the flying requirements and especially the good judgment and maturity of the applicant. If these officials have not seen the applicant flying for this 3 year period, additional letters of recommendation must be presented so that the 3 year block of time is covered.

A1

5   Must possess the Bronze Safe Pilot Award (100 flights; there are no points given for this).

CATEGORIES	POINTS	MAXIMUM POINTS ALLOWED
Air time (min. 400 hrs.)	1 pt./hr. (beyond 400 hrs required airtime)	350
No. of flights (Min. 500 flts. 250 must be foot launched)	1 pt./flt. (beyond required 500 flts)	250
Altitude Gains (Only one altitude gain may be used from each flight)	10 pts./2,000' gain 15 pts./3,000' gain 20 pts./4,000' gain 25 pts./5,000' gain 30 pts./6,000' gain	350
Cross Country (10 mi. min. flts.)	1 pt./mi	350
Number of different sites flown	10 pts./site	300
Number of different gliders flown	5 pts./glider	150
Competition	10 pts./fifth 20 pts./fourth 30 pts./third 40 pts./second 50 pts./first	100
Tandem (As pilot in command)	10 pts./flight	100
Towing (Payout Reel, Stationary Winch, Static Line)	5 pts./flight (50 pts. in each of the possible categories)	100

B. The pilot is to present documentation of flight experience, to meet the 1,450 point minimum, to his Regional Director, who confirms completion of the requirements. The Director then approves or denies the application. If the application is denied, the pilot may appeal the denial to the USHGA Board of Directors. A two-thirds vote of the Board is required to uphold the appeal. A Regional Director's award of a Master designation may be rescinded by a two-thirds vote of the Board.

C. Must agree to all the provisions of the USHGA standard waiver and assumption of risk agreement for the Master rating and deliver an original signed copy to the USHGA office.

104.18 - PARAGLIDING SPECIAL SKILL ENDORSEMENTS

A. Special Skills attainable by Novice and above.

1.   Ridge Soaring (RS):

A1

    a. Demonstrates the ability to kite and launch safely on a slope producing sustainable ridge lift

    b. Demonstrates the ability to fly a standard traffic pattern in both isolated and traffic conditions, illustrating the ability to communicate properly with other pilots in the pattern.

    c. Demonstrates the ability to soar in a crosswind without stalling on downwind legs, and demonstrates the ability to fly at minimum sink without stalling in turns.

    d. Demonstrates the ability to perform consistent and safe top landings.

2. Light Wind Cliff or Ramp Launch (CL):

    a. Demonstrates the ability to launch safely from a shallow slope ramp or non-abrupt or overhung cliff top, where running room is severely restricted, drop off is steep, and wind is 5 m.p.h. or less, such that positive attitude control and strong, aggressive sprinting starts are required. Stalled, falling/diving launches are not acceptable demonstrations, even if flight is achieved.

3. Flat Slope Launches (FSL):

    a. Demonstrates ability to launch in less than 10 m.p.h. wind from slopes which approach the maximum L/D of the glider.

4. Restricted Landing Field (RLF):

    a. Demonstrates a landing using a downwind leg, base-leg, and a final leg approach where the entire base-leg, final, and landing occur within a 100' square.

    b. Demonstrates the ability to plan and execute consistent and controlled side hill landings on various slopes.

    c. Demonstrates the ability to plan and execute consistent and controlled top landings from various approaches.

5. Turbulence (TUR):

    a. Demonstrates controlled and un-panicked flight in conditions requiring quick, deliberate, substantial, and correct control application to reduce pendulum motion.

    b. Demonstrates proper directional control and correction of full (i.e., 50% of the wing span) asymmetric collapses.

    c. Demonstrates sustained flight in moderate thermal conditions without the aid of ridge lift.

    d. Demonstrates smooth and correctly timed surge control.

    e. Must have logged five 30-minute thermal flights without sustaining ridge lift.

6. High Altitude Launch (HA):

    a. Demonstrates the ability to launch unassisted with strong, running forward-inflation launches in winds less than 5 m.p.h.

    b. Demonstrates launches from sites with density altitude of 6000' or higher.

    c. Demonstrates understanding of high altitude conditions (e.g., air density, cloud suck, anabatic and catabatic conditions, hypoxia, hypothermia).

7. Surface Tow (ST)

Reprinted with permission of the United States Hang Gliding and Paragliding Association

a. Must demonstrate tow system set up and preflight, including a complete discussion of all of the factors which are particular to the specific tow system used, and those factors which are relevant to towing in general. Must demonstrate complete understanding of both normal and emergency procedures, including checklists for normal procedures and the indications of an impending emergency, and convince the instructor of his/her ability to recognize and execute emergency procedures.

b. Demonstrates successful, confident, controlled launches and flight under tow to release altitude, with a smooth transition to flying. Such demonstrations may be made in ideal wind conditions.

c. Has discussed all Towing Discussion Topics with the issuing ST official

8. Platform Launch (PL)

a. Must demonstrate tow system set up and preflight, including a complete discussion of all of the factors that are particular to the specific tow system used, and those factors that are relevant to towing in general. Must demonstrate complete understanding of both normal and emergency procedures, including checklists for normal procedures and the indications of an impending emergency, and convince the instructor of his/her ability to recognize and execute emergency procedures.

b. Demonstrates successful, confident, controlled launches and flight under tow to release altitude, with a smooth transition to flying. Such demonstrations may be made in ideal wind conditions.

c. Has discussed all Towing Discussion Topics with the issuing PL official

B. Special Skills attainable by Intermediate and above.

1. Assisted Windy Cliff or Ramp Launch (AWCL):

a. Demonstrates ability to launch with assistance in windy conditions from a non-abrupt or overhung cliff or ramp that exhibit strong lift at takeoff. Must show proper use of release signals and confident, aggressive launch.

2. Cross Country (X-C):

a. Must hold A.4 and A.5 above.
b. Demonstrates ability to recognize a safe landing area from the air and determine and execute a safe approach and landing, accounting for wind direction, rotors, obstacles, power lines, ground slope, vegetation, etc.
c. Demonstrates significant altitude gains (1000' or greater) above launch.
d. Demonstrates flight at a site where the landing area is not visible from launch, is not the normal landing area, and cannot be reached in a glide. The flight must demonstrate the pilot's ability to locate and link thermals to reach a destination.
e. Demonstrates knowledge applicable to cross-country flight (e.g., downwind rotors, cloud streets, detecting wires and other obstructions from the air, advancing storm fronts, convergences and shears, etc.).

A1

Reprinted with permission of the United States Hang Gliding and Paragliding Association

3. Para-Ski (PS)

    a. Must hold A.4 above.
    b. Demonstrates the ability to correctly set up and self launch with skis on. This is a no wind skill. Pilot must have the ability to inflate the canopy in forward launch position first try.
    c. Explains conditions, weather, equipment and protocols peculiar to flight in a ski area environment.
    d. Demonstrates light wind, high altitude launches and landings with skis.

104.19 - PARAGLIDING TANDEM REQUIREMENTS

19.01   Administration

A. The USHGA has established a 3-tiered system of requirements for tandem ('two-place' or 'dual') flying: Tandem 1 and Tandem 2 for recreational tandem flying, and Tandem Instructor for instructional tandem flying. These requirements are in addition to those established by the Federal Aviation Administration tandem exemption.

B. All necessary information will be distributed and administered by designated USHGA Tandem Administrators and Tandem Instructors. Tandem Administrators are appointed by the Tandem Committee. A study guide and both flight and written examination requirement information packages are available from the office of the USHGA.

    1. New appointment requests for Tandem Administrator shall be recommended and presented to the Tandem Committee by the applicant's Regional Director.
    2. Regional Directors may not issue Tandem ratings unless the Regional Director is also a Tandem Official.

C. The Tandem 1 rating involves minimal requirements and regulation, as this form of flying takes place between qualified and consenting USHGA rated pilots. This rating is authorized by Tandem Instructors after administering the written examination and witnessing the proper flight skills utilizing the designated launch method.*

    1. Attendance in a tandem training program or USHGA Tandem Certification Clinic is mandatory.

D. Tandem 2 rating requirements are much more stringent, and require a substantial amount of tandem experience, as they allow flights with USHGA Student rated passengers of limited experience, who have in their possession a USHGA Student Membership Card. This rating is authorized only by the office of the USHGA, after the applicant pilot submits proof of complying with all requirements.

    Tandem 2 rated pilots may not accept any form of remuneration for their flight service.

E. Tandem Instructor Rating requirements include those requirements for a Tandem 2 rating as well as specific written approval from the applicant's Regional Director and a Tandem Administrator for the Tandem Instructor rating.

    1. Tandem Instructors may charge fees for lessons. Tandem Instructors may issue Student ratings and Tandem 1 ratings.

F. USHGA Tandem Instructor Certification Clinics shall be administered by designated Tandem Administrators, trained in USHGA clinic procedures, and using text, study, and examination materials provided by the USHGA.
Tandem Administrators are appointed by Tandem Committee, with the approval of their Regional Director.

G. The designated launch methods will be Foot Launch (FL), or Surface Tow (ST). All Tandem pilots, Tandem Instructors, and Tandem Administrators qualified in one launch discipline will operate only in that discipline for which they are rated.

    * Designated launch method is the term given to the 'foot launch' sign-off (FL), and 'surface tow' sign-off (ST).

H. All Tandem ratings are valid for 3 years from the date of issuance.

  1. Tandem 1 rating renewal requires that the pilot either:

    a. Submit documentation to a Tandem Instructor showing a minimum of 10 flights of 2 minutes duration or longer per year over the previous three year period; or,
    b. Take and pass a check flight exam with a Tandem Instructor.
    c. Submit to the USHGA a USHGA Tandem renewal form, signed by a Tandem Instructor, attesting to the above requirements being fulfilled.

  2. Tandem 2/Tandem Instructor rating renewal requires that:

    a. The pilot prove currency by either:

      i. Submitting documentation to a Tandem Administrator showing a minimum of 10 flights of 2 minutes duration or longer per year over the previous three year period; or,

      ii. Take and pass a check flight exam with a Tandem Administrator.

    b. The pilot present proof to a Tandem Administrator of a current first aid card;

    c. The Tandem Administrator get approval orally or in writing from the pilot's Regional Director;

    d. The Tandem Administrator verify that the pilot is complying with the (30 day or full) membership and waiver requirements for his/her tandem students; and

    e. The Tandem Administrator submit to the USHGA a signed USHGA Tandem renewal form, attesting to the above requirements being fulfilled

I. NOTE: The USHGA has a procedure to rescind a Tandem rating.

J. Tandem Administrator appointments are conducted in the following manner:

  1. New appointment requests for Tandem Administrator shall be recommended and presented to the Tandem Committee by the applicant's Regional Director.
  2. Tandem Administrator candidates must exhibit an intense desire to administer the program.
  3. There must be a need in the area for a Tandem Administrator, or, the Tandem Administrator candidate must be willing to travel to conduct tandem clinics in other areas.

A1

4. Each Tandem Administrator candidate must assist as an Administrator trainee on a Tandem Clinic and receive recommendation from the Administrator with whom he/she works prior to petitioning the Regional Director for their recommendation.
5. The Tandem Committee will have the final authority to grant a Tandem Administrator appointment.
6. The Tandem Committee will review all Tandem Administrator appointments at each BOD meeting.

19.02 Pilot Rating Requirements

A. Tandem 1:
   1. Current USHGA Advanced Rating, Turbulence sign-off, AND;
   2. Minimum 200 hours of logged airtime, OR 100 hours with 500 flights of at least 500' vertical descent, OR 100 hours with 500 flights of 2 minutes or longer.
   3. Ability to consistently perform zero-wind and light crosswind launches, and zero-wind and light-wind landings culminating in zero ground speed at the moment of the flare and when the pilot's feet first contact the ground.
   4. At least 2 logged tandem flights as a passenger with a USHGA Tandem rated pilot using the designated launch method.
   5. 4-10 flights as pilot in command with a current USHGA Tandem Instructor as passenger. Flights must originate from a minimum altitude of 500' AGL or a minimum duration of 2 minutes. These flights should include one light wind (0 - 5 m.p.h.) launch using a forward inflation, one high wind (10 - 15 m.p.h.) launch using a reverse inflation, and landing.
   6. Successful completion of a flight skills test to be administered by the USHGA Tandem Instructor. This test will include, as a minimum, a passenger briefing, a successful tandem launch and a successful tandem approach and landing with the candidate as tandem pilot in command, observed by a USHGA Tandem Instructor (who must be the tandem passenger on this flight) utilizing the designated launch method. The Tandem Instructor then signs off the pilot for the flights in (4) and (5) on the application form.
   7. Successful completion of a written test administered by the USHGA Tandem Instructor.
   8. Neither flight skills (and test) or written test is to be administered prior to completion of pilot rating requirements.
   9. Must agree to all the provisions of the USHGA standard waiver and assumption of risk agreement for the Tandem 1 rating and deliver an original signed copy to the USHGA office.

B. Tandem 2:

   1. Current USHGA Tandem 1 rating
   2. At least 25 logged tandem flights of at least 500' vertical descent or at least 2 minutes duration as pilot in command using the designated launch method.
   3. Successful completion of a 1-2 day tandem exam clinic and pass a written exam and flight test with a Tandem Administrator. Attendance in the exam clinic cannot precede the requirements above.
   4. Endorsement by the candidate's Regional Director.
   5. Must agree to all the provisions of the USHGA standard waiver and assumption of risk agreement for the Tandem 2 rating and deliver an original signed copy to the USHGA office.

C. Tandem Instructor:

   1. A current Tandem rating.

A1

2. At least 25 logged tandem flights of at least 500' vertical descent or at least 2 minutes duration as pilot in command using the designated launch method.
3. Successful completion of an FOI test (Fundamental of Instruction), a 1-2 day tandem exam clinic and pass a written exam and flight test with a Tandem Administrator. Attendance in the exam clinic cannot precede the requirements above.
4. Endorsement of the candidate's Regional Director.
5. Must agree to all the provisions of the USHGA standard waiver and assumption of risk agreement for the Tandem Instructor rating and deliver an original signed copy to the USHGA office.
6. Present proof of a current first aid card to a Tandem Administrator.

19.03 Operating Restrictions and Limitations

A. Tandem 1:

1. May fly tandem recreational flights only with passengers in possession of a current USHGA Beginner Rating (or higher) card, and utilizing their designated launch method (FL or ST).
2. When flying with cross-discipline pilots, a novice rating is recommended for the passenger.
3. Maximum allowable wing loading must be within the placards of the glider.

B. Tandem 2:

1. Pilot may offer recreational tandem flights only, utilizing their designated launch method (FL or ST).
2. Pilot may not accept any form of remuneration for his/her services.
3. Passenger must have in their possession a current plasticized USHGA Student (or higher) rating card. Temporary rating forms are not acceptable.
4. Maximum allowable wing loading must be within the placards of the glider.

C. Tandem Instructor:

1. May offer recreational or instructional flights, utilizing their designated launch method (FL or ST).
2. Student must have in their possession a USHGA Student rating (or higher).
3. Maximum allowable wing loading must be within the placards of the glider.
4. A Tandem Instructor rating only authorizes issuing Tandem-1 ratings, not any other rating or Special Skill.

D. Prior to all tandem flights, the passenger or student must be informed that such flights are conducted under an exemption granted by the FAA, and that the ultralight vehicle does not meet aircraft certification standards set forth by the FAA.
E. When present at a flying site, a Tandem Paragliding Instructor shall personally ensure that all tandem flying requirements and the site requirements are being strictly followed. He shall personally inspect the USHGA ratings of both tandem passengers and pilots, and shall have the authority to halt those tandem flights that are in non-compliance. Noncompliance shall be reported to the Regional Director.
F. Possession of the FAA's Part 103, FAR Grant of Exemption #4721 is mandatory while flying tandem.
G. This exemption expires on October 31, 2006 unless sooner superseded or rescinded.
H. All tandem accidents should be reported by the tandem pilot involved and any other tandem pilot aware of the accident.

19.04 Equipment Requirements

A. The glider is recommended by the manufacturer for two-place flight.
B. At least one backup reserve parachute rated for the gross load being flown is required on flights where any possibility of successful deployment exists.
C. Appropriate helmets are required for both occupants during flight.
D. Suitable harness on both people.
E. Hook knife on pilot.
F. Although choice of other equipment is up to the individual pilot-in-command, ankle supporting boots, knee pads, gloves, and clothing appropriate to the site conditions are recommended.
G. Steel carabineers for the main connection point where the spreader bar meets the riser.
H. A reserve bridle that connects the reserve parachute to the spreader bar and not to the tandem pilot.

A1

FAA EXEMPTION No. 4721

A reprint of the operational parameters of this exemption are listed below:

" . . . individuals authorized by the United States Hang Gliding Association, Inc., are hereby granted an exemption from the . . .

Federal Aviation Regulations to the extent necessary to permit them to operate unpowered ultralight vehicles with another occupant for the purpose of sport and recreation. The exemption is subject to the following conditions and limitations:

1. Each operation must comply with all sections of Part 103, except §103.1 (a) of the FAR.

2. For training purposes, this exemption applies only to flights for the purpose of giving instruction in two-place unpowered ultralight vehicles from USHGA-approved launch sites.

3. Both occupants on all two-place training flights must possess a current pilot rating issued by the USHGA and at least one occupant must possess a current USHGA instructor rating.

4. Prior to all two-occupant training flights, the student must be informed that the flight is conducted under an exemption granted by the FAA and that the ultralight vehicle does not meet aircraft certification standards set forth by the FAA.

5. Both occupants on all two-place flights, other than for training purposes, must possess a current pilot rating issued by the USHGA and at least one occupant must possess a current Advanced hang gliding rating issued by the USHGA.

6. For identification purposes, the USHGA shall issue an individual authorization to each person allowed to conduct operations under this exemption. Each authorization shall include an identification number and a copy of this exemption. The USHGA shall also have a procedure to rescind this authority when needed.

7. Each individual who operates an ultralight vehicle under the authority of this exemption must be familiar with the provisions contained herein and must have in his or her personal possession a copy of the authorization issued by the USHGA and a copy of this exemption. These documents shall be presented for inspection upon request by the FAA.

This exemption terminates on October 31, 2006, unless sooner superseded or rescinded.

Thomas C. Accardi
Acting Director of Flight Standards
Issued in Washington, D.C. on October 9, 1986

Reprinted with permission of the United States Hang Gliding and Paragliding Association

NOTES

_____

_____

_____

_____

_____

_____

_____

_____

_____

_____

_____

_____

_____

_____

A1

PART 103: FAA REGULATIONS FOR ULTRALIGHT AIRCRAFT

RULES FOR OPERATION

The Parma Park LZ (left) overlooks the town of Santa Barbara, California. On good days it is possible to pass thousands of feet above the LZ and fly to the coast. A careless or unknowing pilot could easily pick the wrong route and violate two federal and one city regulations, jeopardizing the site for others.

Part 103 - Federal Aviation Regulations For Ultralight Vehicles

NOTE: FOR CURRENT INFORMATION GO TO WWW.FAA.GOV

PART 103—ULTRALIGHT VEHICLES

Subpart A—General

§ 103.1   Applicability.

§ 103.3   Inspection requirements.

§ 103.5   Waivers.

§ 103.7   Certification and registration.

Subpart B—Operating Rules

§ 103.9   Hazardous operations.

§ 103.11   Daylight operations.

§ 103.13   Operation near aircraft; right-of-way rules.

§ 103.15   Operations over congested areas.

§ 103.17   Operations in certain airspace.

§ 103.19   Operations in prohibited or restricted areas.

§ 103.20 Flight restrictions in the proximity of certain areas designated by notice to airmen.

§ 103.21   Visual reference with the surface.

§ 103.23   Flight visibility and cloud clearance requirements.

Subpart A—General

Sec. 103.1 Applicability.

This part prescribes rules governing the operation of ultralight vehicles in the United States. For the purposes of this part, an ultralight vehicle is a vehicle that:

(a)   Is used or intended to be used for manned operation in the air by a single occupant;

(b)   Is used or intended to be used for recreation or sport purposes only;

(c)   Does not have any U.S. or foreign airworthiness certificate; and

(d)   If unpowered, weighs less than 155 pounds; or

(e)   If powered:

  (1)   Weighs less than 254 pounds empty weight, excluding floats and safety devices which are intended for deployment in a potentially catastrophic situation;

  (2)   Has a fuel capacity not exceeding 5 U.S. gallons;

  (3)   Is not capable of more than 55 knots calibrated airspeed at full power in level flight; and

  (4)   Has a power-off stall speed which does not exceed 24 knots calibrated airspeed.

Sec. 103.3 Inspection requirements.

(a)   Any person operating an ultralight vehicle under this part shall, upon request, allow the Administrator, or his designee, to inspect the vehicle to determine the applicability of this part.

(b)   The pilot or operator of an ultralight vehicle must, upon request of the Administrator, furnish satisfactory evidence that the vehicle is subject only to the provisions of this part.

Sec. 103.5 Waivers.

No person may conduct operations that require a deviation from this part except under a written waiver issued by the Administrator.

Sec. 103.7 Certification and registration.

(a)   Notwithstanding any other section pertaining to certification of aircraft or their parts or equipment, ultralight vehicles and their component parts and equipment are not required to meet the airworthiness certification standards specified for aircraft or to have certificates of airworthiness.

(b)   Notwithstanding any other section pertaining to airman certification, operators of ultralight vehicles are not required to meet any aeronautical knowledge, age, or experience requirements to operate those vehicle or to have airman or medical certificates.

A2

(c)   Notwithstanding any other section pertaining to registration and marking of aircraft, ultralight vehicles are not required to be registered or to bear markings of any type.

Subpart B—Operating Rules

Sec. 103.9 Hazardous operations.

(a)   No person may operate any ultralight vehicle in a manner that creates a hazard to other persons or property.

(b)   No person may allow an object to be dropped from an ultralight vehicle if such action creates a hazard to other persons or property.

Sec. 103.11 Daylight operations.

(a)   No person may operate an ultralight vehicle except between the hours of sunrise and sunset.

(b)   Notwithstanding paragraph (a) of this section, ultralight vehicles may be operated during the twilight periods 30 minutes before official sunrise and 30 minutes after official sunset or, in Alaska, during the period of civil twilight as defined in the Air Almanac, if:

    (1)   The vehicle is equipped with an operating anticollision light visible for at least 3 statute miles; and

    (2)   All operations are conducted in uncontrolled airspace.

Sec. 103.13 Operation near aircraft; right-of-way rules.

(a)   Each person operating an ultralight vehicle shall maintain vigilance so as to see and avoid aircraft and shall yield the right-of-way to all aircraft.

(b)   No person may operate an ultralight vehicle in a manner that creates a collision hazard with respect to any aircraft.

(c)   Powered ultralights shall yield the right-of-way to unpowered ultralights.

Sec. 103.15 Operations over congested areas.

No person may operate an ultralight vehicle over any congested area of a city, town, or settlement, or over any open air assembly of persons.

Sec. 103.17 Operations in certain airspace.

No person may operate an ultralight vehicle within Class A, Class B, Class C, or Class D airspace or within the lateral boundaries of the surface area of Class E airspace designated for an airport unless that person has prior authorization from the ATC facility having jurisdiction over that airspace.

Sec. 103.19 Operations in prohibited or restricted areas.

No person may operate an ultralight vehicle in prohibited or restricted areas unless that person has permission from the using or controlling agency, as appropriate.

Sec. 103.20 Flight restrictions in the proximity of certain areas designated by notice to airmen.

No person may operate an ultralight vehicle in areas designated in a Notice to Airmen under §91.137 (Temporary flight restrictions in the vicinity of disaster/hazard areas), §91.138 (Temporary flight restrictions in national disaster areas in the State of Hawaii), §91.141 (Flight restrictions in the proximity of the Presidential and other parties), §91.143 (Flight limitation in the proximity of space flight operations) or §91.145 (Management of aircraft operations in the vicinity of aerial demonstrations and major sporting events) of this chapter, unless authorized by:

(a) Air Traffic Control (ATC); or

(b) A Flight Standards Certificate of Waiver or Authorization issued for the demonstration or event.

Sec. 103.21 Visual reference with the surface.

No person may operate an ultralight vehicle except by visual reference with the surface.

Sec. 103.23 Flight visibility and cloud clearance requirements.

No person may operate an ultralight vehicle when the flight visibility or distance from clouds is less than that in the table found below. All operations in Class A, Class B, Class C, and Class D airspace or Class E airspace designated for an airport must receive prior ATC authorization as required in Sec. 103.17 of this part.

A2

AIRSPACE	FLIGHT VISIBILITY	DISTANCE FROM CLOUDS
CLASS A	NOT APPLICABLE	NOT APPLICABLE
CLASS B	3 STATUTE MILES	CLEAR OF CLOUDS
CLASS C	3 STATUTE MILES	500 FT BELOW, 1000 FT ABOVE, 2000 FT HORIZONTAL
CLASS D	3 STATUTE MILES	500 FT BELOW, 1000 FT ABOVE, 2000 FT HORIZONTAL
CLASS E BELOW 10,000 FT MSL	3 STATUTE MILES	1000 FT BELOW, 1000 FT ABOVE, 2000 FT HORIZONTAL
CLASS E ABOVE 10,000 FT MSL	5 STATUTE MILES	1000 FT BELOW, 1000 FT ABOVE, 1 STATUTE MILE HORIZONTAL
CLASS G 1200 FT OR LESS AGL	1 STATUTE MILE	CLEAR OF CLOUDS
CLASS G MORE THAN 1200 FT AGL AND LESS THAN 10,000 FT MSL	1 STATUTE MILE	500 FT BELOW, 1000 FT ABOVE, 2000 FT HORIZONTAL
CLASS G MORE THAN 1200 FT AGL AND MORE THAN 10,000 FT MSL	5 STATUTE MILES	1000 FT BELOW, 1000 FT ABOVE, 1 STATUTE MILE HORIZONTAL

FAA EXEMPTION #4721

This exemption to Federal Aviation Regulation 103.1(a) and 103.1(b), permits pilots to operate an unpowered ultralight vehicle with another occupant for the purpose of sport, recreation and/or training. This exemption is subject to the following conditions and limitations:

1) Each operation must comply with all sections of Part 103, except section 103.1(a) of the FAR.

2) For training purposes, this exemption applies only to flights for the purpose of giving instruction in two-place unpowered ultralight vehicles from USHGA approved launch sites.

3) Both occupants on all two-place training flights must possess a current pilot rating issued by the USHGA and at least one occupant must possess a current USHGA Instructor rating.

A2

4) Prior to all two-occupant training flights, the student must be informed that the flight is conducted under an exemption granted by the FAA and that the ultralight vehicle does not meet aircraft certification standards set forth by the FAA.

5) Both occupants on all two-place flights, other than for training purposes, must possess a current pilot rating issued by the USHGA and at least one occupant must possess a current Advanced hang glider rating issued by the USHGA.

6) For identification purposes, the USHGA shall issue an individual authorization to each person allowed to conduct operations under this exemption. Each authorization shall include an identification number and a copy of this exemption. The USHGA shall also have a procedure to rescind this authority, when needed.

7) Each individual who operates an ultralight vehicle under the authority of this exemption must be familiar with the provisions contained herein, and must have in his or her personal possession a copy of the authorization issued by the USHGA and a copy of this exemption. These documents shall be presented for inspection upon request by the FAA.

This exemption was extended to terminate on October 31, 2006, unless sooner superseded or rescinded.

A2

NOTES

A2

WILLS WING PARAGLIDING INSTRUCTION TRAINING SYLLABUS OUTLINE

A3

The following is an outline for a suggested instructional syllabus for paragliding. Your instructor's syllabus may differ from this one, but this syllabus will give you a look at the major elements that will be included in your instruction.

1. ON SITE - INSTRUCTOR DEMO. Instructor demonstrates forward pull up and "launch" on flat ground, in zero to 3 mph wind. Demonstrates proper "horseshoe" layout of canopy for light wind launch, proper pre-launch line clearing technique, proper way to hold risers and brakes, use of front risers to pull up and inflate canopy, control of canopy using brakes, and by running under canopy, keeping canopy inflated, over head, directionally controlled, and loaded, keeping weight on seat, while running for 50 yards or more.

2. ON SITE - STUDENT PRACTICE. Students practice #1 above under direct instructor supervision.

3. ON SITE - INSTRUCTOR DEMO. Instructor demonstrates reverse pull up in 3 - 12 mph wind (6-10 mph preferred). Demonstrates control of the canopy using brakes, risers, and by moving under the canopy. Demonstrates use of outside A lines to fold in canopy tips, and use of brakes to re-inflate. Demonstrates use of one brake to collapse canopy quickly and completely, to prevent drag-back.

4. ON SITE - STUDENT PRACTICE. Students practice #3 above under direct instructor supervision.

5. ON SITE - INSTRUCTOR DEMO. Instructor demonstrates forward pull up and launch technique on a suitable slope in 0 to 8 mph wind, including launch abort technique, and demonstrates straight flight and landing, including proper use of brakes and proper position in the harness for landing.

6. ON SITE - STUDENT PRACTICE. Students practice #5 above under direct instructor supervision.

7. IN CLASSROOM - GROUND SCHOOL - USING VIDEO AND SIMULATOR

Instructor covers basics of:

Equipment (including nomenclature)

a. Canopy. Including classes of canopies, and suitability of the various classes to different levels of pilot experience

b. Helmet

c. Harness

d. Boots

e. Reserve Parachute

f. Spinal Protection

Aerodynamics and Meteorology

a. Lift and how it is produced

b. Drag

c. L/D

d. Stalls and what causes them

e. Airspeed and groundspeed, dangers of downwind flying.

f. Flight heading and ground track, crabbing

g. Wind, rotors, thermals, gradient, effects of turbulence

Preflight Operations

a. Canopy

b. Preflight of harness

c. Preflight of reserve

d. Putting On and Adjusting Harness

e. Clipping harness into canopy, attaching reserve

f. Line clearing procedure

g. How to hold brakes

A3

Canopy Control on the Ground

    a.   Forward inflation and launch

    b.   Reverse inflation and launch

Canopy Control in the Air (Perform all on simulator)

    a.   Speed control with brakes

    b.   Speeds to fly - use of airspeed in different conditions

    c.   Using brakes to control pitch oscillations

    d.   Use of front risers

    e.   Turning control with weight shift

    f.   Turning control with brakes

    g.   Turning control with risers

    h.   Landing technique

    i.   Constant stall (parachutage)

    j.   Full stall

Deliberate Collapses

    a.   Big Ears

    b.   One Side Collapse

    c.   Front Collapse

    d.   Front Horseshoe Collapse

    e.   Recovering from turbulence induced collapses

    f.   Directional control

    g.   Re-Inflation

Turning Maneuvers

    a.   Spirals

    b.   Spins

A3

Flight Plans - Why you need one and how to make one

Emergency Procedures— Rescue Parachute Deployment; When to deploy, How to deploy — Practice in a simulator

Canopy Packing and Maintenance

8. ON SITE - FLIGHT WITH TURNS - REVERSE LAUNCHES

   a. Student practices flight with turns of 90 degrees change of heading, maximum 45 degrees from straight into wind.

   b. Student practices flight with turns of 180 degrees change of heading, maximum 90 degrees from straight into wind.

   c. Student uses turns to set up approach for landing accuracy.

   d. Students practice reverse launches

   e. Student makes and executes a specific flight plan

9. ON SITE - ALTITUDE FLIGHTS

   a. Student practices turns of 180 degrees change in heading, with headings up to 180 degrees from wind direction.

   b. Student practices aircraft approach, with landing accuracy.

   c. Student practices controlling glide path for landing accuracy.

   d. Student practices flight across the wind direction, controlling ground track by crabbing.

   e. Student practices canopy control maneuvers:

      1) Big ears

      2) Asymmetric tip folds with opposite brake to control direction

      3) Asymmetric tip folds allowing turn and correcting

      4) Wing collapse using front riser, with opposite brake to control direction.

A3

5) Wing collapse using front riser, allowing turn and correction.

6) Brakes induced pitch oscillations and recovery

10. IN CLASSROOM - GROUND SCHOOL - SOARING SKILLS AND METEOROLOGY USING VIDEO AND WRITTEN MATERIALS

a. Meteorology - including weather, sources of wind, stability and instability in atmosphere, thermals, gradient, turbulence, rotors, gusts.

b. Right of way rules

c. FAR Part 103

d. USHGA basic safety recommendations

e. Assisted launch techniques - communication

f. Crosswind Launch

g. Cliff / platform launch both calm and windy

h. Speeds to fly - airspeed control - flight at minimum sink - danger of parachutage stall and accidental stall and spin

i. 360 degree turns

j. Thermalling techniques - how to thermal with other paragliders, how to thermal with hang gliders

k. Ridge soaring techniques - rules of the ridge - ridge soaring with other paragliders - ridge soaring with hang gliders

l. Side hill landing techniques

m. Top hill landing techniques

11. ON SITE - ALTITUDE FLIGHTS - SOARING

a. Students practice crosswind launches

b. Students practice assisted launches as pilots and launch assistants

c. Students practice cliff launches, calm and windy (optional at this stage)

d. Students practice airspeed control in flight

e. Students practice 180 degree turns in significant wind, controlling ground track

f. Students practice 360's

g. Students practice thermal soaring away from the hill in mild conditions.

h. Students practice ridge soaring in moderate smooth winds

i. Students practice side hill landings

j. Students practice top hill landings

12. IN CLASSROOM - GROUND SCHOOL

a. Review of canopy Owner's Manual - including operating limitations

b. Written exam

A3

NOTES

RECOMMENDED REFERENCE SOURCES

Mitch McAleer banks it up over Telluride, Colorado — Dean Stratton photo

On Weather

Pilot's Handbook of Aeronautical Knowledge from the FAA

Available from pilot's supply shops

On Federal Aviation Regulations and Procedures

FAR / AIM Federal Aviation Regulations and Airman's Information Manual

Available from pilot's supply shops

USHPA Address:

United States Hang gliding and Paragliding Association

PO Box 8300

Colorado Springs, CO 80933-8300

The internet offers a plethora of sites for education and soaring:

For good explanations regarding the science of weather:

`http://www.usatoday.com/weather/wworks0.htm`

For more technical explanations (more than you will likely care to ever know):

`http://www-das.uwyo.edu/~geerts/cwx/notes/notes.html`

A4

For free, real-time online weather information:

`http://www.intellicast.com/`

`http://www.wunderground.com/`

`http://www.weather.com/`

For specific aviation weather:

`http://aviationweather.noaa.gov/`

`http://www.aviationweather.com/`

For weather specific to hang gliding and paragliding:

`http://www.usairnet.com/cgi-bin/launch/code.cgi`

The RUC website for local atmospheric profiles is:

`http://maps.fsl.noaa.gov/`

Once there, click on the "interactive/java" soundings link.

Dr. Jack Glendening's BLIPMAP site provides valuable information on the thermalling potential to include the predicted best locations, intensity, height of the thermals; their buoyancy to shear ratio, areas of local convergence and thunderstorm potential. The hourly-updated BLIP forecasts are available on the web at:

`http://www.drjack.net/BLIP/index.html`

A4

Additional local weather information is available at the weather underground web site at

`http://www.wunderground.com/.`

A good generic weather site for forecasting the potential for overdevelopment and thunderstorms is:

`http://www.intellicast.com/`

For Notices To Airman (NOTAMS):

`https://www.notams.jcs.mil/`

LIST OF FLYING SITE WIND TALKERS
(dial up and listen to current conditions)

Alaska:

Eagle River, AK (20 sec ring) 907-694-3017

California

Candlestick Park,CA 415-467-7287

Crestline Peak, CA 909-338-3362

Ed Levin Pk, CA 408-946-9516

Fort Funston, CA 415-333-0100

Millerton Lake, CA 209-822-6276

Oceanside, CA 619-754-WIND

Palos Verdes, CA 310-544-4387

Rancho Seco Lk, CA 209-748-5158

Santa Barbara, CA 805-963-4422

A4

San Francisco Airport (Coyote Pt), CA...............650-877-3585

San Luis Res, CA 209-826-9019

San Luis Res park station, CA 209-826-1196

Santa Clara Model Aircraft Skypark. 408-776-0101

Sherman Island, CA...916-777-7007

SkySailing Airport,CA 760-782-9055

Sylmar, CA (Kagel Pk) 818-362-9604

Colorado

Boulder Res, CO 303-581-WIND

Denver Res, CO 303-766-0020

Lookout Mountain (Mt. Zion), CO 303-526-5600

Florida

Hugenot Pk, FL 904-251-3674

Shell Pt Beach, FL 904-926-8802

Tampa Bay, FL 727-430-6403

Georgia

St Simons Island, GA 912-634-SURF

Michigan

Holland St Park, MI 616-786-9871

North Carolina

Cape Fear, NC 910-458-3272

Lake Norman, NC 704-892-7853

A4

New Mexico

Albuquerque, NM 505-891-1733

Cochiti Lake, Pena Blanca, NM 888-700-9279

Sandia Pk, Albuquerque, NM 505-243-8664

Nevada

Echo Bay, Las Vegas, NV 702-394-4440

Lake Mead, NV 702-294-2400

New York

Bristol MT, NY 716-396-3245

Padgham Hill, NY 716-924-9610

South Carolina

Charleston, SC 803-883-9817

Washington

Lake Wenatchee, WA 509-763-2831

Wisconsin

Lake Monona N, WI 608-266-5266

Canada

Rustico Bay, PEI CAN 902-963-2618

Appendix 5

UNDERSTANDING SOUTHERN CALIFORNIA WEATHER PATTERNS

Bo Criss studies the sky as he prepares to launch from Pine Mountain, north of Ojai, California — Mike Preston photo

Nearing cloudbase, Dean Stratton heads over the back for a long XC flight — Bo Criss photo

Southern California is renowned for its year-round soaring. There are numerous flying sites but the majority of paragliding tends to cluster around the Los Angeles basin (Kagel Mt., Crestline/Marshall Mts., and Lake Elsinore sites), San Diego (coastal cliff and other inland thermal sites), and Santa Barbara (also with coastal cliff and inland thermal sites).

All of the inland sites are heavily influenced by the daily onshore flow of the cool, moist, and stable marine air and the nightly offshore flow of the drier, colder, and unstable desert air. The major differences between the various sites are the geographical distances from the ocean and the specific orientation to the sun and mountain ranges. Sites on the eastern side of the L.A. basin (Kagel and Crestline/Marshall) are far enough inland that the approaching marine layer is usually readily visible by the additional smog component of the natural haze. The incoming marine layer is less obvious at sites that are closer to the ocean and downwind of less populated areas such as Santa Barbara or Santa Maria (Plowshares Mt.). The depth of the marine layer is typically 2-4,000 feet in the basin areas and, depending upon the amount of solar heating, will rise up to 6-7,000 feet in the mountains.

Marshall Launch

On days with good solar heating, it is possible to find late morning thermals that rise up to 6-7,000 feet prior to the marine influx. The approaching marine layer acts like a small cold front, pushing the warmer air upward as it approaches. The thermal intensity will increase at the junction of the two air masses and it is possible to gain thousands of feet in the local convergence. Such convergence flying is common at the Eastern-facing Lake Elsinore sites where pilots soar the upslope offshore morning flow and wait for the convergence line to pass from behind. Once the marine layer moves past, the winds switch to downslope conditions but pilots can often boat around in the convergence and follow it out across the lake for miles.

The L.A. basin sites are soarable year-round but are most consistent during the summer months. The best soaring days are typically post-frontal days in the spring and fall after passing cold fronts have cleared out the warm inverted air mass. The sun is still at a high enough angle and the days sufficiently long for good solar heating, enabling a high lapse rate with thermals that can reach to 10-12,000 feet.

Late in the summer season there are normally several weeks of "monsoonal flow" where tropical moisture is carried inland from Baja California and can lead to strong vertical development and cloud streeting in the desert. Outstanding flights have occurred on days immediately following monsoonal weather (when the prevailing westerly winds reestablish themselves). Special attention needs to be paid to the possibility of over development and localized high desert winds.

After Labor Day, a unique winter weather system begins to occur with increasing regularity. Santa Ana winds occur when an inland high pressure area couples with an offshore low pressure system, causing a strong inversion-clearing offshore flow. Winds within the L.A. basin are normally too strong for flying but the day after the end of the Santa Ana conditions is often a great soaring day. Lake Elsinore is often flyable on Santa Ana days if the winds are not too strong.

Skyport Launch,
Santa Barbara

The Santa Barbara mountain sites are renowned for excellent winter soaring conditions. It is common for the rest of the L.A. basin to be grounded by strong Santa Ana winds while the southern slopes of the Santa Ynez Mountains are basking in calm, clear air and setting up a strong thermal block. Often the lower level flow is from the west enabling long XC flights in the wind shadow of the higher mountains. Summer brings stable, inverted air and increasing low altitude cloud coverage to Santa Barbara. This is when the Ojai mountain sites are often best with their clear skies and high altitude inversion-free flying.

The Plowshares site, near Santa Maria, is renowned for its spring and fall high altitude sea-breeze convergence flying. During the summer, the greater inland heating causes the sea breeze front to move inland earlier (prior to the coastal areas developing thermals) and thus moving the convergence zones further east. During these months, convergence flying is possible in the San Fernando Valley, the Mojave Desert, and Lake Elsinore.

San Diego is perhaps best known for the Torrey Pines glider port in La Jolla which offers a 350-ft cliff face with ridge soaring possible for several miles in either direction. Year round thermal flying is also possible at several inland sites.

Torrey Pines

NOTES

_____

_____

_____

_____

_____

_____

_____

_____

_____

_____

_____

_____

_____

_____

_____

_____

Glossary:

COMMON TERMS AND ABBREVIATIONS

Enjoying excellent soaring conditions at Mission Ridge, near Fremont, California — Andy Stocker photo

GLOSSARY

COMMON TERMS AND ABBREVIATIONS

A

Active Piloting — a method of countering the effects of minor turbulence by sensing small changes in the pressure in the brake lines and risers and making continuous corrections.

Accelerator — a system to increase the trim speed of the paraglider by altering the relative lengths of the forward risers, normally activated by a foot stirrup.

AGL (Above Ground Level) — height as measured above the ground.

Aircraft Approach — a landing pattern based on the conventional aircraft pattern, consisting of a downwind, base, and final leg.

A-lines — the forward most lines leading from the A-risers to the first set of attach points near the leading edge of the canopy.

Altimeter — an instrument used to measure height, normally based on static air pressure and referenced to mean sea level (MSL) altitude.

Airmass — a body of air covering a relatively wide area, exhibiting approximately uniform properties through any horizontal section.

Anabatic — an uphill wind produced by the effects of local heating.

Angle of Attack (AoA) — angle between the chord of the wing and the direction of the relative wind.

A-Risers — the forward most risers.

Aspect Ratio — the relationship of the wing span to the wing area (actual formula is the square of the wingspan divided by the wing area). Higher aspect ratios infer higher performance but reduced stability.

Attitude — the inclination of the three axes of an aircraft relative to the ground.

B

Bank Angle — the inclination of the roll axis relative to the horizon.

B-lines — the lines extending from the B-risers to the second set of chord line attach points.

Base leg — a portion of an aircraft approach that is downwind of the intended landing spot and perpendicular to the wind. Normally flown after the downwind leg and prior to the final leg.

Best Glide Speed — the speed that achieves the maximum glide ratio. Normally referenced to glide ratio through the air not over the ground.

Brake — the handle on the end of the brake line used to modulate the speed, bank, or angle of attack by altering the trailing edge deflection.

Brake line — the lines from the brake handle to the trailing edge of the canopy.

C

Camber — the rise of the curve of an airfoil, usually expressed as the ratio of the rise to the length of the chord.

Canopy — the portion of the paraglider constructed from cloth (i.e. the wing).

Carabiner — a D-shaped ring with a spring catch on one side, used for attaching the risers to the harness.

Catabatic — an air current moving down slope due to cooling, especially at night.

Cell — a section of the canopy defined by the volume bounded from the leading to the trailing edge between the longitudinal ribs on each side.

Center of Gravity (CG) — the center of mass of the paraglider, pilot, harness and all equipment. The CG is located near the pilot and is the point through which the resultant of gravitational forces passes.

Chord — the length defined by a straight line joining the trailing and leading edges.

Class A - G Airspace — Refer to airspace classification discussion in Chapter 14.

G

Cloudbase — the bottom of the clouds, normally used in relationship to cumulus clouds, defining the top of usable soaring lift.

Cloud Street — when cumulus clouds align in a downwind row, often followed for long distance soaring.

Cold Front — the zone separating two air masses, of which the cooler, denser mass is advancing and replacing the warmer.

Convection — the vertical transport of atmospheric properties.

Convergence — a net flow of air into a region, often a source of wide spread lift.

Coriolus Effect — the apparent deflection of wind due to the earth's rotation.

Crabbing — a method of compensating for drift by heading partly into the wind to achieve the desired ground track.

Cravat — when a portion of the canopy becomes entangled in the lines.

Cross Country — flying done with the intent of landing at a distant, often undetermined destination.

Cumulus Clouds — a cloud class characterized by dense individual elements in the form of puffs, mounds, or towers, with flat bases and tops that often resemble cauliflower.

Cumulonimbus Clouds — a cloud class indicative of overdeveloped cumulus clouds with thunderstorm conditions, characterized by large, dense towers that often reach altitudes of 30,000 ft.

D

Deep Stall — see parachutage.

DHV — the German Hang gliding and Paragliding Federation responsible for the testing and certification of both types of aircraft.

Downwind — flying in the direction toward which the wind is blowing.

Downwind Leg — the portion of an aircraft approach that is flown offset from and parallel to the intended final approach leg.

Drag — the aerodynamic force exerted on an aeronautical body that tends to reduce its forward motion.

Dynamic Pressure — the pressure due to the movement through the air. The pressure measured by common non-spinning airspeed indicators (e.g. floating disk airspeed meters). Increases with the square of the velocity.

E

F

Figure 8 Approach — an approach pattern commonly used to lose altitude in moderate winds. Characterized by a series of reversing turns perpendicular to the wind and downwind of the intended landing spot.

Flaring — a smooth and relatively large deflection of both brakes to cause a short-term reduction in descent speed and angle so as to land as slowly and softly as possible. Flaring is not practiced at altitude because recovery from it could involve pitch surges and/or stalling.

Forward Inflation — the process of inflating the canopy by facing forward into the wind with the canopy to the rear. Normally reserved for calm winds with shallow slopes.

G

G Forces (G's) — the apparent gravitational force due to maneuvering accelerations.

Glide Ratio — the ratio of the forward horizontal vector to the downward vertical vector with respect to the ground (i.e. how far you fly over the ground based upon your height). Often mistakenly interchanged with lift to drag (L/D) ratio (which references your forward movement with respect to the air).

Ground Handling — controlling the canopy on the ground. See Kiting.

Ground Speed — the speed with respect to the ground (the speed portion of the vector summation of your airspeed and heading vector with the wind speed and heading vector).

Ground Track — the path the glider covers over the ground (the bearing vector summation of your airspeed and heading vector with the wind speed and heading vector).

G

H

Heading — the angle between the axis from front to rear of the glider and magnetic north.

Headwind — a wind coming from in front of the glider, opposed to your heading.

Helicopter Landing — an advanced landing technique in which the canopy is spun at the last second. Sometimes used in a very restricted LZ to drop vertically the last few feet.

Horseshoe — laying out the canopy so the center of the wing is further away from the pilot than the wingtips. Done to encourage the center section inflating first, reducing the chances of one wing rising more than the other.

House Thermal — a thermal that is repeatedly present at a specific location.

I

Induced Drag — aerodynamic drag due to the production of lift. Normally thought of as the drag due to the wingtip vortices.

Inflation — the process of lofting the canopy overhead from the ground.

Initial Point — the entry point for a landing pattern.

Inversion — when the temperature profile is inverted, that is, the temperature increases with an increase in altitude. Indicative of stable atmospheric conditions that counter thermal convection.

J

K

Kiting — The method of practicing glider control by inflating the canopy and keeping it airborne while the pilot stays on the ground.

L

Landing Pattern — an approach pattern followed with the intention of landing. See aircraft approach, figure 8, and overhead key approach patterns.

Landing Zone (LZ) — an area on the ground where the intended landing spot is contained. A good LZ is large, flat and void of obstacles.

L/D — see Lift to Drag ratio.

Lapse Rate — the change in temperature with respect to altitude. Normally referenced to the dry adiabatic lapse rate, meaning the layer of the atmosphere from the surface to cloudbase. A lapse rate higher than standard (3 deg C / 5.4 deg F) infers a thermal will rise through that altitude.

Leading Edge — the forward edge of the canopy. The inlets are located on the leading edge.

Leeward — pertaining to, situated in, or moving in the direction which the wind blows (opposed to windward).

Lift (aerodynamic) — the component of the aerodynamic force exerted by the air on an airfoil, having a direction perpendicular to the direction of motion and opposing the force due to gravity

Lift (atmospheric) — a rising parcel of air. Paragliders can exploit lift in order to extend their flight.

Lift to Drag (L/D) Ratio — the ratio of the lift force to the drag force. Normally referenced to the airspeed where the ratio is at its maximum (L/D max). This ratio equals the glide path through the air and in calm winds is equal to the glide ratio over the ground. L/D max occurs at the airspeed that parasitic drag is equal to induced drag. Most paragliders are trimmed to achieve L/D max with the brakes up.

Lines — the suspension lines connecting the risers to the canopy.

Lockout — a dangerous condition that can occur during towing if the glider is allowed to get too far off-axis with from the towline. Lockouts are avoided by keeping the glider's longitudinal axis parallel to the tow rope.

M

MSL (Mean Sea Level) — a height referenced to pressure altitude above sea level.

Meteorology — the atmospheric conditions and weather of an area.

G

Micrometeorology — local and small-scale atmospheric phenomena confined to the within a shallow stratum of air adjacent to the ground.

Minimum Sink Speed — the speed that achieves your minimum vertical speed through the air. Normally requires some brake application and is approximately 75% of the speed for best glide (L/D max).

N

Negative Spin - see Spin.

NOTAM (Notice To Airman) — a message issued by the FAA to alert aircraft pilots of any hazards en route or at a specific location.

O

Overhead Key Approach — a relatively close-in approach pattern in which a helical flight path is used to spiral down around the landing aim point. Applicable to restricted landing zones in calm or light winds.

P

Parachutage — see Stalls.

Parasitic Drag — the component of drag caused by skin friction and the shape of the surfaces not contributing to lift (essentially a measure of the frontal area of the glider, lines, pilot and equipment).

Pattern — term commonly used to refer to the landing pattern

Penetration — the ability to fly forward against the wind (forward ground speed).

Performance — the measure of a paraglider's efficiency and flight envelope. Common performance measurements include L/D max, minimum sink rate, and minimum and maximum airspeeds.

Q

Quicklinks — metal ring connectors used to secure the lines to the risers.

R

Rating — a method of certifying pilot skill level. USHPA ratings include P-1 (novice), P-2 (beginner), P-3 (intermediate), P-4 (advanced), and P-5 (master). Regulated flying sites often have requisite minimum rating requirements.

Relative Wind — the wind speed and direction opposite to the flight path through the air.

Reverse Inflation — the process of inflating the canopy in which the pilot first turns away from the wind or slope to face the canopy. After inflation the pilot would turn to face forward into the wind prior to launching.

Ribs — Internal vertical cloth webs that connect the upper and lower surfaces of the canopy and define an individual cell

Ridge Soaring — the process of staying aloft by working the orographic lift caused by the wind flowing up and over the terrain.

Right of Way — rules used to predetermine the orderly flow of aircraft that are in close proximity to each other

Riser — a length of webbing that collates the lower ends of the lines and distributes them to the harness.

Root — the center cell or seam of the canopy

Rotor — swirling, turbulent air normally downstream of an object

S

Scratching — flying close to the terrain while working light lift

Sectional — an aeronautical chart that depicts topographical information overlaid with airports, airways, and controlled airspace.

Sink (atmospheric) — a descending parcel of air. Paragliders normally avoid sink or increase speed when encountering it, in order to maximize their flight time.

Soarable — when sufficient lift exists to maintain altitude indefinitely.

Soaring — the practice of putting soarable conditions to proper use.

Speed Bar (Stirrup) — a rigid member that the pilot pushes on with his feet to actuate the accelerator system (see Accelerator).

Speed-To-Fly — the concept of flying an optimal airspeed based upon the vertical and horizontal air components and the anticipated strength of the next lift encounter.

Spin — a dangerous maneuver in which the paraglider descends at a stalled angle of attack in a vertical direction along a helical path. The yaw rate and helical path is due to one wing being more stalled than the other. In paragliding it is sometimes referred to as a "negative spin." Depending upon the entry conditions, either a banked or flat (helicopter) spin can result.

Spiral — a maneuver in which the paraglider descends at a normal angle of attack in a vertical direction along a helical path. A spiral is entered by an extended brake application and is characterized by the glider over banking until it rotates leading edge down, carving an accelerated, high-G downward helical path. An advanced maneuver used to generate high rates of descent. Sometimes referred to as a "positive spin."

Stability (aerodynamic) — once disturbed, the ability of a paraglider to return to its equilibrium flying condition.

Stability (atmospheric) — a measure of the propensity for convection. A stable atmosphere inhibits convection.

Stall — when the paraglider exceeds the critical angle of attack and lift can no longer be generated. Glider behavior and appearance is dependant upon the type of stall.

B-line Stall — a maneuver in which the pilot pulls downward on the B-risers, distorting the airfoil to the point that the paraglider descends vertically. A B-line stall can be an effective way to lose altitude without turning.

Constant Stall — see Parachutage.

Full Stall — a stall normally entered by a symmetrical, excessive, and extended brake application. The canopy collapses and momentarily falls behind the pilot. Quickly releasing the brake pressure at this point can result in an extreme and dangerous forward surge. The glider is not controllable in a full stall and the rate of descent is extreme. Full stalls can result in spins, twisted risers, and cravats.

Parachutage — a term used to describe a stable stalled descent that can occur without pilot input. The glider is unresponsive when in parachutage and the rate of descent exceeds that of a normally-sized reserve parachute. Parachutage is rarely encountered on modern paragliders but is possible due to aggravating conditions such as a wet canopy and turbulence.

Static Pressure — the pressure due to the weight of the atmosphere above. Commonly referred to by weather forecasters as barometric pressure.

Stratus Clouds — a cloud characterized by a gray, horizontal layer with a uniform base, found at a lower altitude. Denotes stable atmospheric conditions.

T

Tailwind — a wind coming from behind the glider.

Tandem — a paraglider that can carry two people, normally a student in the front and the instructor slightly higher and to the rear.

Thermal — a rising air current caused by surface heating.

Tip Vortices — the swirling eddy that extends behind the glider's wingtips caused by the lateral movement of higher pressure air beneath the wing towards the lower pressure air above the wing. The strength of these vortices is indicative of the amount of induced drag.

Track — see Ground Track

Trailing edge — the rearward most part of the canopy. Normally covered by a ribbon of reinforcement webbing. The brake lines attach to the trailing edge.

Trim Speed — the speed at which the glider will naturally fly without any control (brake or accelerator) input. Most paragliders are trimmed to fly at L/D max.

U

Unstable (aerodynamic) — when a paraglider diverges away from its equilibrium flying condition.

Unstable (atmosphere) — when the lapse rate exceeds the standard adiabatic rate, promoting convection.

Upwind — moving or situated in the direction from which the wind is blowing.

USHPA — the United States Hang gliding and Paragliding Association (formerly knows as the Untied States Hang Gliding Association (USHGA)

V

Variometer — an instrument that measures the rate of change in static pressure to determine vertical rate of climb or descent.

Visual Flight Rules (VFR) — rules that govern the operation of aircraft in visual meteorological conditions.

Venturi Effect — the acceleration of wind that occurs due to the shape of terrain, specifically in funnel-shaped canyons or near the lateral edges of ridges.

V-ribs — internal cloth webs used to distribute loads between the lines and the internal cells. By using V-ribs the designers can maintain a clean aerodynamic ship and reduce the number of external lines.

V-tabs — small tabbing reinforcements used to distribute the loads from the lines to the canopy attach points.

W

Wake Turbulence — turbulent flow behind an object

Wind Dummy — term given to someone who launches early so that others can better evaluate the flying conditions.

Windward — pertaining to, situated in, or moving in the direction from which the wind blows (opposed to leeward).

Wind Gradient — the slowing of the wind due to friction near the earth's surface.

Wing Loading — wing area divided by total flying weight (pilot, glider, and all equipment), the measure of how much weight is lifted by unit area of the wing.

Wingover — an aerobatic maneuver that involves a steep, climbing turn to a near stall, then a reversing turn with a steep dropping of the nose. Wingovers are often linked together in a series of deceptively simple maneuvers. A properly flown wingover is a difficult maneuver involving critical timing and application of braking and weight shift. An improperly flown wingover has caused many a collapse, cravat, and reserve parachute deployment.

X

XC — abbreviation for Cross Country flying

Y

Yaw — rotation of the wing about the vertical axis

Z

G

NOTES

BONUS DVD

The saying goes that a picture is worth one thousand words. Complex ideas are best learned with more than text and words. The enclosed DVD contains 90-minutes of menu-driven instructional video that mirror the major sections of this book. The video is in NTSC format for ready viewing in DVD players used in most North, Central, and South American countries, Japan, South Korea, and the Philippines. It may also be viewable in other countries by using a personal computer.